Understanding Islam

Shoes in the entryway of a mosque in Cairo, Egypt. Photo: © 2006 Megan J. Thorvilson.

Understanding Islam

An Introduction

C. T. R. Hewer

Fortress Press

Minneapolis

UNDERSTANDING ISLAM
An Introduction

First Fortress Press edition 2006.

Cover image: Waterfront mosque at sunset. Jiddah, Saudi Arabia. 1997–1998 © Wolfgang Kaehler/Corbis.
Cover design: James Korsmo

A study guide and other helpful materials for readers and teachers are available at www.understandingislamtext.com

The publishers and author gratefully acknowledge Oxford University Press and Yvonne Y. Haddad and Jane I. Smith for their permission to reprint and help in updating "Muslims in the United States of America," Yvonne Yazbeck Haddad and Jane I. Smith, *The Oxford Encyclopedia of the Modern Islamic World*, John L. Esposito, ed. Oxford University Press, 1995.

Library of Congress Cataloging-in-Publication Data
Hewer, C. T. R., 1952-
  Understanding Islam : an introduction / C.T.R. Hewer.
    p. cm.
  Includes bibliographical references and index.
  ISBN-13: 978-0-8006-3791-0 (alk. paper)
  ISBN-10: 0-8006-3791-7
  1. Islam—Essence, genius, nature. 2. Islam—Doctrines. I. Title.
  BP161.3.H49 2006
  297—dc22
                              2006009204

The paper used in this publication meets the minimum requirements of American National Standard for Information Sciences—Permanence of Paper for Printed Library Materials, ANSI Z329.48-1984.

Manufactured in the U.S.A.
10 09 08 07 06   1 2 3 4 5 6 7 8 9 10

Contents

To Professor Dr. Khalid Alavi,

*Imam Khatib of the Faisal Masjid and Director of the Da'wah
Academy, International Islamic University, Islamabad, and sometime
Professor of Islamic Studies at the University of the Punjab, Lahore,
and Director of Birmingham Central Mosque, who was the first teacher
to open my eyes to the contents of the Qur'an.*

To the Reverend Dr. Sigvard von Sicard,

*Lecturer on Islam in Africa at the Center for the Study of Islam and
Christian-Muslim Relations, University of Birmingham, who taught
by example that the teacher's door must always stand open to students.*

*And finally to the thousand people who followed the course on which
this book is based, who by their interest and challenging questions
shaped the content into what it is today.*

Illustrations

Shoes in the entryway of a mosque.
Pakistani students recite the holy Qur'an in Hyderabad, Pakistan.
The Dome of the Rock in Jerusalem.
The Mohammed Ali Mosque in Cairo, Egypt.
A *minbar* and *mihrab* in the 'Amr Ibn al-'As Mosque in Cairo, Egypt.
Muslim men from Palestine perform Friday midday prayers.
Dome and minaret of the Al-Azhar Mosque in Cairo, Egypt.
Women pray in a mosque in Mumbai, Bombay, India.
A man reads the Qur'an in the Al-Azhar Mosque in Cairo, Egypt.
Page from the Qur'an in Kufic script, 10th century.
Afghan school children with their teacher.
Mosque in Al-Jimi, Al-Ain, United Arab Emirates.
Page from an Iranian copy of the Qur'an, 12th century.
Muslim women in Indonesia.
A muslim student in the Netherlands.
The Sultan Agung Mosque in Medan, Indonesia.
Muslim children in the village of Sheik Yasin, Afghanistan.
Muslim farmers near the village of Minya, Egypt.
Dome over the mausoleum of the Mamluke Sultan Qaytbay in Cairo, Egypt.
The Mecca Masjid in Hyderabad, India.
Turkish prayer rug, 17th century.
An Egyptian dance troupe performs their "whirling dervish" Sufi dance.
Interior of the mausoleum and khanqa of Ibn Barquq in Cairo, Egypt.
Courtyard of the of the 'Amr Ibn al-'As Mosque in Cairo, Egypt.
A man performs *wudu'* outside the Suleyman Pasha Mosque in Cairo, Egypt.
Tawaf, or circumambulation, around the Ka'ba in Makka during the *Hajj*.
A *dikka* in the Sultan Barquq Mosque in Cairo, Egypt.
A *mihrab* in the Suleyman Pasha Mosque in the Citadel. Cairo, Egypt.
Mosque Maryam in Chicago, Illinois.
The Mother Mosque of America in Cedar Rapids, Iowa.
The Madina Mosque in Cardiff, Wales.

Acknowledgments

I must record my gratitude to two of my teachers, Professor Khalid Alavi and Dr. Sigvard von Sicard, both for allowing me to dedicate this work to them and for reading and commenting on the manuscript. Professor Yahya Michot did me a great service by meticulously scrutinizing a late draft, and his many helpful suggestions and comments profoundly improved the final outcome. I am grateful to Christian friends and colleagues for their comments, including Dr. Elizabeth Harris, the Rev. Dr. Toby Howarth, the Rev. John Trenchard, and the Rev. Dr. Pat McCaffrey. A wide range of Muslim scholars have read and corrected all or part of the manuscript, including Ali Akhtar, Abdullah Bawhab, Dr. Jabal Buaben, Shaykh Mohamed Amin-Evans, Maulana Tariq Kamal, Chaudary Abdul Rashid, and Abdul Karim Saqib. Two Christian theologians, Bishop Mark Santer and David McLoughlin, rendered considerable assistance to correct and improve chapter 9. Three colleagues with particular expertise in the field, Yahya Birt, Dilwar Hussain, and Professor Dr. Christian Troll, gave assistance by reading and commenting on chapter 10. Finally, it was a joy and a challenge to receive the critical comments of four former students: Sadaf Ali, Mubeen Azam, Nourallah Chakroun, and Nicola Maier. Grateful thanks must also go to Canon Matthew Joy for agreeing to do the final proofreading. As always, the final text is my responsibility alone, and following the Muslim custom, I seek the correction of the learned and the forgiveness of God for any mistakes contained therein.

I am grateful to Dr. Yvonne Yazbeck Haddad and Dr. Jane I. Smith, as well as to Oxford University Press, for their helpful discussion of Muslims in the United States in chapter 10.

Readers will find other helpful learning tools for the volume—including chapter summaries, study questions, Web resources, a research paper guide, and testing materials—at www.understandingislamtext.com.

Pakistani Dawar-e-Islami students recite the holy Qur'an in Hyderabad, Pakistan.
Photo: © Nadeem Khawer/epa/Corbis.

Introduction

The journey of a thousand miles, we are told, begins with a single step. This book is intended to be the first ten steps in the endless journey of understanding Islam. As a tradition of more than one billion followers worldwide and with a body of scholarship stretching back over fourteen centuries, Islam is indeed very rich in its self-understanding. What follows is the merest taste of the riches contained within that tradition.

It is written for people in the West with limited understanding of Islam and perhaps some misunderstandings based on current perceptions and our Western experience of Islam as something "foreign." It aims to tell the story of Islam in a way that is accessible and so does not contain quotations from other scholars. It is the product of many years of study and teaching Christians and other people about Islam, but it is still the perspective of one person. In order to try to ensure that it is as faithful as possible to the Muslim tradition, the text has been read through by a number of Muslim scholars and by others who are involved in communicating about Islam in the West. Nevertheless, the author is responsible for the contents and follows the Muslim practice of asking the forgiveness of God for any errors and the correction of the learned.

The author is a Christian, and as such it is clear that he cannot accept everything Islam teaches or see the world in exactly the same way a Muslim does. Were that so, then the author would have to become a Muslim immediately or risk being condemned as a hypocrite. To accept that the Qur'an is the ultimately revealed scripture from God that corrects all others and that Muhammad was the infallible sinless Prophet of God, in the way that Muslims believe, would make it necessary to leave the Christian faith and become a Muslim. Nevertheless, the author's position is that Muslims are cousins in faith in the one God, and this requires that we take seriously the message of the Qur'an and the lived example of Muhammad and ask what Christians might learn from this. The Qur'an is held by Muslims to be guidance for all humanity and not just for Muslims; similarly, Muhammad was sent with a universal mission to all humankind (Q. 34:28).

Several principles underlie this approach. First, the eighth commandment given to Moses requires us not to bear false witness against our neighbor, and so the story of Islam is retold with fidelity to that tradition. Second, just as Moses took off his shoes at the burning bush because the ground on which he was to step was holy, so due respect is given to Muslims on whose holy ground we are about to step. Third, there is a significant difference between the ideals proclaimed by a religion and the realities of the ways in which it has been lived out through the centuries by followers who do not always live up to those ideals; this work errs on the side of the ideals of Islam because that is the way that any religion would like first to be understood. Fourth, not every follower of a faith has had the opportunity to study it in depth, and so we need to acknowledge that we may well meet Muslims who do not see their faith in quite the way that it is portrayed here. Fifth, this does not mean that we have to be uncritical of the story as it unravels; the Qur'an itself calls on people to ask questions and puzzle things out for themselves (Q. 2:266, 3:190-191). Sixth, there is a real urgency for people in the West to come to some understanding of Islam, given that over the last fifty years substantial numbers of Muslims have been born or come to live in the West. Seventh, communication is a two-way process, and so at times elements of Christian thought are presented in a way that tries to communicate accurately to readers for whom this may not be familiar.

This book is divided into ten chapters, the ten steps, each of which builds on what has gone before. It is intended to be read from the beginning, so that the foundations can be laid before looking at the details that are based upon them. Once the first three chapters have been absorbed, it is then possible to follow through different aspects, but without these foundations there is the possibility that later themes will be misunderstood. It can be used for self-study, and further books are listed in the bibliography for those who want to engage more deeply. It can also be used by a group of people, who can read and explore each chapter in turn and thus together explore the whole picture. A glossary of Islamic words used in the book is given at the back so that readers can refresh their memories about things that occurred earlier on.

Whenever dates are given, they are according to the Common Era (C.E.). In terms of years, this is the same as A.D., but that stands for *Anno Domini*, or "in the Year of Our Lord," so only a Christian properly can use that. In religious studies we now use C.E. instead. Most of the key words and names of people and places in Islamic studies are taken from Arabic. Arabic is written with its own alphabet, so we need to find a way of using English letters to make the same sound as the Arabic word. Most modern authors use one of the standard forms to do this. I have chosen I. R. Netton, *A Popular Dictionary of Islam* (London: Curzon, 1992). Some words have become common in older forms and among them are: Muslim (Moslem), Qur'an (Koran), Muhammad (Mohammed), 'Id (Eid), Makka (Mecca), and Madina (Medina). Many references are given to the Qur'an in parentheses so that readers can become familiar with the Qur'an itself; such references begin with Q., followed by the chapter number, then a colon followed by the verse number: (Q. 2:156). Sometimes older translations of the Qur'an had a slightly different numbering system for verses. The references given in this book are from the Abdullah Yusuf Ali translation, as updated by a team of contemporary scholars, published by the King Fahd Complex for the Printing of the Holy Qur'an in Madina, and revised by the Islamic Foundation of Leicester, England (used by permission).

Page from an Iranian copy of the Qur'an.
Photo: © Minneapolis Institute of the Arts.

A muslim student in the Netherlands. Photo: © 2006 Anke Leunissen.

1

The Wider Picture:
Creation from a Muslim Perspective

God is one – creator – sustainer – creation is in harmony through obeying God's will – the natural God-given way of life – free will – we are the servants of God and the stewards of creation – guidance – accountability – revelation sent in Books and in creation – a chain of Prophets from Adam onward – all guidance essentially the same – Qur'an is the criterion – role of Prophets – a code by which to live – a sense of the closeness of God – the practices of Islam

Everyone sees things from a particular angle. If we think of a football game, the supporters of the losing side often tell the story of the match differently from the winners. The same would be true if we think about an event in history like a war. The victors always seem to write the history books. If we don't know how the other person sees something, then it is easy to misunderstand.

The same is true when looking at a religion. Jews and Christians grow from the same roots but read their histories in different ways. Each religion has its own way of seeing the world; its own story to tell. When we grasp the big picture, we can make sense of the details. Most people in the West know very little about Islam. Probably they have heard that there was a prophet called Muhammad. A few may have heard about a holy book called the Koran (or Qur'an, as it normally is spelled now). Apart from that, most of what we know about Islam and Muslims is what we hear on the news. We have no framework to make sense of it. To build such a framework, we need a starting point. The Muslim starting point goes back before the creation of the world, before time began.

Before the world was created, God always existed because God has no beginning and no end. God is beyond our created universe. God is outside time and outside space. God created time like everything else. There is no place that we can say, "God is there." To sum this up, we say that God is transcendent, meaning beyond everything that is created. This does not mean that "God is very old" or that "God lives in a place a long way away." God is beyond all that. It means also beyond our understanding and beyond our ability to speak accurately about God. Our language, our understanding, our ability to imagine simply does not stretch far enough to be able to handle the transcendent world of God. Even to call it a world is wrong. God is beyond everything.

The fundamental understanding of Islam is that God is one and unlike any created thing or being (Q. 112:1-4). God alone exists without the need for anything else. God was never created. God always simply existed. God cannot be divided up into parts nor can any created thing or person share in the being of God. The English word "God" is used for this one supreme being, and similar words occur in a variety of languages. In Arabic, God is Allah, meaning simply "the one and only God." This Arabic word for God is used by Arabic-speaking Jews and Christians as well as by Muslims worldwide. Just as the English word "God" with a capital G cannot have a plural, so in Arabic Allah has no plural form. This defends the absolute uniqueness of God.

God chose to create by a free act of the will. God did not need to do it but chose to create. God simply creates by a word of command. God says, "'be' and it is!" God is the creator of everything that exists and all is dependent on God (Q. 2:255, 36:81-82, 54:50). God is perfect, and a perfect being cannot create imperfection; therefore the whole of the creation was created in a state of perfection. Or better to say, it was as perfect as it could be (Q. 32:7, 39:5). God exists outside time and space but the creation is within time and space. This means that everything that is created had a beginning and so must grow older and eventually cease to exist. From the very moment that we are born, we are getting older and will in the end die. Every created thing is limited also by space. I am here and not there. Therefore, to be created in time and space carries with it certain limitations. The creation can only be the best of all possible worlds.

God is the sustainer of the whole universe (Q. 11:6). God did not create it and then cease to be involved. Without the ongoing, sustaining presence and interest of God, the whole of creation would cease to be any more. Nothing can exist without being in a relationship with the creator (Q. 2:255).

Christians may be asking: What about Adam and Eve, the fall, and original sin? The Qur'an speaks of the existence of Adam and Eve as the first two human beings and of their error of judgment in thinking that something evil was good. This led to their being cast out from Paradise. Eventually they repented and were reconciled to God. Christians maintain that this shattered the perfection of creation in a way that could not be fully repaired. This led to the development of the doctrine of Original Sin to speak about this fundamental flaw in creation. From the Muslim perspective, God can do anything and so is capable of restoring the creation to the state of perfection that was lost. When Adam and Eve repented and sought God's mercy, they were forgiven and returned to a state of harmony with God (Q. 2:30-39).

The key word here is "harmony." God creates the world in a state of harmony (Q. 32:7, 95:4). That harmony exists between every individual created thing and God. If everything is in harmony with God, then the whole of creation must be in harmony within itself. Each human being, for example, is created in a state of harmony with God, with all humankind and with every other element in creation. Now, harmony between the creator and the creation is not a partnership of equals. Who knows best how the creation should run? Surely the creator who designed it and brought it into being. Therefore, harmony with God requires that every element of creation knows its place and obeys the will of God. So all creation, including every human being, is called to be the obedient servant of God. Only then can there be true harmony or peace.

This idea of fundamental harmony with God and within the creation is contained in the word *islam*. Arabic is a language built up on three-letter roots. Words are made by adding to these three letters. Every word built on the same root is part of one family and shares a set of common meanings. Take, for example, the Arabic root S L M. From this we can make three words all belonging to the same family: *islam*, *muslim*, and *salam*.

s l m

is **lam**

mus **li m**

salam

See the way in which the root letters appear in each word? The word *islam* means that state of perfect harmony that exists between God and the whole of creation, and within creation itself, which is the way that God created it. It contains also the idea of submission, because this harmony can come about only when everything submits to the will of God and acts according to the plan of the creator. This will lead to the state of absolute peace, which can come about only when everything is in harmony and obedience to God.

The word *muslim* describes something in the state of *islam*. In this way, we can say that God created everything in the state of *islam*, that is, God created everything *muslim*. This goes right back to the dawn of creation itself. The planets, sun, and stars all were created *muslim*. Mountains, rivers, and minerals all are *muslim*. Trees, plants, flowers, and vegetables are *muslim*, and so are animals, birds, and fish. The natural condition of the whole of creation is to be in a state of potential perfect harmony with God and with everything else, that is to be *muslim* (Q. 17:44, 24:41). In the same way, every human being is created *muslim* and we are most completely at peace when we submit to the will of God in all things (Q. 57:1, 64:1). This brings us to the third of our words made from the same root: *salam*. This word is used in the traditional Arabic greeting between Muslims: *salam alaykum*. This is normally translated "Peace be with you," but it really means "may you come ever more completely into that state of perfect harmony and peace with God that is meant by *islam*." When people finally reach heaven, one of the names for which is Dar al-Salam (The Land of Peace), this will be the greeting that they will use there (Q. 33:44).

When the disciples of Jesus asked him to teach them to pray, he taught them the words of what today is called the Lord's Prayer. This contains the line, "Your kingdom come, your will be done on earth as in heaven." This leads Christians to speak about the kingdom (or reign) of God. In the reign of God, the will of God will be obeyed by every element of creation. It is worth thinking about this in relation to the definition of *islam* in the last paragraph.

When human beings are living this way of life, which is in total harmony with God, that is, *islam*, they are said to be following the *din al-fitra* (the natural God-given way of life) (Q. 30:30). The human being is now living like a flower or a bird in the sky, fully and completely the way that God intended. The difference between a human being and a flower or a bird is that we have received the revelation from God in the form of Books of guidance. We have thus been called to live an ethical life following the revealed will of God. It is in this way that we come to a state of harmony with God, and, as we can rationally comprehend and morally implement the divine will, we can bring out the full potential harmony that is latent in all creation.

When a mountain, tree, or dog is in its natural state, it is *muslim*, but it has no choice in the matter. That is how it was created and that is how it is. Human beings are different. We are the pinnacle of creation. What makes us unique is that we are able to receive direct revelation from God and that we are given the gift of free will with which to put it into practice. This means that we are free to submit to the will of God and thus find perfect harmony and peace. The opposite is also true. Part of God's plan in giving us free will is that we also have the ability to rebel against God's will. This is sin. Why then should God give us free will? Consider the different values of these two acts. First, if I program my bedside tea-maker to make tea in the morning, I hardly feel the need to reward it when it does the job for which it was made. Second, if I rise ten minutes before my wife and creep downstairs to make her tea, then I stand likely to receive a reward for an act of thoughtfulness and love. Only a free being can act out of love, compassion, and overriding concern for the other, and therefore the value of a free act is different from one that is programed. Only a human being can choose to become the servant of God in everything, to live a life of obedience to the divine will, a life of ethical service to God, and freely to rely totally on the mercy of God. This is the duty and the dignity of human beings, and this is why God gave human beings free will.

The role of each human being in God's plan is summed up in two words. The first of these is *'abd*, the human being as the slave or loving servant of God. We can see how central this is in Islamic thinking as the man's name that we often hear, Abdallah, means the Servant of God. The servant is the one who obeys the master's will and lives it in practice. This leads to the second concept of *khalifa*. This means to be the Regent of God upon the earth (Q. 2:30). The regent is the one who is given all power and authority under God. Every human being is called to the high dignity of being *khalifa* and thus is called to tend the whole of creation, to cherish it, and to bring it into a state of perfection. The Qur'an tells us that God created human beings for the sole purpose that we would worship God (Q. 51:56).

The Islamic understanding of creation is that it is dynamic and not static. Once something is created in time, it never stands still. It is like walking against the flow on a moving walkway; one needs to keep moving just to keep one's place. Standing still means that one goes backward. So, even though God created the best of all possible worlds, it needs to be tended in order to maintain that state and to develop its full potential. This is the role of every human being.

Human beings have always been in a relationship with the rest of creation. We have formed artificial lakes to provide water supplies and generate electricity. Every rose that grows in our gardens is the result of generations of breeders striving to bring out the full potential of the perfection of roses. All our breeds of dogs have been bred for specific purposes by human beings. Similarly with all our domestic animals, they are far from the original forms of cows or sheep centuries ago. This is all part of human beings acting as *khalifa* on the earth. This should mean that ecology, care for the environment, is a natural part of being human, of being the Regent of God upon the earth (Q. 31:20). We are not at liberty to pollute or abuse the earth for our own selfish ends. That would be rebellion against God's will, and that is sin.

If someone is sent as the regent of a higher authority, as the servant of a master, that person is not free to do as he or she pleases. The regent always receives guidance on how to act from the higher authority and will be held to account for the way in which she or he has discharged her or his duty of obeying God in all things. Notice here that all human beings are called to be *khalifa*. This is not just something for rulers or the rich. It applies equally to all men and women. This is the dignity and duty of being human. Not surprisingly then, God will hold all human beings to account at the end of their lives for the way in which they have discharged this duty to be the Regent of God on earth (Q. 2:48, 6:21-31, 22:17, 99:7-8). Depending on this, judgment will be eternal reward in heaven or punishment in hell.

To send a servant without guidance and then to hold that person to account would be fundamentally unjust. When God sends guidance to the earth, we call that revelation (Q. 3:73, 7:203, 16:64). In an Islamic understanding, guidance comes from God in two forms. The first is in the form of Books or Scriptures that have been sent by God to explain how human life should be lived. The second is in the form of the creation itself, which is full of the signs of God. By exploring the handiwork of the creator, we come to an understanding of how the creator intended that everything should be organized. We are used to thinking of the religious scholar or theologian as someone who serves or worships God by seeking to understand the revealed books. The scientist too, who seeks to understand the workings of creation, is likewise serving or worshipping God by so doing. All exploration of the revelation of God is an act of worship.

According to this model, both the Books revealed by God and the created order revealed by God have their origins in the same source, namely God. This means that ultimately they must agree. In this way, there is no tension between religion and science in Islam. Both have their source in God and ultimately must agree. If it appears that science and religion do not agree, then we either are not understanding our Books properly or we have more work to do on our science so that we understand the creation better. Again and again in the Qur'an, we read that we should use our heads to puzzle things out, to reason and question, so that we more perfectly understand the world around us "in which there are signs from God" (Q. 6:98-99,105).

Now, if every human being stands in need of this guidance from God, then guidance must have come right from the very beginning of human life on earth (Q. 2:30). God is the source of all revelation, and without it we would not be able to know the will of God and obey it. Revelation is an essential element in God's plan. Through revelation we are lifted up into an ethical state of living a moral life. Through revelation we are able to know the path that human beings should follow. In the Islamic system, morality, the way of life that pleases God, is revealed. It is the duty of the human being to listen to revelation and obey it. From the beginning, human beings were created with a predisposition to acknowledge the Lordship of God (Q. 7:172). Now, we are all called to serve God through obedience and love. As one well-known statement of God related by Muhammad (*hadith qudsi*) puts it:

> My servant keeps on coming closer to me through performing good deeds beyond what are commanded, until I love him. When I love a man, I am the hearing with which he hears, I am the sight with which he sees, I am the hands with which he holds and I am the feet with which he walks.

Adam and Eve, as the first human beings, needed guidance from God. Thus Adam was the first human being to receive revelation from God; he was the first Prophet of the *islamic* way of life. But guidance is needed by every human being, and so the Qur'an tells us that revelation has been sent to every people on earth so that none are left without a Prophet to help them live an *islamic* way of life (Q. 25:51, 35:24).

By definition there is only one God and all human beings are equally called to be the servants of God upon earth; we are all one family (Q. 7:189). This means that all the guidance sent by God on how to live human life was *in essence* the same (Q. 6:92, 17:107-109). God would not guide one group of people to live in one way and another group to live in essentially a different way. All peoples, wherever they live on earth and whenever human life began in that place, have received essentially the same guidance on how to live according to God's plan for creation. This should affect the way in which people react when they "discover" a new civilization. Often when Europeans went out to discover the world, they thought that it was their task to bring civilization and religion to those people because it was not there beforehand. According to this Islamic model, exactly the opposite is the case. Whenever a new civilization is "discovered," we should be aware that God has been there before us and that those people have received revelation from God (Q. 10:47, 16:36). This ought to bring about a sense of deep respect rather than a feeling of supremacy.

How then are we to judge what remains from the original revelation sent by God and what has been added or lost down through the centuries? From a Muslim perspective, the Qur'an is the final revelation sent by God that has been preserved intact from the time of Muhammad (Q. 41:42). This was not a new revelation but *in essence* the same as all that had gone before (Q. 2:41, 3:81, 5:48, 16:36, 41:43, 43:45). The Qur'an serves as the benchmark or the criterion by which all other earlier revelations are to be judged (Q. 25:11, 86:13). When a new people are encountered, their way of life can be measured against the Qur'an. Those things that agree with the message of the Qur'an, such as a profound respect for the natural order in creation, are a cause for rejoicing, because Muslims believe this new community is guided by the revelation sent to them. Those things that go against the fundamental revelation of the Qur'an, like human sacrifices, for example, can be seen not to have come from God. Wherever such practices came from, if they are contrary to the guidance in the Qur'an, they did not come from God but must be the result of human misunderstanding or rebellion against the will of God. In this way, the Qur'an can be seen coming to confirm earlier revelations but also to correct contemporary errors and practices based on them, given that the Qur'an is always to be regarded as the preferred text. Similarly the example of Muhammad, based on the Qur'an, acts as a universal model for a life lived in submission to God.

If every people on earth has been sent revelation through a Prophet, how many Prophets were there? What were their names? What were the Books that were sent to them? We don't know all the answers to these questions. The criterion is the Qur'an that was sent to the Prophet Muhammad. Whatever disagrees essentially with the Qur'an and whatever example is contrary to the example of Muhammad are not from God. The Qur'an tells us the names of twenty-five Prophets of God and names five Books that were sent. Of these we can be sure, but this is not an exhaustive list. There were other Prophets and other Books whose names are not known to us (Q. 40:78). Every Book sent by God must be respected by Muslims as a revelation from God. Similarly, every Prophet sent by God must be respected, and his or her example is an example of a godly life that could be followed. The problem for a Muslim is that those earlier Books are no longer intact in such a way that we can rely on them entirely. The lives and teachings of those Prophets have not been preserved like the life and teaching of Muhammad and so cannot be relied on in the same way. However, the principle is clear. Every earlier Book and Prophet must be respected, but the criteria of authenticity are the Qur'an and Muhammad (Q. 2:285, 4:150-152).

For Jews and Christians especially, this has a profound message. Of the twenty-five Prophets named in the Qur'an, twenty-one are biblical figures. A Muslim is required to believe that Abraham, Moses, and Jesus, among others, were Prophets sent by God to teach essentially the same message as Muhammad and the Qur'an. Islam never sees itself as a new religion revealed to Muhammad in the Qur'an in the seventh century of the Common Era. Islam is part of that ongoing revelation from God that goes right back to Adam and Eve and encompasses every human being who has ever lived. The Qur'an is a restatement of the essentially identical revelation, which is there to reinforce and clarify earlier revelations. To the extent that earlier revelations have been lost or misunderstood, the Qur'an comes to correct those errors and restate the revelation of *islam*.

You may have noticed the careful way in which the words "Islam" and "Muslim" have been used until now. Capital-I Islam and capital-M Muslim can be used only to refer to that revelation that was contained in the Qur'an and exemplified in the teaching of Muhammad in the seventh century. As such, it is fixed in time, and one cannot speak of Islam and Muslims before this date. At the same time, *islam*, that is the never-changing way of life that has been revealed by God, has existed from the time of Adam and Eve. They were the first *muslims*, that is, those who lived according to the guidance given by God. In this way, Abraham, Moses, and Jesus, and all the earlier Prophets, were *muslims* too, exemplifying that perfect life of submission to the will of God.

The term Prophet, with a capital P, is used repeatedly in this book. This has a special meaning in Islam, which is different from the way in which the term is used by Jews and Christians. In Islamic usage, Prophets have three functions: first, to receive revelation from God and articulate it in their own society; second, perfectly to exemplify that revelation in their own lives and teachings; third, to lead a community of people to live according to that message. Let's take each of these in turn.

In an Islamic understanding, the Books of revelation were sent down by God and are not the product of human authors. The Prophets received the Books as a literal, verbal revelation from God (Q. 32:2, 41:2, 46:2, 55:1-2). God is the author of the Book and the Prophet the one who receives it and passes it on to others. This means that the Books are guaranteed to be free from error and from human weakness or misunderstanding in their reception.

The Prophets not only received the Books but also molded the whole of their lives around them. They exemplified the message that they had received (Q. 33:21,46). Two things flow from this. First, the

Prophets had to be human beings, nothing more and nothing less (Q. 6:50, 14:11, 25:7-8, 41:6). If they had been super-human in some way, then we would never know whether we ordinary mortals were capable of living out the message fully in our lives. If they were somehow less than human, for example if they did not have the gift of free will and so were not subject to the temptation to rebel, then they would be equally useless as exemplars for us. In this way, the life example of the Prophet is described as a model (Q. 33:21) and a guiding lamp (Q. 33:46). Second, the Prophets needed to be sinless in the way that they lived their lives (Q. 43:43). If sometimes they sinned and sometimes they obeyed God's will, then we never would know when to believe them. Their lives had to be sinless so that they could be an example in everything they said and did. It cannot be that they were incapable of sin—then they would not share our common humanity—but they were preserved from sin by God.

The message that was given to the Prophets was not for them alone (Q. 43:44). They were called to lead a community of people into a way of life that was in accordance with the will of God. Some of the Prophets were in positions of authority within their societies, and so they were able to establish a path or way of life that embodied the guidance from God. Others were sent to call people back to the way of life that had been established by earlier Prophets. It stands to reason that if the Prophets had the recipe for a fully human and perfectly happy way of life that will lead to fulfilment in this life and the reward of eternal life in heaven, then they would want to share it with others and encourage others to live by that guidance.

This model can be seen in the life of the Prophet Muhammad. He received the Qur'an from God as a literal, verbal revelation. He then modeled his whole life perfectly on the guidance that he had received and taught others to do the same (Q. 4:80). The things that Muhammad did, what he said and taught, and the things of which he approved become important for all subsequent generations. What he did—how he conducted his personal, family, business, and community life—can serve as a model to be followed. Everything that he said and taught, the way in which he dealt with questions or cases that were brought to him, acts as a source for implementing the revelation of the Qur'an in daily life. Muhammad was not born onto a blank page of history but into a society that already had established ways of doing things. This means that if he approved of some customary practice, it agreed with the guidance of God. Anything in the Arabian society of his time that was against God's guidance, he changed. The records of Muhammad's actions and teaching, and the things of which he approved, are collected in the Hadith, or the Traditions of Muhammad. These form a crucial source for living a Muslim way of life. This way of life, based on the Qur'an and Hadith, was gradually drawn up into the Shari'a, which is a clearly drawn pathway through life and a complete code for living according to this guidance.

Let us take stock of the assistance provided by God for every human being to live as the Regent of God on earth. There is first the guidance that was given in the Books and in the signs contained in creation. There are the lives of the Prophets, human beings like us, who perfectly exemplify that guidance and act as role models (Q. 33:21). All that guidance has been drawn into codes of life to guide human beings on the straight path. What more is needed?

Each human being needs to develop a deep sense of their closeness to God and a spiritual communion with God that can help them to make the right decisions in life and bring all this guidance into every fiber of their own daily living. At the end of the day, each and every human being is called to be the Regent of God, and all will be answerable directly to God for the way in which they have fulfilled their duty (Q. 6:94). This profound sense of the presence of God is summed up in the Islamic term *taqwa*, which can be translated as "God-consciousness" and carries with it aspects of the traditional "fear of the Lord" and a sense of protection before the awesomeness of God (a word from the same root is used in Arabic for "vaccination"). This does not just occur naturally but must be built up by living according to the guidance of God. This is where the practices of Islam come in.

Each of the principal practices of Islam is good for the human being and leads her or him into a deeper sense of *taqwa*. They lead the Muslim into an awareness of God through the way in which every element of life is lived. Everything that one does should be done in a spirit of *taqwa*, and everything should lead to a deeper awareness of oneself as the creature of God, called to be Abdallah, the Loving Servant of God, in everything.

These principal practices are summed up in what are generally called the "five pillars of Islam." We will look at these in much more detail later, but here we need to see how they contribute to this growing sense of *taqwa*.

The first of these pillars is *shahada*; this is the principal statement of belief in Islam. It reads: "I bear witness that there is no god (that is, nothing worthy of worship) save God; Muhammad is the Messenger of God." This calls for a constant examination that it is God alone who is worshipped and that nothing else is permitted to get in the way of perfect obedience to and worship of God. It is through the message sent to Muhammad, the Qur'an, and the lived example of the Prophet that Muslims are able to know how to live such a God-centered life. In earlier generations, that is, before the coming of Muhammad, the equivalent of the *shahada* would have read: "There is no god save God; Abraham (or Moses or Jesus, etc.) is a Messenger of God."

The second pillar is that of *salat* or formal, liturgical prayer. These are the prayers required of all Muslims after the age of puberty five times each day, timed according to the passage of the sun. They build up *taqwa* by bringing the believer to listen once more to the guidance of the Qur'an when it is recited and then to respond by submitting all to God and seeking mercy and forgiveness. These formal prayers are supplemented by informal prayers called *du'a* (prayers of supplication) and *dhikr* (the remembrance of God in the heart). In this way, the believer is called to raise up the mind and heart to God continuously.

Zakat is the third pillar of Islam and is part of the whole social, welfare, and economic system of Islam. The foundation of this system is *sadaqa*, or bearing one another's burdens. This is a reminder that all we have is given by God's providence and must be used for the benefit of all humanity. The system includes important principles such as the prohibition of *riba*, or usury, and economic exploitation, and the importance of *infaq*, or the principle of the circulation of wealth. At the summit of this system comes *zakat* itself, which acts as a purification of wealth. Muslims are required to pass on two and a half percent of their surplus wealth each year to set categories of people who need it. This is in addition to charitable giving, in which one is encouraged to give generously according to one's means.

Fourth among the pillars of Islam is *sawm*, or fasting during the month of Ramadan. This practice requires that every adult Muslim not eat, drink, or have sexual relations during daylight hours for a month. It does not suggest that these things are bad, far from it, but they are among the most fundamental of human urges. If one can take control of these things for a month, then one has a good training in *taqwa*, to remember God in every aspect of life and live accordingly.

The final pillar of Islam is the *hajj*, the annual pilgrimage to Makka, which is compulsory for all Muslims once in their lifetimes, if they have sufficient wealth and good health. This draws the pilgrim back into the Abrahamic chain of revelation by remembering practices associated with the earlier Prophets. It emphasizes the oneness of all humanity and brings the believer face to face with their judgment, from which there is no escape.

This chapter set out to paint the wider picture of creation and the place of every human being within it according to the Muslim perspective. We have seen that Islam sees itself as the last revelation in a series that goes back to Adam and spreads out to encompass all humanity. We have seen the need for revelation as guidance from God and for Prophets to receive and exemplify that guidance in every aspect of their lives. We have explored the Qur'an and Hadith of Muhammad as the sources for the Muslim way of life and concluded by touching on the key concept of *taqwa* in leading the individual into a life lived consciously in the presence of God. All these elements will be explored in much greater depth in forthcoming chapters, but now we should have the wider picture of how creation looks from a Muslim perspective.

Muslim children in the village of Sheik Yasin, Afghanistan. Photo: Linda Wiehl.

2

Muhammad, the Last in
the Chain of Prophets

Prophethood – a chain of Prophets – biblical Prophets – the role of a Prophet –
Abraham – the building of the Ka'ba – test of obedience to God – the *Hajj* – 'Id
al-Adha – birth and early life of Muhammad – the first revelation – early years
of Muhammad in Makka – some Muslims seek asylum with the Christians of
Abyssinia – the miraculous ascent to heaven – migration to Madina – beginning
of a settled community life – exemplary life of Muhammad – death and succession: the Sunni view – the Rightly-Guided Caliphs – the Shi'a view – history of
the Imams – the martyrdom of Imam Husayn

As we saw in the first chapter, Prophets are an essential part of the
Islamic worldview. The Qur'an tells us that a Prophet has been sent to
every people on earth (Q. 10:47, 16:38). They all brought in essence
the same message, guidance for every human being on how to live
a life perfectly in harmony with the will of the creator, that is, *islam*.
The Prophets received revelation from God, exemplified it in their
lives, and led communities on the straight path that leads to human
fulfilment through obedience to the divine will.

The sinlessness of the Prophets is worthy of further mention. If the
whole of the life of a Prophet is to be a role model for human beings,
then it follows that he or she cannot be sinning some of the time and
obedient to God's will at other times. If that were the case, we would
never know when we should follow a Prophet and when not. The
scholars of Islam have discussed this. Were Prophets sinless in every
aspect of their lives or just in those things that they did as Prophets?
The majority have said in all things, but a minority have said just in
those things that relate to being a Prophet. Some scholars have held
that Prophets might commit minor sins prior to the call to prophethood; even then, they immediately repented when they became aware
of such sins and so for us are an example of repentance too. This sinlessness is a gift or protection from God and not something of which they
could boast. Even Muhammad, as an act of humility, was told to seek
the forgiveness of God (Q. 4:105-106, 40:55). What sort of protection
from sin was this? Scholars have seen this as being through the gift of

knowledge from God. It was a kind of enlightenment that meant they saw things in a perfectly clear light.

We need to think a little more about the incident of Adam's fall from Paradise. We might ask: If Adam was a Prophet and all Prophets are sinless, then what happened with Adam? The scholars have spoken about this in three ways. First, they speak of Adam and Eve, who were totally innocent and had no experience of evil, making an error of judgment in mistaking evil for good rather than speaking of this act as a sin. Notice that God actually pointed out the location of the forbidden tree to them (Q. 2:35-39). Second, it seems that the fall of Adam and Eve was always in God's foreknowledge as God created both heaven and earth beforehand, but it was only after their fall that they were sent to the earth. Third, God is revealed in the Qur'an to be merciful, compassionate, and forgiving. This means that God "needed" (of course God does not *need* anything) to be able to show compassion and mercy to them in order that the full extent of God's character might be known. In this way, the error of judgment of Adam and Eve allowed the full wonder of God to be manifest in a way that would not be possible without it.

A chain of Prophets

The first Prophet sent to humankind was Adam, the first human being. In order to fulfil his duty of being the *khalifa*, or Regent of God on earth, he needed to receive divine guidance; only then could he freely submit and so become Abdallah, the Servant of God. After Adam there was an unknown number of Prophets, at least one to each of the peoples of the earth. The Qur'an names twenty-five of these Prophets, but this is not meant to be an exclusive list. There were others not named in the Qur'an (Q. 40:78). If we look at the list of those named, twenty-one are figures known in the biblical tradition (Q. 6:84-87, 19:56-57, 38:41-49). They are: Adam, Idris (Enoch), Nuh (Noah), Ibrahim (Abraham), Isma'il (Ishmael), Ishaq (Isaac), Lut (Lot), Ya'qub (Jacob), Yusuf (Joseph), Ayyub (Job), Musa (Moses), Harun (Aaron), Dhu 'l-Kifl (Ezekiel), Dawud (David), Sulayman (Solomon), Ilyas (Elijah), Alyasa' (Elisha), Yunus (Jonah), Zakariyya (Zachariah), Yahya (John the Baptist), and 'Isa (Jesus); of these, those mentioned most frequently (in order) are: Moses, Abraham, Noah, and Jesus. The remaining four are: Hud, who was sent to a South Arabian tribe (Q. 7:65-72, 12:50-60, 26:123-140, 46:21-26); Salih, who was sent to the Arabian tribe of Thamud (Q. 7:73-79, 12:61-68, 26:141-159;

Fig. 1. Prophets named in the Qur'an

Name in the Qur'an	Name in the Bible
Adam	Adam
Idris	Enoch
Nuh	Noah
Hud	
Salih	
Ibrahim	Abraham
Isma'il	Ishmael
Ishaq	Issac
Lut	Lot
Ya'qub	Jacob
Yusuf	Joseph
Shu'ayb	
Ayyub	Job
Musa	Moses
Harun	Aaron
Dhu 'l-Kifl	Ezekiel
Dawud	David
Sulayman	Solomon
Ilyas	Elijah
Alyasa'	Elisha
Yunus	Jonah
Zakariyya	Zachariah
Yahya	John the Baptist
'Isa	Jesus
Muhammad	

27:45-53); Shu'ayb, an Arabian Prophet sent to the people of Madyan (he has sometimes been associated with the biblical Jethro) (Q. 7:85-93, 12:84-95, 26:176-191, 29:36-37); and Muhammad, although the Qur'an is clear that Muhammad's coming was foretold by Jesus (Q. 61:6, 7:157) (Figure 1).

Several points must be mentioned in connection with these biblical identifications. First, the Bible would not necessarily refer to all these men as Prophets; some would be called Kings, like David or Solomon, or Patriarchs, like Abraham, Isaac, and Jacob, or the Lawgiver, Moses. When the Qur'an uses the term "Prophet," this is the highest dignity that can be given to any human being. The important point to note here is that just because a certain term is used in both biblical and Islamic traditions, it does not necessarily mean that it has the same meaning.

Second, the biblical tradition is capable of living with the sin of characters such as David, who according to the Bible wanted the wife of Uriah the Hittite and so planned for him to be killed in battle so that he could have her (2 Sam. 11–12). Such a sinful act is unthinkable in the Islamic tradition. That is not the way that Prophets behaved. This means that Islam does not accept this biblical account of David's sin. It must have been something that was later added into the biblical tradition, as it could not be an accurate account from David's life. Jews and Christians might find this a difficult point, as the Bible is clear that David sinned and the child he had with Bathsheba died as a result. To understand this from an Islamic perspective, it might be helpful for Christians to think how they would react if an ancient manuscript was dug up in the deserts of Sinai that said that Jesus had several mistresses and children by them. Christians would immediately want to disregard this manuscript as inauthentic on the grounds that it goes against everything we know and believe about the character of Jesus.

Third, several important biblical prophets, such as Isaiah, Jeremiah, and Amos, are unknown in the Qur'anic account, although, as the list in the Qur'an is not exhaustive, there is room to think that they may have been Prophets. Fourth, Jesus is listed as one of the Prophets in the Qur'an and thus accorded the highest dignity among human beings. While there are several unique aspects to the life of Jesus, which we will explore later, in the Qur'an he is not in any sense a divine person but a human being like the rest of humankind (Q. 3:59, 5:17, 9:30). Finally, the biblical tradition accepts that the later Prophets were sent to call people back to the original message of Moses when they had gone astray. Christians think of Jesus as coming to fulfil the earlier message and take it forward a significant additional step. In the same way, Muslims see Muhammad and the Qur'an as coming to reinforce and clarify the earlier revelations and correct the errors that had crept into the way that the followers of these earlier Prophets had interpreted their teaching, which was originally pure *islam* (Q. 5:15).

The Qur'an uses two terms when speaking of Prophets. The first is *rasul*, which is sometimes translated as "Messenger." These were Prophets who had been given a revealed Book or Scripture from God. Five of the above list are referred to as *rasul*: Abraham, Moses, David,

Jesus, and Muhammad. The second term is *nabi*, generally translated as Prophet and here referring to those who were sent to reinforce the earlier Books but did not receive a particular Book of their own.

Even given this distinction between *rasul* and *nabi*, Islam is clear that on the level of being a Prophet, all Prophets are equal. None is greater than the others (Q. 4:152). This does not prevent some Prophets from having particular characteristics. Moses had the distinction of being spoken to directly by God (Q. 4:164). Abraham is given the title Friend of God (Q. 4:125). Elijah was by tradition taken up into heaven while still alive (Q. 37:123-132). Jesus uniquely was born of a virgin by the command of God, without any father (Q. 3:47). Muhammad is also known as the Friend of God and is called the Last and the Seal of the Prophets. He was the Last, in that the Qur'an makes clear that there will be no more Prophets after him. And he is the Seal, in that he confirmed and validated all that had gone before him; he was the universal Prophet and for all time (Q. 33:40). Some scholars have spoken of the Light of Muhammad, that is, the essential Light of Prophecy, dwelling in all the earlier Prophets but then coming to its perfection in the person of Muhammad himself (Q. 4:174). Other scholars speak only of Muhammad being present in the original plan of God for creation, through him came the final revelation; and he was the final conveyor of guidance and the bringer of the final Shari'a.

The importance of Abraham

Abraham (Ibrahim) is the key link between the three faiths of Judaism, Christianity, and Islam. Scholars have spoken of these three as the Abrahamic faiths. In the biblical book Genesis (especially Gen. 16 and 21), we read of Abraham being called by God from Ur of the Chaldeans, in modern Iraq, to travel in faith to a new land where God would make a covenant with him and his descendants. Abraham and his wife Sarah grew old together childless, and so Sarah suggested to Abraham that he take her Egyptian maid, Hagar, as a second wife and have children with her. Abraham and Hagar together had a son called Ishmael (Isma'il). Later Sarah received a message from God that in her old age she too was to have a son. Then Abraham and Sarah together had Isaac. It was at this stage that Sarah started to suggest to Abraham that he send away Hagar and Ishmael as she, Sarah, now had a son. Abraham was reluctant to do this, but a message came from God to say that Abraham should send them away and that God would protect them and raise up a great nation from Ishmael. After this,

Fig. 2. The descendants of Abraham

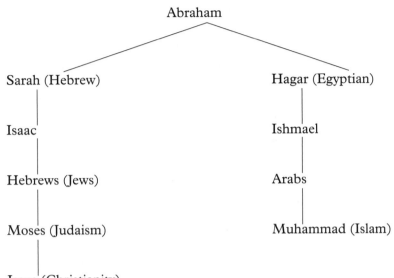

Judaism, Christianity, and Islam are cousins in the faith of
Abraham or the three Abrahamic faiths.

the biblical message remains silent about the future of Hagar and
Ishmael, except to say that both sons were present at the burial of
Abraham and that Ishmael's descendants settled in the lands between
Egypt and Syria (Gen. 25). The Talmud, the scholarly body of wisdom and commentary built up by the Jewish scholars through the
centuries, tells us that Abraham kept contact with Hagar and Ishmael
and used to visit them periodically. Many elements of the story of
Abraham are contained in the Qur'an (Q. 2:127-129, 6:75-83, 14:35-
41, 37:100-111).

The Islamic tradition takes up the story by recording that Hagar
and Isma'il (Ishmael) journeyed south into the Arabian desert until
they came to the site of the present day city of Makka (also sometimes written Mecca). Here their water supply was running short,
and so Hagar left the young Isma'il to go in search of water. There
were two small hills nearby, and so she ran to the top of each in turn
and scanned the horizon for any sign of water. Finding none, she
became more frantic and ran back and forth between the two hills.

Fearing the worst, she returned to where Isma'il lay, only to find that he had dug his heels into the ground and God had caused a spring of water to well-up in that place. That spring flows to this day and is called Zamzam.

Some years later, on one of his visits to Makka, Ibrahim and Isma'il together built the Ka'ba, the cuboid building that stands to this day at the center of Makka (Q. 2:125-127). This is held by Muslims to be the first building on earth built for the worship of God (Q. 3:96). At the time of its building, a white stone was brought by Gabriel from heaven and was incorporated into a corner of the Ka'ba. Over the centuries that followed, during which the Ka'ba became a place of idol worship before Muhammad, this stone turned black. This black stone is particularly reverenced by visitors to the Ka'ba today. When they had completed the building, Ibrahim and Isma'il walked around the Ka'ba praising God.

In both biblical and Qur'anic accounts, Ibrahim was put to the test by God to see if he would submit absolutely everything to the divine will. He was asked to sacrifice his son. In the Bible, it is Isaac who was to be sacrificed, but in the Islamic tradition it was Isma'il. The Qur'an is not explicit that the son to be sacrificed was Isma'il, but the overwhelming Muslim tradition interprets it that way (Q. 37:102-113). Here lies an important difference between the Jewish and Islamic traditions. Of course, for Muslims, the Qur'an is always to be preferred because it was sent down by God and has been preserved intact from that time onward. This means that Muslims must see the biblical version of the story as having become corrupt at some stage in its history. Another important difference is that, in the Bible, Isaac did not know what was about to happen, but in the Qur'an, Isma'il knew that he had been called by God to be sacrificed by his father, and so it was a double test of obedience. Would Ibrahim sacrifice his son, and would Isma'il agree to be sacrificed, at God's command?

According to the Islamic sources, on their way to the place of sacrifice, Ibrahim and Isma'il were tempted by the devil to rebel against God's command and not go through with the sacrifice. They are reported to have thrown stones at the devil to drive him away. The three traditional sites of these temptations are marked today with stone pillars. Ibrahim and Isma'il arrived at the place of sacrifice, but just before the act was committed, God stopped them, as they had proved their obedience in this ultimate test. A ram was provided for the sacrifice instead.

The *Hajj*

The self-understanding of Islam as standing in the line of the earlier Abrahamic tradition is made explicit in the annual pilgrimage of the *Hajj*. This key element in Muslim faith and practice shows clearly that Islam never sees itself as a new religion but rather as a continuation and completion of the revelations to earlier Prophets. Almost all the rites of this pilgrimage, which we will now explore, are primarily associated with Ibrahim, Hagar, and Isma'il. They were endorsed and given a definite form by the Prophet Muhammad in his own time, but the tradition dated back to the time of Ibrahim and Isma'il. During the centuries between this time and Muhammad, the rites had been corrupted by the Arab peoples who had become idol worshippers, but even up to the time of Muhammad's youth, some of these practices remained.

The *Hajj* is one of the five pillars of Islam and thus stands at the heart of the Islamic way of life (Q. 22:26-38). Every adult Muslim should make the *Hajj* once in his or her lifetime, provided that he or she has sufficient money and good health to do so (Q. 3:97). Having sufficient money is important because Islam is always practical: the balanced, middle way. It does not place on people a burden that would be impossible to bear (Q. 2:286). Even though around three million Muslims make the *Hajj* each year, most of the one billion Muslims alive today are unlikely ever to make the *Hajj* because of a lack of funds. One must not only have the cost of travel and accommodation but also be able to provide for one's family while away from home. Those who have insufficient funds or have family responsibilities that cannot be avoided are not obliged to make the *Hajj* unless and until their circumstances change. The same applies to those who cannot make the journey and perform the rites because of ill health or old age. The fact that people need to have financial security and be out of debt means that many who make the *Hajj* do so in their later years.

The *Hajj* takes place only once each year on five days in the Islamic month of Dhu 'l-Hijja. In these days of jet travel, it is easy to time the journey to coincide with the right days, but in earlier centuries when people had to travel for months or years on foot or riding on camels, it was always possible to arrive too late and have to remain in Makka until the next *Hajj* season. There is also a minor pilgrimage called *umra*, which only follows some of the rites, but this can be performed at any time of the year. This is not compulsory. Many people never make *umra*, while others perform *umra* many times in their lives.

The areas surrounding Makka, and the city to which Muhammad migrated to the north, now called Madina, are reserved for Muslims only as they are regarded as the holy places of Islam (Q. 9:28). Before the pilgrims making the *Hajj* enter the area surrounding the Ka'ba itself, they are required to take off their customary clothes and wear special garments. For men, these consist of two white unsewn cloths, one wrapped around the lower body and the other around the upper body. Women are required to wear a plain dress and head-covering but without any jewelery or ornamentation. This clothing is called *ihram*, and once it is put on, the pilgrims have entered into the spirit and rites of the *Hajj*; they must do no harm to any living creature and refrain from all aggressive speech and sexual relations. It would be immodest for women to dress in loose-fitting sheets, but the spirit of *ihram* applies equally to them clothed in their simple dresses. Many men follow the custom of keeping their *ihram* to act as their shroud when they are buried.

The importance of *ihram* is that it symbolizes the absolute equality of human beings before God. Muslims from every culture, ethnic group, language, and part of the world, rich and poor alike, are dressed identically to stress their common humanity before God. The American Muslim civil rights leader in the 1960s, Malcolm X, was originally a member of an extremist black Muslim group that taught black racial supremacy over white people. It was only when he went on the *Hajj* that he encountered for the first time this spirit of the absolute oneness of human beings. It completely changed his life. When he returned from the *Hajj*, he left the extremist group and embraced mainstream Islam, where he had found the oneness of the human family before God, which is color-blind.

The Ka'ba is the earthly focus of Muslims worldwide whenever they pray. Five times each day, Muslims all around the world are required to turn in the direction of the Ka'ba for their formal prayers (Q. 2:144). Now during the *Hajj*, their bodies follow that daily direction so that they pray surrounding the Ka'ba itself. The Ka'ba is generally covered by a black cloth, the *kiswa*, with verses from the Qur'an embroidered into it with gold thread. This is raised during the days of *Hajj* to reveal the stone walls beneath. Each year it is renewed at the time of *Hajj*, and the old one is cut into pieces, which become the treasured mementos of some of the pilgrims.

The first rite of the *Hajj* is called *tawaf*. During this rite, pilgrims walk around the Ka'ba seven times in a counterclockwise direction, that is from right to left, as did Ibrahim and Isma'il, praising God. When they pass the Black Stone, they salute it by raising their right hands. Those close enough will touch it or reverence it with a kiss. This respect to the Black Stone was part of the practice of Muhammad. Beside the Ka'ba, a stone marks the Place of Ibrahim, where tradition has it that Ibrahim used to pray. If possible, pilgrims will try to pray at this special place.

Next comes the *sa'y*, or the running between the two small hills of al-Safa and al-Marwa. This commemorates the search by Hagar for water for Isma'il. Pilgrims perform this "running," actually a mixture of walking and jogging, seven times. The stress here is on seeking the providence and mercy of God. After this, Hagar returned to Isma'il, who had been blessed with the waters of Zamzam. Pilgrims drink this water and take bottles of it home to friends and relatives.

The next day, pilgrims make their way to a plain surrounding the Mount of Mercy about twenty kilometers from Makka called the Plain of Arafat. Tradition has it that this was the site where Adam and Eve were reconciled to God and forgiven. This was the site of the Farewell Sermon of Muhammad, when he made the *Hajj* shortly before his death. This is the high point of the *Hajj*. The Islamic understanding is that God has imposed upon himself the law of mercy (Q. 6:12). The responsibility lies upon the individual to take advantage of the mercy of God, which is on offer always to those who seek it with a sincere heart. The pilgrims will have been preparing for this moment for a long time. They will have searched their hearts and brought all their sins before God on this day for forgiveness. Four elements are required in seeking the forgiveness of God. First, the person must recognize and acknowledge their sin. Second, there must be an end to this sinful practice. Third, the person must resolve that, with God's help, they will not sin again. Fourth, if it is possible, recompense must be made to put right the effects of the sin. If people have a pure *niyya*, or intention, and seek God's mercy, then they may be sure that all their sins are forgiven (Q. 4:116).

The pilgrims stand on the Plain of Arafat in prayer for some hours. It is as though they were anticipating the Day of Judgment itself when all will stand before God for the final judgment that will result in reward in Paradise or punishment in hell (Q. 6:21-31, 22:17). This is the most intense moment when each individual stands before God in deepest humility, with profound trust in God's mercy. Here prayers will be offered for family and friends and for all human beings. Many pilgrims speak of a deep sense of unburdening and peace descending on them on this day. Of course, God is not limited by any particular time or place. The mercy of God knows no bounds. Every Muslim is taught to seek forgiveness from God immediately wherever they are as soon as they become aware of some sin in their lives. The standing on the Plain of Arafat only writes in large letters what is there in every time and place. The Muslim who is prevented from making the *Hajj* for some good reason is in no way deprived of the mercy and forgiveness of God, provided they seek it wherever they are with a pure intention.

The pilgrims begin their return journey from Arafat with a sense that now they are truly *muslim*, that they have submitted all to the will of God and stand in great humility before their Lord. They take a few hours of rest in the open at Muzdalifa, part-way toward Makka. Here they collect pebbles for the last rite of the *Hajj*, the stoning of the pillars in a place called Mina, which recalls the temptation of Ibrahim and Isma'il. Having been forgiven by God on Arafat, the pilgrims gather at each of the pillars and throw small pebbles to symbolize their rejection of the temptations of the devil in their lives from this time onward. They are thus reinforcing the spirit of Arafat. On the first day, they throw seven pebbles at one pillar only, but then they return on two subsequent days to stone all three.

This day is 'Id al-Adha, or the Festival of Sacrifice. Traditionally, each pilgrim now took an animal and sacrificed it to God, as did Ibrahim and Isma'il. Given the numbers of pilgrims today and the need to ensure that animals do not suffer, these sacrifices are now mostly performed by trained slaughtermen who act in the name of each pilgrim. During recent years, huge abattoirs have been built to ensure hygiene, and the meat is butchered and loaded into freezer trucks or canned for later distribution among the poor in various countries. Prayers are said; pilgrims clip their hair or shave their heads and take off their *ihram*. They return to Makka to repeat *tawaf*.

The pilgrims can now put the title *al-Hajj*, for men, or *al-Hajjah*, for women, in front of their names. Most will make the journey to Madina to visit the grave of the Prophet Muhammad, who is buried there. Then begins the homeward journey. For most, this will be the journey of a lifetime, and they will never return to make an additional *Hajj*. For those who can afford it, it is possible to make the *Hajj* in future years. Sometimes people who have the intention of making *Hajj* but cannot do so for a good reason, such as poor health, pay the expenses of someone who already has made the *Hajj* to go again to make the pilgrimage on their behalf. The physical strain of the *Hajj* is considerable, especially for those who live in cooler climates and are not used to the sun. Wherever three million people are gathered in one place, especially when a high proportion of them are elderly, there are bound to be deaths each day through natural causes. To die while making the

Hajj is considered a great blessing. Traditionally pilgrims are required to put all their affairs in order and make their will before setting off for the *Hajj*. Should they die in Makka or Madina, they then would have the privilege of being buried there. The fact that pilgrims are dressed in their burial clothes and that nearly every one of the five daily prayers during *Hajj* is followed by the funeral prayers of someone who has died keeps the focus on our human mortality and our accountability before God.

The *Hajj* can only be performed in Makka on the set days each year, but 'Id al-Adha is celebrated throughout the Muslim world. It is a great festival with each Muslim sacrificing an animal and distributing some of the meat to the poor and needy. This sacrificed meat is called *qurban*. In countries where there is no shortage of food, the custom has grown up of sending a sum of money (also sometimes called *qurbani*) to a poor country, which can be used to buy an animal, have it sacrificed in the name of the donor, and the meat distributed to the poor in that place. This can be organized by families, Muslim associations, or relief agencies operating in disadvantaged countries.

In traditional societies, the whole town or quarter of a larger city would gather together in an open space for 'Id prayers. In the West, these prayers usually take place at the principal mosques in a city, where there may have to be several congregations to accommodate all those who want to pray. People take a full bath (*ghusl*) early in the morning, then wear new clothes. Gifts are exchanged with family and friends, and *sadaqa* is given to those in need. Special *du'a* are recited. Everyone goes on a round of visits to exchange greetings and share in food. Many will go to visit the graves of deceased members of their family. Games and sports are organized.

This study of the *Hajj*, as one of the five principal practices of Islam, has been placed in this chapter for a particular reason. It demonstrates clearly the fact that Islam is part of a much older tradition that goes back through Muhammad, through Ibrahim, to be linked with Adam and Eve and thus the whole human family down through the ages. Islam is part of this Abrahamic family of faiths, of which Muhammad, to whom we now turn, is held by Muslims to be the Last and the Seal of the Prophets.

Fig. 3. Map of the Arabian Peninsula

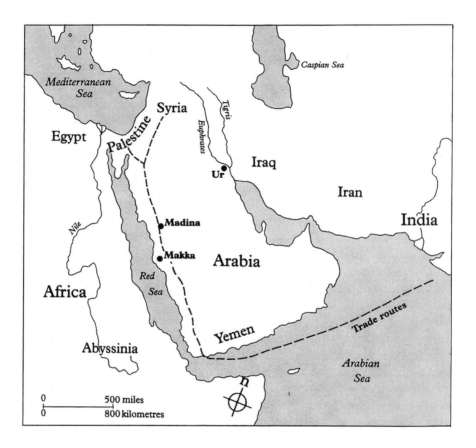

The birth and early life of Muhammad

Muhammad was born in Makka into a merchant family. His grand-father, Abd al-Muttalib, was one of the leading citizens of the city. Shortly before the time of Muhammad's birth, probably in the year 570 c.e., there was an invasion of Makka by an Abyssinian army. This army was special because it included war elephants, which were seen for the first time in Makka on this occasion. It was to be called "The Year of the Elephant." As the invaders were about to attack the Ka'ba to destroy it, a huge flock of birds arrived from nowhere and dropped stones on the invaders to kill them or drive them away (Q. 105). This was taken as the action of God in saving the Ka'ba from destruction.

Muhammad's father died before he was born, and his mother died at the time he was about two years old. Shortly afterward his grandfather died, and so Muhammad was brought up by his uncle Abu Talib (d. c.619). As a boy, Muhammad spent some time minding sheep before he was trained in the business of his uncle as a camel-train merchant. Muhammad would go on trading journeys with his uncle. Makka was on the great trade route that ran up from the coast in Yemen toward Syria and Egypt.

On one of these journeys, when Muhammad was about twelve, they were crossing the Syrian Desert on their way to Damascus. A Christian hermit called Bahira lived in that area. He was well-versed in Christian wisdom. When he saw the camel train approaching, he was inspired to approach it and seek out Muhammad. After questioning him, he told Abu Talib that he had seen the sign of prophecy on Muhammad and that his uncle should take good care of the boy as he was destined for greatness.

Camel-train merchants at that time acted as the agents of the owners of the goods they carried to far off markets. They agreed to a price that they would try to obtain for the goods, but no money would change hands until the merchant returned. If the goods were stolen on the journey or a lower price had to be accepted, it was the owners who suffered the loss. Much depended on the word of the merchant. Not surprisingly, some of them were less than honest and cheated the owners of their money. It is against this background that it is import-ant to note that Muhammad, as a young man involved in trading, was given the nickname *al-Amin*, meaning "The Trustworthy One." He obviously earned this through a reputation for fair dealing.

Muhammad also had a reputation for being a thinker and a source of wise counsel. An incident is reported that, when he was a young man, he was crossing the square in Makka when the Ka'ba was being rebuilt. A dispute had broken out among the leading families as to who should have the honor of replacing the Black Stone in the wall. Muhammad solved the problem by calling for a blanket and placing the stone on it. Then a representative of each of the leading families took hold of the edges of the blanket and thus the Black Stone was jointly carried back to its place in the Ka'ba where Muhammad replaced it himself.

In his early twenties, Muhammad was employed by a wealthy woman named Khadija (d. *c.*619). She had a camel-train business and employed Muhammad as her manager on account of his reputation for trustworthy and honest dealing. When he was around twenty-five, Khadija proposed to Muhammad and married him. They had two sons, who died in infancy. One of their children was Fatima (d. 633), who later married Ali (d. 661).

At this time, most of the clans in the Arabian peninsula were idol-worshippers. There were many of these idols, some belonging to a particular family and some recognized by much wider groups. The Ka'ba itself had become a center for these idols, and it was said that there were some 360 of them in, on, and around the building (Q. 53:19-23). Some of the Arabs would not be associated with idolatry and instead worshipped the one God, but without much knowledge about God. They were called *hanif* (monotheist seeker) and used the Arabic title Allah (the one and only God) for God. Muhammad's family belonged to this group; his father was called Abdallah, the Servant of God. It was in this tradition that Muhammad grew up.

There were also some Jewish clans in Arabia at this time, and several are recorded as living in the city of Yathrib, which would later be known as Madina when Muhammad moved there. Some Christians were also to be found who belonged to various branches of Christianity. A few were probably resident in Makka, and others were to be found in villages in the Arabian peninsula. Some of these had distinctly unorthodox understandings of Christianity, like the Collyridians, who were condemned by the Qur'an for worshipping Jesus and Mary as gods in addition to God (Q. 5:116).

The first revelation

It was the practice of Muhammad to spend time in deep meditation and spiritual retreat. He often took himself off to a cave on Mount Hira just outside Makka, where he would spend days and nights in meditation. The Arabs at this time worked on a lunar calendar with each month beginning with the new moon. One of their months was called Ramadan. In the year 610, on an odd-numbered night toward the end of the month of Ramadan, an event took place that was to change Muhammad's life. As it was near the end of the month, it was a dark night with almost no moonlight.

A light appeared on the distant horizon and drew closer to Muhammad (Q. 53:1-18). Eventually it took on a form and was identified as the Angel Jibril (Gabriel). Throughout the biblical tradition, Gabriel was identified as the angel who brought messages from God. Jibril halted about two bowshots away from Muhammad and spoke the single Arabic word *iqra*, being a word of command with the meaning of "recite" or "speak forth." Muhammad did not know what he was supposed to say, and so Jibril drew closer and again said *iqra*. At this, Muhammad said that he did not know what he was supposed to recite, as he was *ummi*. This term is best translated as unlettered or without book-learning. Like most people at this time, Muhammad had not received formal education in reading and writing. The meaning here is clear. If Jibril is commanding Muhammad to recite something, then it must be given to him by God, as it cannot come from Muhammad's own knowledge. From a Muslim perspective, this is important, as one accusation later to be made about the Qur'an was that Muhammad gathered it together from various books that were in circulation at that time (Q. 10:37-38, 17:88, 52:33-34).

Jibril approached Muhammad and embraced him. During this embrace, the heart of Muhammad, as the seat of all wisdom and knowledge, was purified in receiving the revelation of the Qur'an. Christians might like to consider this purification of the heart of Muhammad, to make it a fitting resting place for the Word of God in the Qur'an, in the light of the virginity of Mary, which is held to have been a sign of her purity so that she might be a repository for the Word of God in Jesus. This time, when Jibril stepped back and commanded Muhammad *iqra*, the first verses of the Qur'an just erupted from the heart of Muhammad and were there on his lips. These words are recorded in the Qur'an (Q. 96:1-5). These were the first verses that were revealed in the process of the revelation of the Qur'an that went on for the next twenty-three years. We will look at this in more detail in the next chapter.

After Jibril had left, Muhammad went home to Khadija, his wife, who comforted him. When she learned the story, she sent for her cousin Waraqa, a Christian. When he heard of Muhammad's encounter with the angel, he confirmed that in his Christian tradition such things were known and that Muhammad had been called by God to carry a message into the world. Khadija realized that Muhammad had been called by God and became his first follower.

This incident in 610 is celebrated collectively each year on the twenty-seventh night of Ramadan as the Night of Power (*Laylat al-Qadr*). According to the Qur'an (Q. 97:3), this night is "better than a thousand months," when angels are sent throughout the earth seeking those who are at prayer so that their requests might be granted by God. It is a widespread Muslim custom to spend the whole of this night in worship. Some Muslims will observe the Night of Power on each of the last five odd nights of Ramadan, as the precise night is uncertain.

The early years in Makka

For some time after this first revelation, Muhammad was left without further revelations from God. This period ended with the revelation of Q. 93:1-8. The early verses of the Qur'an revealed in Makka have the quality of calling people to the worship of God alone and for an end to worshipping idols. People were called to live ethical lives and to take particular care of the weak in society. All this was to be done in the knowledge that human beings face judgment by God after their earthly lives. When Muhammad began to repeat these verses in public and call upon people to follow them, he faced opposition from the Makkans. One reason for this was that they held fast to their idol-worship and made money out of the pilgrims who came to worship their idols at the Ka'ba. The first male converts to Islam were Ali, the cousin and son-in-law of Muhammad, and Abu Bakr (d. 634), later to become the first Caliph, followed by Uthman (d. 656), later the third Caliph. In these early years, the number of converts was small, and they faced persecution for following the message of Muhammad.

Muhammad and his immediate family were spared the worst excesses of this persecution because they were protected by the Prophet's uncle, Abu Talib. Others were beaten, denied food and drink, and given other tortures. One of those tortured was Bilal, a black slave. He eventually was set free and later took on the responsibility for calling the Muslim community to attend regular prayers.

In 615 C.E. the persecution was such that Muhammad sent a party of the Muslims to seek refuge in Abyssinia, where there was a Christian king. When they arrived and told their story, they were asked by the king to recite some of the verses of the Qur'an that had so far been revealed. When the king heard them, he recognized that they were a message from God and said that the Muslim belief was very like his own Christian belief. He gave the Muslims refuge in his land for as long as they needed it. They remained there until after Muhammad moved north to Madina. Back in Makka the persecutions continued and indeed became worse after the death, probably in 619, of Muhammad's uncle and protector, Abu Talib. In the same year, Khadija died. She had been a great support and strength to the young Muslim community.

During these later years in Makka, Muhammad underwent a miraculous night journey (*isra*) and ascent into heaven (*mi'raj*) (Q. 17:1). Muhammad was woken one night in his sleep by an angel and seated on a wonderful and mysterious mount called *al-buraq*. Thus he rode as far as Jerusalem. He stepped down from *al-buraq* on the Temple Mount and was taken up to heaven from that place, known as the Rock, as in the Dome on the Rock. Muhammad travelled up through the heavens until he came into the presence of God, where an audience took place. It was at this time that Muhammad, among other things, received the instruction that his followers should say their formal prayers at five set times each day. He then descended from heaven, returned to the Temple Mount, and was taken by *al-buraq* back to Makka. The scholars are divided as to whether this was a physical journey or a spiritual one. It is clear that it was mysterious in that it all happened in one night. Some sources have it that in rising, Muhammad knocked over a pitcher of water, and when he returned, the splash thus caused was just hitting the floor. It is this association with the *mi'raj* that makes Jerusalem, along with Makka and Madina, one of the three holy cities of Islam. The Dome on the Rock has long been a site of visitation for Muslims. Each year, the *mi'raj* is celebrated as the *Laylat al-Mi'raj*, the Night of the Ascension of the Prophet, on the twenty-seventh night of the month of Rajab.

The migration to Madina

In the year 620, a group of leaders from the city of Yathrib, about three hundred miles north of Makka, came to the Prophet to listen to his teaching and report back to their people. This led to a large delegation from Yathrib coming to Makka in 622 to invite Muhammad to come to live in their city as their leader. They would convert to Islam, and he would establish an Islamic way of life in Yathrib, which from now on would be called *Madinat al-Nabi*, the City of the Prophet, or just Madina. There had been disputes between the clans there, and they felt the need for wise leadership and a new way of life.

Small groups of Muslims moved north to Madina during the first part of 622. The Makkans by this time had decided to assassinate Muhammad but were outwitted when Ali slept in the Prophet's place so that he could not be found. Muhammad hid for three days in a cave on his way to Madina. Tradition has it that a spider spun a web over the mouth of the cave while he was inside so that the attackers believed that no one could have passed to hide within (Q. 9:40). In September of that year, Muhammad arrived in Madina to take up the responsibility of leading the community. This event, known as the Hijra, or migration, is so important in the history of Islam that it marked the start of a new system of dating. This is normally referred to as A.H., from the Latin, *Anno Hegira*, "in the Year of the Hijra." As Islamic years are made up of twelve lunar months, they are about eleven days shorter than solar years. This makes the calculation of dates from A.H. to C.E. quite complicated. In many books on Islam both dates are given, e.g. 633/1236.

Those who migrated from Makka were known as the *muhajirun*, or migrators, and those in Madina who had converted to Islam were called the *ansar*, or helpers. These two communities mixed well together, with the *ansar* sharing their lands and businesses with the *muhajirun*. This was a practical example of there being one single community, or *umma*, of Muslims, who should bear one another's burdens (Q. 9:71, 49:10, 21:92). So as not to show favoritism to any one family or group, when he arrived in Madina, Muhammad allowed his camel to wander around freely. Where the camel stopped, he built his house and the first mosque in Madina, the spot now marked by the Masjid al-Nabi, or the Prophet's Mosque.

This was a time of rapid change for the young Muslim community. They were now settled, relatively free from persecution, and able to establish a regular community rhythm. The verses of the Qur'an revealed from this time onward also evolved. These verses are often described as being more constitutional, that is, laying down the pattern of life for a settled community. An important document dates from this time, often referred to as the Constitution of Madina. This acknowledged Muhammad as the leader and final judge under God. There was to be a mutual defense treaty between all the parties in Madina. The Jewish communities that lived in that city were regarded as an *umma* alongside the Muslims, sharing in the duties and rights of fellow citizens.

There were battles with the Makkans, who still feared that Muhammad would harm their trade and way of life. Three battles are remembered particularly: the Battle of Badr in 624, the Battle of

Uhud in 625, and the Battle of the Ditch or Trench in 627. Some of the Jewish clans in Madina had strong trading and economic links with the Makkans. This led to a conflict of loyalties. After the Battle of Badr it appeared that one Jewish clan had been openly hostile and treacherous toward the Muslims. The clan was besieged by the Muslims until they surrendered. The Arab custom in cases of treason was that the men should be executed, the women and children sold into slavery, and all property confiscated. Muhammad decided to show leniency and sent them into exile with most of their goods. After the Battle of Uhud, another Jewish clan was openly hostile and had conspired with the Makkans. Again they were shown clemency and sent into exile with their property. Finally, in the Battle of the Ditch, the largest remaining Jewish clan openly conspired with the enemy; perhaps they thought that the Makkans would win and wanted to be on the victorious side. This time Muhammad followed the Arab custom of going to arbitration. The decision was reached that no more leniency should be shown but the customary punishment should be applied; the men were executed, the women and children sold into slavery, and all their goods were forfeit. These treacherous acts provided the context for some of the harsh verses about Jews in the Qur'an (Q. 2:40-42, 5:41-42,82, 9:30).

Muhammad's influence had begun to spread much wider than just the city-state of Madina. Many of the local Arab clans came to him to make treaties so that they could all live in peace, and a good number of these Arabs embraced Islam. One group that came in 631 were from the Christian village of Najran, to the south of Makka. This delegation comprised both community and religious leaders, including their bishop. They were received with courtesy by Muhammad in his mosque and, when the time came for them to pray, they were allowed to offer their prayers in his mosque. This was an important sign. Even though Muhammad entered into a detailed discussion with them about the person of Jesus and invited them to convert to Islam, he still acknowledged that they were worshipping God, or else he would not have allowed them to pray in his mosque. Many verses from the Qur'an were revealed at this time relating to the earlier revelation to the Christians (Q. 3:1-80), and Muhammad challenged them to a mutual cursing to see who was telling the truth before God. The Christians accepted that Muhammad was sent by God and so did not want to engage in the challenge. They agreed to leave in peace and follow their Christian way of life in Najran. They had such respect for Muhammad and his young Muslim community that they asked him to appoint a wise Muslim to live among them to settle any disputes that they could themselves not resolve.

Fig. 4. The direction of prayer in Makka and Madina

Early years in Makka

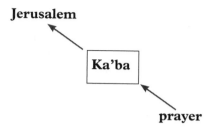

First sixteenth months in Madina

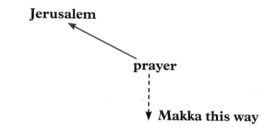

The *qibla* established

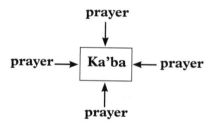

Although the young Muslim community now had moved to Madina, Makka still remained the spiritual focus of Islam. The early Muslims in Makka used to offer their prayers at the Ka'ba so that they were also facing Jerusalem. When they moved to Madina, for the first sixteen months they faced Jerusalem for prayer. Then verses were revealed commanding the faithful to change their direction for prayer so that they faced toward the Ka'ba in Makka (Q. 2:142-145,149-150). This direction is observed by Muslims worldwide and is called the *qibla*, or direction.

Muhammad made a treaty with the Makkans that he could lead a group of Muslims from Madina to make the *Hajj* or annual pilgrimage in 629. So that there would be no trouble, Makka was evacuated for three days. The same peaceful situation occurred in 630, but in 631 someone was killed, and so Muhammad marched south with an army. The Makkans surrendered almost without bloodshed or loss of property. They agreed to embrace Islam, and a Muslim government was installed. The first act of Muhammad in the Muslim city of Makka was to smash all the idols in, on, and around the Ka'ba so that it would be purified for the worship of God. Muslims were now free to live in Makka and make their pilgrimages in peace. Muhammad made only one more *Hajj*, in 632, shortly before his death, at which he gave what is often called his Farewell Sermon on the Plain of Arafat.

The exemplary life of the Prophet

Muhammad was not only the conveyor of the Qur'an; he also perfectly put it into practice in his own life and in all that he said and did. One of his wives, A'isha (d. 678), was once asked what it was like to live with the Prophet. She said that if one reads the Qur'an, one knows about Muhammad, and if one sees Muhammad, one knows about the Qur'an. Everything about Muhammad was an interpretation of the message of the Qur'an for human living. This means that the biography of Muhammad, or *sira*, was extremely important, and many accounts of his life have been compiled through the years. Through the purifying gift of knowledge from God, Muhammad, like all the Prophets, was rendered sinless. This meant that his every word and action became an example. This did not mean that he was an expert on everything. There was a famous occasion when a date farmer asked him for guidance on agricultural practice and was told that he had been growing dates all his life and so knew more about it than the Prophet.

As long as Khadija lived, Muhammad was married to her alone. In the years after her death, Muhammad contracted twelve marriages with women from various Arab clans. Sometimes these were political unions to cement good relations with a particular clan. Sometimes they were acts of kindness to take in and care for a widow whose husband had been lost in battle. The Qur'an permits a Muslim man to marry up to four wives, provided he can treat them all equally (Q. 4:2-3), but the case of Muhammad was a singular exception, explicitly allowed by the Qur'an to provide practical guidance on how to treat all sorts of women fairly (Q. 33:50-52). In a culture of monogamy, even though many people have several partnerships in their lives, polygamy seems somehow shocking. It must be remembered that when contrasted to earlier generations, including examples in the Old Testament, Muhammad had far fewer wives than many other leaders.

The way in which Muhammad lived has become a role model for Muslims down through the centuries (Q. 33:21,45-46). He set the example of hospitality and trustworthiness in all his dealings. He showed humility in his relations with other people and always claimed only to be the Servant of God. In practical ways, too, he was a role model. He often dressed in white, and so many Muslims now dress in white, especially for prayers. He wore his beard and hair at certain lengths, and so men imitate him in this. He often wore a turban with one end hanging loose, cleaned his teeth with a particular fibrous piece of wood, sat to drink, slept in a certain position, and so on; all these actions are imitated by pious Muslims in various cultures around the world.

Because of their great love and respect for Muhammad, Muslims react with great sensitivity to any insult or bad word spoken about him. Whenever his name is mentioned, it is immediately followed by saying "peace and blessings be upon him" (Q. 33:56). Such respect is applied to all the Prophets, and compliments are added to all their names. It was out of respect for Jesus that Muslims in Britain objected strongly to a contemporary film about him that they felt showed him disrespect. They could not understand why British Christians did not object in the same way. There is a saying among Muslims that "one word against the person of the Prophet is a thousand times worse than the vilest insult against my own mother." It is no surprise then that when Muslims saw Salman Rushdie's book *The Satanic Verses* as insulting Muhammad and other Prophets, they wanted to have it taken out of circulation and the author censored.

Some Muslims celebrate the Birthday of the Prophet, *Mawlid al-Nabi*, every year on the twelfth of the Islamic month of Rabi' al-Awwal. There are often processions and speeches in honor of the Prophet. Poems are written and recited, and lectures are given to make his life and teaching better known.

Muhammad died in June 632 and was buried in his house in Madina. Later a tomb was built over his grave, and eventually this was incorporated into his mosque. The mosque was hugely extended through the centuries, and now Muhammad's tomb can be found in the Masjid al-Nabi. Many Muslims go there on visitation and pray near his tomb in the belief that he can hear them and lend his prayers to theirs.

Death and succession: The Sunni view

It is no surprise to us in any culture that sometimes the events of history are told differently by different groups. Shortly before the death of Muhammad in 632, his last remaining son, Ibrahim, the son of Mary the Copt, died so that he had no surviving sons. Soon after the death of Muhammad, a division arose over the question of his succession. The group that became the majority among Muslims is called the Sunnis, that is, those who follow the tradition of Muhammad (as they see it). They account for about ninety percent of Muslims today and are found all over the world. This group held that Muhammad did not say who was to succeed him after his death nor did he lay down a procedure for selecting his successor. Three things were clear. Muhammad was the last of the Prophets, and so they were looking for a leader and not another Prophet. There was to be a single focus of leadership within the Muslim community; this person was to be the spiritual leader, the final judge of disputes, and the political or military leader (and therefore had to be male). This leader was of course to rule under God and according to the guidance of the Qur'an, but leadership was open to any man based on his piety and wisdom. Leadership was to be a meritocracy and not limited to any one family or clan.

After the death of Muhammad, one of his closest companions and one of the earliest converts to Islam, Abu Bakr (d. 634), was selected as the leader or Caliph. A group of the leading figures in Madina simply got together and selected him. He was presented to the people and accepted but not without some dissenting voices. Abu Bakr did not live long as Caliph (632–634), but before his death he nominated his successor, Umar (d. 644), who was accepted by the majority of people and ruled as Caliph from 634 to 644. Toward the end of his life, Umar nominated a group of leaders who were to act as an electoral college after his death. They chose Uthman (d. 656) as the third Caliph to the acclaim of most people. Finally he was followed by Ali (d. 661), the son-in-law and cousin of Muhammad, who was elected by the people. It is important that all these Caliphs, even though they were selected by different methods, were acclaimed by the people who accepted their leadership. This was a golden age, and these four leaders are generally referred to as the Rightly Guided Caliphs, the *Rashidun*.

They are contrasted with the dynasties of rulers who came after them. These were more secular in their lifestyles, and the tradition grew up of keeping the Caliphate within a certain clan or family, like the Umayyads, who held the Caliphate from 661 to 750.

Death and succession: The Shi'a view

The minority group among the Muslims, the Shi'a, saw things differently. They base their understanding on a particular verse of the Qur'an (Q. 33:33), which speaks of the Family of the Prophet, the *Ahl al-Bayt* (literally "the Family of the Household"), as being made pure and spotless. This verse is held by the Shi'a to refer to an incident in which Muhammad, his daughter Fatima and son-in-law Ali, and their two sons Hasan (d. *c.*669) and Husayn (d. 680) were all called "under the blanket" and purified by God. This rendered them the highest of creation, and from this family must come the legitimate successors of Muhammad.

On the return journey from the last *Hajj* that Muhammad made, in March 632, he halted the Muslims with him at the oasis of Ghadir al-Khumm. Here he publicly raised the hands of Ali and said that whoever held Muhammad as their leader should regard Ali in a similar way. This is held by the Shi'a to be evidence of the divine selection, supported by the action of Muhammad, to say that Ali should be his successor. All the leading members of the Muslim community of Madina, including the three men who were later to be acclaimed as the first three Rightly Guided Caliphs, were present at this time. They all then pledged allegiance to Ali as the legitimate successor of Muhammad.

Immediately after the death of Muhammad, in June 632, Ali was engaged in the preparations for the burial of the Prophet's body. It was at this time that the group of leaders met and decided to select Abu Bakr as their Caliph. When Ali found out what had happened, he did not protest, as it would be unworthy for him to claim leadership for himself, although he made his position clear. Similarly, he remained silent when Umar and later Uthman were selected to succeed Abu Bakr. It was not until 656, with the death of Uthman, that Ali assumed his rightful place.

In Shi'a terminology, the leaders of the community in succession to Muhammad are called Imams. Therefore Ali was the first legitimate Imam, and the first three Rightly Guided Caliphs were in fact usurpers who had no right to this position. Those who supported Ali were called the Party of Ali, or *Shi'a Ali*, hence the name Shi'a.

The understanding of Imams among the Shi'a has developed considerably, stemming from the close relationship between Muhammad and Ali. Muhammad is reported once to have said, "Ali is my *nafs*." The term *nafs* has many shades of meaning including soul, spirit, inner self, and mind. The understanding grew up that Ali was of the same inner light as Muhammad and thus inherited from him this light of divine knowledge. As such, an Imam is held to be infallible in interpreting the Qur'an and the Islamic way of life. He does not receive revelation from God (*wahy*) as Muhammad did when the Qur'an was sent down to him, but the Imam receives a divine inspiration (*ilham*), which gives him the supreme authority and guidance to issue laws that are binding on all Muslims. The Imams are sinless guides of the community and possess both spiritual and political authority.

As the Imams are infallible and divinely guided, they have the duty to nominate their successors, and they must be accepted by the community as God's choice. All Imams must come from the Family of the Prophet, descended through Fatima and Ali. The selection does not necessarily pass to the eldest son, as in a monarchical system, but each Imam must nominate his successor on the basis of piety and wisdom according to the guidance of God. Ali was followed by Hasan, the second Imam, and then by Husayn as the third Imam.

Not all the Muslim community agreed to the appointment of Hasan as Ali's successor, and so it was at this point that the division really took place. The majority followed Mu'awiya (d. 680) as the fifth Caliph. He was the founder of the Umayyad dynasty, which ruled from 661 to 750. The Shi'a accepted Ali's nomination of Hasan as the second Imam. Mu'awiya's base was in Damascus, while the Shi'a were strongest around the city of Kufa in Iraq, which Ali had made his base and in which he was killed. The Shi'a objected to the corruption that they saw among the Umayyads and wanted to keep away from such practices to follow the pure Islamic way of life as taught by Muhammad and Ali.

After the death of Hasan, the Imamate passed to his brother Husayn. In 680, Husayn was leading a party of Shi'a believers from Madina toward Kufa when they were ambushed at Karbala in Iraq, where a siege and battle took place. The Umayyads vastly outnumbered the Shi'a, and a massacre took place in which Husayn and his followers were killed and their bodies desecrated. This was seen as a martyrdom in the cause of right, and the events at Karbala play a most significant part in the lives of Shi'a Muslims until today.

Husayn's death took place on the tenth of the month of Muharram 680. It is commemorated today by ten days of intense mourning culminating in Ashura Day, the tenth of the month. The period of mourning continues for a further thirty days. In the days leading up to Ashura, the events of each day are remembered, for example the heroic attempts by some of the party to bring back water to the others, and the attempt by Husayn to plead for the life of his infant son, who was eventually killed by the Umayyads in his father's arms. Ashura Day itself is marked with the most intense mourning, the reenactment of the final battle and the death of Husayn. The spirit of the commemoration is to call on Shi'a Muslims to rededicate themselves to absolute obedience to the divine will, even if this should mean accepting martyrdom in the cause of right. "If only we had been with you on that day, we would have remained firm and died martyrs alongside you." This spirit of mourning is often accompanied by beating the chest in anguish and, in its more extreme form, can lead to people cutting themselves to show their willingness to shed their blood if called upon.

One of Husayn's sons, Ali ibn Husayn (*ibn* means "the son of"), also known as Zayn ul-Abidin (d. 712 or 713), was ill on the day of his father's death and so took no part in the battle and survived to become the fourth Imam. There are three major branches of Shi'a Muslims today; the smallest of them, the Zaydis, take their name from Zayd ibn Ali (d. 740). He was the eldest son of the fourth Imam. The Zaydis hold him to have been the true fifth Imam and therefore follow him. They are sometimes called Fivers for this reason. They took their Imams from the Family of the Prophet, descendants of both Hasan and Husayn, but did not allow the Imamate to descend by inheritance so that dynasties could not develop. Today they are mainly found in Yemen, where they continue a line of Imams and held political power until 1962.

The majority of the Shi'a accepted Muhammad al-Baqir (d. uncertain between 732 and 743) as the fifth Imam. He was the grandson of the third Imam, Husayn. He was succeeded by Ja'far al-Sadiq (d. 765), who became a renowned scholar and developed the particular Shi'a code for living, called the Ja'fari School. After Imam Ja'far, another split took place among the Shi'a. A group among them recognized the eldest son of Imam Ja'far, called Isma'il (d. 762), as the rightful successor, but he died before his father. They then took Isma'il's son as the true Imam, Muhammad ibn Isma'il, and so they are called Isma'ilis, or Seveners. They later splintered further, one group being the Bohras, predominantly in the Indian Subcontinent, but the largest of these groups today are the Nizari Isma'ilis, who have maintained the tradition of having a living Imam who is always available to guide the community. The present Imam of these Isma'ilis is the Aga Khan.

They give great emphasis to the hidden meaning behind the words of the Qur'an (*batini*, or esoteric), which can be interpreted rightly only by the Imam. This gives them a powerful focus of authority, which guides them to develop their Islamic understanding in new ways. The practice of many of these Isma'ilis today is significantly different from other groups of Muslims. These Isma'ilis are to be found largely in Central Asia, the Indian Subcontinent, East Africa, and throughout the West.

The majority of the Shi'a took Musa al-Kazim (d. 799) as the rightful seventh Imam. He was the younger son of Imam Ja'far. He was succeeded in turn by Ali al-Rida (d. 818), Muhammad al-Taqi (d. 835), Ali al-Naqi (d. 868), and Hasan al-Askari (d. 874). On the death of the eleventh Imam, Hasan al-Askari, his young son Muhammad al-Qa'im became the twelfth Imam at the age of six. He appeared at his father's funeral and then immediately went into a sort of hidden existence or *ghayba* (occultation). This condition is held to have had two phases. For the first sixty-seven years, he was in lesser occultation during which he could be contacted for guidance, but from 941, he entered the greater occultation, in which he is beyond reach, where he will remain until the beginning of the Last Days. At this time, he will return as Imam al-Mahdi and begin the ultimate struggle for good over evil that will mark the end of the world.

As the twelfth Imam is still alive, there can be no question of a continuation of the line of Imams, and so this majority group amongst the Shi'a are called Ithna Asharis, or Twelvers. They are to be found as the official religion of Iran (since the sixteenth century), as the majority of the population of Iraq, especially in the south, in Bahrain and Lebanon, and as minorities in Kuwait, Syria, Pakistan, and India. In the course of centuries, a considerable body of scholarship was developed. Their theology had a strong philosophical basis, and the various ranks of scholars formed into a kind of hierarchy. Authority now rests with the body of Ayatollahs (literally "sign of God"), who give guidance in the name of the Hidden Imam until his return.

Fig. 5. Table of Shi'a Imams

Muhammad (d. 632) + Khadija (d. 619)

1st Imam	Ali (d. 661) + Fatima (d. 633)
2nd Imam	Hasan (d. *c.*669)
3rd Imam	Husayn (d. 680)
4th Imam	Ali ibn Husayn [Zayn ul-Abidin] (d. 712/3)
5th Imam	Muhammad al-Baqir (d. 732/743)
	Zayd ibn Ali (d. 740) (Zaydis or Fivers)
6th Imam	Ja'far al-Sadiq (d. 765)
7th Imam	Musa al-Kazim (d. 799)
	Muhammad ibn Isma'il (Isma'ilis or Seveners)
8th Imam	Ali al-Rida (d. 818)
9th Imam	Muhammad al-Taqi (d. 835)
10th Imam	Ali al-Naqi (d. 868)
11th Imam	Hasan al-Askari (d. 874)
12th Imam	Muhammad al-Qa'im (occultation 874, then 941) (Ithna Asharis or Twelvers)

3

The Qur'an, the Revealed Word of God

Qur'an revealed to guide all humanity – process of revelation – an Arabic Qur'an – the *Kalam Allah* – earlier Books and their Messengers – the unreliability of earlier Books today – Qur'an needed as the reliable Book – structure, compilation, and preservation of the Qur'an – translation – interpretation – translations and commentaries in English – respect for and pious use of the Qur'an – memorization and recitation – calligraphy

Toward the end of Ramadan in the year 610, the revelation of the Qur'an first came down to the Prophet Muhammad. The Qur'an is absolutely central to Islam; the name means "the recitation" (Q. 2:129). Muslims believe it to be the literal, verbal revelation from God and as such is like no other literature in existence today; it is of divine authorship and so is literally the Word of God. It was sent down as guidance for all humanity, to show human beings the way to live in accordance with the will of God (Q. 81:26). Only by living according to the revealed will of God can human beings find true happiness and fulfillment in this life and live in such a way that they will be found worthy of a place in heaven after death.

The Qur'anic term for this process of revelation is *wahy*, which is linked to the term *tanzil*. Together they mean the "sending down" of the Qur'an from the transcendent world of God into our human world in a human language, Arabic (Q. 12:2). In this system, Muhammad is the recipient and conveyor of the revelation and not in any sense the author (Q. 52:33-34). The actual verbal form of the Qur'an was sent down upon his heart without his creative faculties being engaged in the process. He did not make it up or choose words to express the revelation; it was given to him by the power of God (Q. 53:3-4). As it was sent down on the heart of Muhammad, he did not have to memorize it as we might do. It was simply "there" in his heart and he knew it.

The Qur'an came down to Muhammad in a series of revelations that lasted throughout the rest of his life. Thus the Qur'an was revealed over a period of twenty-three years (Q. 17:106, 25:32). Several reports have been retained in the *sira*, or biography of Muhammad, that explain how it appeared when he was receiving revelation. Sometimes it was sudden,

like the ringing of a bell, and at other times Muhammad was seen to be
absorbed or taken up in the process of revelation. On occasion he was
seen to sweat and appeared to be in a kind of trance. Muhammad was
the pure channel through which the revelation passed into this world.

One model used by some Muslims to try to describe this process
can be likened to a loud speaker. When a loud speaker is coupled to
an amplifier and a tape recorder, it lends its diaphragm to the process
of making the sounds that we hear. In no way would one say that the
loud speaker is the author of those sounds. It is merely the mechanical
instrument that responds to the impulses from the tape recorder and
amplifier. In the same way, Muhammad lent his voice to the process
of revelation. He was no more the author of the revelation than the
loud speaker is the author of the sounds that it emits. Authorship was
God's, and Muhammad conveyed the revelation that was sent down
to him. This example is not intended to be disrespectful to the Prophet
but rather to make it clear that God, not Muhammad, is the source of
the Qur'an.

Other more mystical or philosophical models have been used to try
to describe this process. The highest element in the human makeup
of Muhammad was completely filled with knowledge or light by the
lowest emanation of the divine. Thus Muhammad was enlightened or
purified by his being filled with light or knowledge so that a pure resting place in his heart was made to receive the revelation. In this way,
it could be sent down upon his heart without any fear of corruption
or interference. The Qur'an says of itself that it was sent down upon
the heart of Muhammad (Q. 2:97). The passage from the heart of the
Prophet to his lips was under the guidance of the "Trusted Spirit" or
the Agent of Revelation, which is one way in which the philosophers
spoke about the role of the Angel Jibril. This preserved from any error
the passage from the heart to the lips.

Naturally the words in which the Qur'an was revealed had to be in
the language that Muhammad knew and used, Arabic. As the Prophet
was to be the interpreter of the Qur'an, he had to understand it, and
so the language used had to be within his grasp. It would have been
useless to reveal the Qur'an to an Arabic-speaking Prophet in Chi-
nese (Q. 41:44)! In this way we can see that the Arabic words in the
Qur'an had to be those used by Muhammad and his people. It is part
of our human makeup that any idea we have needs to form into images
and these images need words in order that they can be expressed.
It is as though the Word of God hit the heart of the Prophet with
such force that it clothed itself in words in order to find expression

Fig. 6. Muslim and Christian understandings of the revelation of the Speech or Word of God

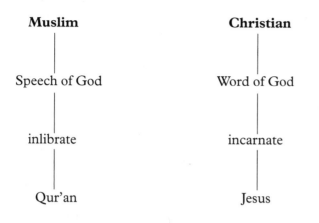

Muslim	Christian
Speech of God	Word of God
inlibrate	incarnate
Qur'an	Jesus

and be articulated by his lips. Scholars have differed on whether the Qur'an was actually sent down upon the heart of Muhammad as a whole or "piecemeal." In either case, the verses were brought forth from his lips in stages over the period of twenty-three years through the Agent of Revelation.

It is important for Christians especially to grasp this Qur'anic theology of revelation, because it differs from common Christian theologies. For a Muslim to say that the Qur'an is the Word of God is not to use that expression in the same way that most modern Western Christians normally use it when speaking of the Gospels or any other part of the Bible. In Islam, God speaks, and what God speaks cannot be defined as a separate reality. In this case, it is better to think of the speech of God, which cannot be separated from the speaker. In the Qur'anic model, the Qur'an is literally the Speech of God in book form, or *inlibrate*, as one might say, to use a Latin term. This may be contrasted to the Christian theological understanding of Jesus as the Word of God *incarnate*, that is, in human form. For Christians to gain a better understanding, there needs to be an equivalence between the Qur'an, as the Speech of God inlibrate, and Jesus, as the Word of God incarnate. The Gospels, which are the inspired theological constructions of the Evangelists based on the recorded teaching of Jesus, are not equivalent to the Qur'an but are better paralleled to the Hadith, which are the recorded sayings of Muhammad.

The *Kalam Allah*

The Qur'an is the earthly deposit of the Speech of God in Arabic, but Arabic is an earthly language. In the transcendent world, the world of God, there exists the *Kalam Allah*. This is the speech or self-communication of God. It exists only in the transcendent world and not here on earth. A traditional understanding is that the *Kalam Allah* is contained on the Preserved Tablet, *al-Lawh al-Mahfuz*, in the transcendent world (Q. 85:21-22). From here it has been sent down to various Prophets in various languages throughout human history. The relationship of God to the *Kalam Allah* has been the subject of much theological discussion. Is the *Kalam Allah* eternal or created? If one says "eternal," then there is a danger of two eternal beings: God and the *Kalam Allah*. If one says, "created," then it exists in time and space and so is only the best form of the self-communication of God that was possible at that moment. This is not easy, but the Islamic tradition has used the term "uncreated" to indicate the relationship between the *Kalam Allah* and the single eternal reality, namely God. God and the *Kalam Allah* cannot be separated; God is "the speaking speaker" and the *Kalam Allah* is the speech. God is the sole eternal self-existent reality.

Christians will be familiar with a similar problem in Christian theology when speaking about the relationship between God and the Word of God. In Greek the Christian theologians used here the philosophical understanding of the *logos* for the self-communication of God. The first verse of the Fourth Gospel represents this idea by saying: "In the beginning was the Word, and the Word was with God, and the Word was God." This Word, or *logos*, was the self-communication of God through which all was created. In Gen. 1:3, for example, God says, "Let there be light," and "there was light." The Word was the operative cause of all that God made or did (see also Ps. 33:4). The Qur'an has a similar understanding when it says that when God created, God said, "'be,' and it is" (Q. 2:117).

God is one and is speaking the Speech of God in the transcendent world. This timeless self-communication of God was sent down to all the Prophets who have ever received revelation. The same process of revelation that we have explored with reference to the Qur'an was used in all earlier revelations too. So the Qur'an says that revelation was sent down to Moses (in Hebrew), to Jesus (in Aramaic), and to Muhammad (in Arabic). The source of all these revelations, and there were others about which we know nothing, was God through the speaking of God, the *Kalam Allah*. In this way, Muslims are not troubled

Fig. 7. Relation of the *Kalam Allah* to earthly Books

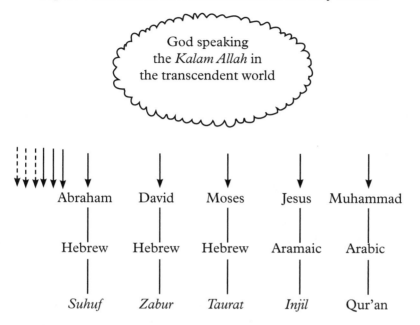

The number of revelations, the languages in which they were sent, the identities of all the Prophets who received them, and the names of these Books are not known; the Qur'an is explicit only about these five.

by the fact that the Qur'an mentions earlier revelations or episodes in the lives of earlier Prophets, such as the accounts of Abraham or Moses. This knowledge was with God, and so it is not surprising that God should choose to make mention of these events in the Qur'an. Not only was the same process of revelation at work in all earlier Books but also the same Agent of Revelation, the "Trusted Spirit" or the Angel Jibril.

The earlier Books and their Messengers

The *Kalam Allah* is one, and so the guidance sent in all Books must be in essence the same. The particularities of the way in which that message was to be lived out differed; for example, Jews were commanded to pray three times each day and Muslims five times, but the essence of the message was the same: all are commanded to pray in a regular daily rhythm. We do not know how many Books were sent in human history, nor the names of them all, nor the identities of all the Prophets to whom they were sent. We have seen in the last chapter that the Qur'an lists twenty-five Prophets of whom we can be sure. In the same way, the Qur'an lists five Books in which all Muslims must believe.

The Messengers listed in the Qur'an who were sent with Books or Scriptures are: Abraham, who was sent with a Book about which we know little but is referred to in the Qur'an as *Suhuf* (sheaves or leaves) (Q. 4:163); Moses, who was sent with the *Taurat* (Q. 6:91-92); David, who received the *Zabur* (Q. 17:55); Jesus, to whom was sent the *Injil* (Q. 5:46); and Muhammad, who was given the Qur'an. An immediate question must be whether these Books mentioned in the Qur'an correspond to the writings associated with these figures in the Bible.

Many Christian scholars would look on the Book of Psalms as the hymnbook of the Temple in Jerusalem. Some of these Psalms can be traced back perhaps to the time of King David, but many are later additions that were added to the hymnbook through the ages. From a Muslim perspective, this means Christians admit that they do not have the writings of David intact as they came from him originally. This means that the Book of Psalms may contain some of the original *Zabur* but not necessarily all of it preserved from the Prophet David onward. This makes it an unreliable source for the complete guidance of how to live a fully human life following the will of God.

Regarding the *Torah*, or the first five books of the Hebrew Bible, which Orthodox Jews hold to have been given to Moses on Mount Sinai, there are other problems. Some discrepancies when compared to the Qur'an already have been uncovered in these pages, for example: the problems over the sacrifice of Abraham; David was not a sinner; accounts of the pattern of creation; episodes in the lives of Abraham and Moses; and so on. This must mean that, while the *Torah* as it currently is preserved in the Hebrew Bible might contain some, perhaps much, that was originally given to Moses in the *Taurat*, it is incomplete and contains some errors. The presence of some errors means that it is unreliable as a complete guide to human living. How do we know how many other errors there might be, once we admit there are some?

The Qur'an accuses the Jews of being careless with the text of the *Taurat* that was given to Moses (Q. 2:75-79). These errors must have resulted from carelessness in copying the text or in preserving the manuscripts intact, or perhaps there have been deliberate changes written into the text of the *Torah*, such as the substitution of the name

Fig. 8. Messengers with Books mentioned in the Qur'an

Ibrahim Abraham	*Suhuf* leaves or sheaves
Musa Moses	*Taurat* Torah
Dawud David	*Zabur* Psalms
'Isa Jesus	*Injil*
Muhammad	Qur'an

of Isaac for the firstborn Isma'il. These are very serious charges, and, not surprisingly, Jews are not happy with such an accusation. The situation is worse for many Christian scholars and Progressive Jews, who see the *Torah* as the human compilation of a whole variety of traditions and documents that circulated in early Judaism. From a Muslim point of view, this renders the text of the *Torah* in the Bible as being an unreliable source of guidance.

Christian tradition knows nothing of the existence of a Book called or resembling the *Injil* as mentioned in the Qur'an. Various attempts have been made by Muslim scholars to explain this. Perhaps Christians have been careless and mislaid it or deliberately have suppressed it. Perhaps parts of it have been preserved in the direct speech of Jesus as recorded in the four Gospels. Perhaps it was the mysterious Q, or *Quelle* (German for "source"), which modern Christian scholarship has seen as being a deposit of the teaching of Jesus upon which the four Gospel writers drew as one of the sources for their own writings. Whatever might be the truth, the fact remains, from a Muslim perspective, that contemporary Christians do not have the *Injil* and thus are lacking the guidance from God necessary to live a truly *muslim* life.

Christians should know about the existence of a work called the Gospel of Barnabas. Some Muslims have held that this is the closest thing we have to the *Injil*. Christians will know that there were many writings that did not make it into the New Testament when it was compiled by the early church in the second to fourth centuries. These included several Gospels, such as the Gospel of Thomas. These are generally preserved in what is called the Apocryphal Writings. Scholars use these works as containing some authentic teaching from Jesus but for a variety of reasons did not come up to the standards set by the early church for inclusion in the New Testament. Was the Gospel of Barnabas one of these? Nowadays scholars of linguistics are capable of analyzing a text and saying with considerable reliability in which language it originally was composed. When such scholars have examined the Gospel of Barnabas, they have concluded that the original was written in Medieval Italian, probably in the fifteenth century. As far as such scholars are concerned, the Gospel of Barnabas definitely does not date back to the first century after Jesus. Why is this work important? The Gospel of Barnabas agrees with most of the things the Qur'an says of Jesus, including those points at which the four Gospels and the Qur'an differ. If it could be shown that the Gospel of Barnabas dated back to the time of Jesus, then it could be the best deposit of the *Injil*, and this would mean that Christians have either suppressed it or been extremely careless with it.

Christians also must consider whether the Christian understanding of Jesus as the Word of God incarnate is compatible with Jesus receiving a scripture from God of which he is in no way the author, as the Islamic understanding of revelation would require. Can Christian theology of Jesus make room for such a text? This is a Christian problem, not a Muslim one. One way in which this question has been discussed is to understand the *Injil* not as a written text that was given to Jesus but as the oral tradition that was contained in his teaching. The word *Injil* is usually understood as being taken from the Greek (*evangel*), from which we get "gospel." However there is also an Arabic root *n j l*; thus *najala* is "to beget," *najl* is "the offspring," and so *Injil* would be "that which issues forth." This would make the *Injil* the self-communication of God.

From a Muslim point of view, it is now clear why the Qur'an was needed and why it is to be preferred over all other earlier Scriptures. They are simply unreliable as a deposit of the infallible teaching of God to guide human beings on the straight path. At best, the earlier scriptures are only partial deposits of the Books that were sent down, and possibly they have been corrupted deliberately through the ages. In this way, Islam is a successionist religion. The Qur'an has come to correct earlier error and to give certain guidance on matters that are unclear.

The structure, compilation, and preservation of the Qur'an

The Qur'an was brought to the lips of Muhammad through the process of revelation. He articulated it and recited it to his immediate group of followers, who memorized it. In our own times, the function of memory has become terribly weak. In societies where things are not written down, right up to the present day, the power of memory is strong, so that people are able to remember large portions of text and recite them verbatim from memory.

In Arabia in Muhammad's time, the role of poets and storytellers was of great importance. They would memorize hundreds of stories and poems and travel from one city to another reciting their stories for the entertainment and education of their listeners. This process continues to the present time. Experiments have been made by tape-recording stories told in one part of the Arabian peninsula and then asking a storyteller hundreds of miles away to recite the same story. They can tell the same story verbatim. The same feat can be repeated across Africa and in many other parts of the world where oral tradition is still alive. It was quite common in Muhammad's time for people to memorize poems as long as one of our books today.

It was men and women with memories such as these who memorized the Qur'an from the lips of Muhammad. They became the first guardians of the revealed word. Muhammad checked the deposit of Qur'an memorized by his followers, and they cross-checked one another. Several occasions are recorded in the biography of Muhammad when the Angel Jibril came to him, especially during the month of Ramadan, to listen to him recite the verses of the Qur'an thus far revealed. In this way, a secure deposit of the Qur'an was contained in the hearts of the memorizers.

Eventually a man called Zayd ibn Thabit (d. *c.*634) joined the company of Muslims and around him formed a small group of scribes to Muhammad. They wrote down the verses of the Qur'an from the lips of the Prophet as they were revealed. They did not have access to large quantities of material on which to write, so they wrote the verses of the Qur'an on pieces of parchment, skins, leaves, bleached bones, stones, the bark of trees, and pieces of bark-free wood. In this way, by the end of the revelation of the Qur'an, two deposits existed: one in the hearts of the memorizers and one in the writings of the scribes.

Muhammad was taught the order in which the verses, or *aya*, of the Qur'an were to be arranged into chapters, or *suras*. He then gave this order to the scribes and the memorizers. The names of *suras* and the numbering of the *aya* were added later. Eventually a parchment of manuscript length was obtained, and Zayd himself undertook the task of copying the Qur'an on to it. In so doing, he cross-checked the written deposit with the memorizers to ensure that there was no room for mistakes. Scholars are divided about the exact date at which this was completed. Some hold that it was done during the lifetime of Muhammad and some that it was completed shortly after his death under the Caliph Umar (r.634–644). Arabic is written without vowels. It is up to the reader to insert the vowels in the correct places. This requires a considerable degree of knowledge of the text and the language by the reader. If ever there was a question over the voweling, diacritical dots, or pronunciation of the text of the Qur'an, then the dialect of the Quraysh, the tribe to which Muhammad belonged, was preferred. The finished manuscript by Zayd was given into the safekeeping of Hafsah (d. 665), one of the wives of Muhammad.

The third Caliph of Islam, Uthman (d. 656), traditionally is considered to have been responsible for revising and checking the text of the Qur'an. He ordered the writing of a standard version in the best Arabic that could be managed at that time. This still lacked vowels and other technical niceties, but it became the standard text, which then was copied and distributed around the growing Islamic Empire. It took another three centuries before written Arabic had advanced to the state in which a complete voweled form, in standardized grammar and writing and with all the marks of emphasis, could be produced. The earliest existing manuscripts of the Qur'an, which probably date from the early eighth century, are preserved in museums in Tashkent, Sanaa, and Istanbul. It must be emphasized repeatedly that the primary deposit of the Qur'an was and still is in the hearts of the memorizers, for whom any written form acted only as an *aide memoire*. This emphasis prevents any thought of discrepancies from entering into the recited text. This process of memorization and compilation of the written form means that the science of manuscript criticism, which is central to New Testament scholarship, is almost nonexistent in Islam, as almost no variant readings in ancient manuscripts exist.

The Qur'an says of itself that God will preserve it intact without error for all time (Q. 15:9). This is regarded as the primary miracle of Islam. It also challenges those who doubt it to bring forward ten verses of comparable eloquence of their own composition (Q. 2:23, 52:34). Scholars are agreed that this has not been done. The Qur'an is written in a style that is partly poetic but truly unique and unlike any other form of literature in the Arabic language. Because young people were taught to read by using the Qur'an, it became the primary deposit of words in the Arabic language and so changed little through the centuries. In this way, the Arabic of the Qur'an became as central in the formation of the Arabic language as did the Book of Common Prayer or the King James version of the Bible in English. Even when diffrent forms of colloquial Arabic were developed in various parts of the Arabic-speaking world, the classical language of the Qur'an was maintained so that educated Arabs would be able to understand the text today in a way that few can do with medieval English. This constant use of the Qur'an in its original Arabic has had a stabilizing effct on the language, so that classical Qur'anic Arabic is still the scholarly Arabic language of today.

The Qur'an, as the Revealed Word of God, actually exists only in the Arabic language. It is this Arabic Qur'an that is used in all formal prayers, teaching, and scholarship. Arabic is a language that contains many shades of meaning that cannot be caught in any translation. Translations of the Qur'an into other languages, and many exist in English alone, are considered only interpretations. This applies to any great work of literature; if one were to translate Shakespeare into German, one might have a text that caught something of the original, but one would not have the original Shakespeare. While non-Arabic-speaking Muslims and others use translations of the Qur'an for study and general reading, any scholarly discussion must work from the Arabic text alone. Of course this is the same with the Bible, which originally was written in Hebrew and Greek. While there are many translations, no scholarly discussion of the text of the Bible can take place unless one has access to the original languages.

The Qur'an is divided into 114 *suras*, or chapters. These are of hugely varied lengths. The shortest have only three verses, while the longest has 286 verses. The chapters of the Qur'an are not arranged in the order in which they were revealed. Generally the longer chapters are toward the front, and the shorter occur later. The difference in character between the early chapters revealed in Makka, which tend to call people to belief in the one God and to live an ethical life in the knowledge of judgment and life hereafter, and the later Madinan chapters, which tend to be more constitutional, has been noted already. As the Qur'an appeared over a period of twenty-three years, the contexts into which particular verses were revealed is of importance. These contexts are called the *asbab al-nuzul*, or "occasions of revelation." Many of these occasions of revelation have been preserved in the early commentaries on the Qur'an, called *tafsir*. They are of great importance in the interpretation of the Qur'an; it is as though one must ask: What question was asked at that particular time to which these verses of the Qur'an are the answer?

Interpretation of the Qur'an

The first and best interpreter of the Qur'an was the Prophet Muhammad himself. This means that careful attention is paid to the ways in which he put Qur'anic principles into practice in his life, teaching, and judgments. These incidents are recorded in the biographies of Muhammad and the Companions, and the great collections of Hadith, which contain what Muhammad said and did, and the things of which he approved. For Shi'a Muslims, the Imams were also infallible interpreters of the Qur'an and were able to give guidance under divine inspiration. This means that the body of interpretation built up by them, especially the sixth Imam, Ja'far al-Sadiq, is of great importance.

From the early centuries of Islam, great commentaries exist that were written by learned Muslims who were close to the time and context of the revelation of the Qur'an. Such *tafsir* not only contain the occasions of revelation but also give biographical information about the people concerned; trace the origins, grammatical structure, and shades of meaning of Arabic words; list cross-references; and generally help to clarify the teaching of the Qur'an within its context. Some of these tend to be more philosophical or based on the Arabic language, or they use sayings of Muhammad especially to bring out the meaning. Among the great early writers of *tafsir* were: al-Tabari (d. 923), who also wrote history and legal books, al-Zamakhshari (d. 1144), al-Razi (d. 1209), and al-Baydawi (d. *c.*1291).

These great works exist only in Arabic, although one volume of al-Tabari has been translated into English. A most helpful series has been started by the Lebanese scholar Mahmoud Ayoub, called *The Qur'an and Its Interpreters*, in which he surveys the commentaries of nine scholars, classical and modern, on the first three chapters (so far) of the Qur'an. Modern commentaries have been translated into English. These need some classification to understand their perspectives. Those of Maududi (d. 1978, *Towards Understanding the Qur'an*) and Sayyid Qutb (d. 1966, *In the Shade of the Qur'an*) have been influential in the revival of Muslim political movements. The leading Shi'a scholar, Tabataba'i (d. 1981, *Al-Mizan: An Exegesis of the Qur'an*) has about seven volumes translated into English. Standard modern Urdu commentaries with translations into English are available from Mufti Muhammad Shafi (d. *c.*1975, *Ma'ariful Qur'an*), Abdul Majid Daryabadi (d. 1977, *Tafsir-ul-Qur'an*), Abdul Kalam Azad (d. 1958, *The Tarjuman al-Qur'an*), Shabbir Ahmad Usmani (d. 1949, *The Noble Qur'an*), and an interesting Sufi commentary from the contemporary

Fadhlallah Haeri (*Keys to the Qur'an*). Classical commentaries, such as those of Ibn Kathir (d. 1372, *Tafsir ibn Kathir*) and al-Qurtubi (d. 1273, *Tafsir al-Qurtubi*), are being abridged and translated into English; however, one must ask here what guides the scholars who decide which passages to translate and how well they represent all that the original scholar wanted to say.

Different scholars and groups have different understandings of the Qur'anic text. Some scholars treat it very literally; therefore their commentaries tend to belong to the *zahiri*, or literalist school, for example Ibn Hazm (d. 1064). Some Shi'a scholars in particular have stressed the allegorical meaning of the Qur'anic verses and thus have developed commentaries that belong to the *ta'wil*, or allegorical school of interpretation. Among the Isma'ilis and some Sufis, there has been an emphasis on the hidden meanings, hence the *batini*, or hidden school of interpretation.

When someone who reads English but not Arabic comes to read the Qur'an, there are many translations available. The Qur'an is not a piece of narrative, like much of the Bible, and so it is not easy to follow a theme all in one place. Often the same theme is touched on in many different chapters, and all these verses need to be drawn together and understood against their various contexts, so that the teaching of the Qur'an can be understood fully. Two helpful books in this respect are Fazlur Rahman, *Major Themes of the Qur'an* (Bibliotheca Islamica, 1980), and Jacques Jomier, *The Great Themes of the Qur'an* (SCM, 1997). Two useful books draw together Qur'anic passages around key concepts. These are T. B. Irvine, *The Qur'an: Basic Teachings* (Islamic Foundation, 1992) and Kenneth Cragg, *Readings in the Qur'an* (Collins, 1988). Caution must be exercised here, as the last two do not give much of the context of the verses they group together.

When tackling the Qur'an itself, a useful method is to work systematically through the second chapter, *Surat al-Baqarah*. This is often called "The qur'an within the Qur'an," as it touches on all the major themes in the space of one chapter. To do this, a translation with footnotes is strongly recommended. The most widely available translation with footnotes is that of Abdullah Yusuf Ali, *The Holy Qur'an* (first published in 1934 but with many later revisions). More scholarly and requiring harder work and caution is *The Message of the Qur'an*, the translation with footnotes of Muhammad Asad, who spent decades living among the Bedouin to understand better the subtleties of Arabic but who is regarded by many Muslims as being too rationalist in his approach. A translation with footnotes from a Shi'a perspective is that of S. V. Mir Ahmad Ali, *The Holy Qur'an*. Translations of the text without footnotes also exist. An early twentieth-century translation by Muhammad Marmaduke Pickthall, *The Glorious Qur'an*, is widely used, but the language is somewhat dated. Modern English translations also have been written by T. B. Irvine, *The Noble Qur'an* (Amana, 1988); Abdalhaqq and Aisha Bewley, *The Noble Qur'an* (Madina, 1999); and M. A. S. Abdel Haleem, *The Qur'an* (Oxford University Press, 2004).

Respect for and pious use of the Qur'an

To understand why respect is shown for the Qur'an, a useful starting point is to think that it is the Word of God. It is not just "a book," and respect is to be shown to any printed or written verses from the Qur'an. The words of the Qur'an become alive when they are read or recited; therefore particular respect is to be shown at these times. Many Muslims follow the tradition of covering their heads whenever the Qur'an is read aloud or recited, or when they study the text of the Qur'an.

Before a Muslim will handle a copy of the Qur'an, he or she will make the ritual washing, such as is made before prayers (*wudu*). The Qur'an is guidance for all humankind, who therefore need to be able to read it to hear its message, but non-Muslims are not required to wash before handling it. However, it always should be handled with great respect. It never should be laid on the floor or any other unclean place. In a pile of books, it always should be on the top. These rules apply strictly speaking only to the Arabic text of the Qur'an, but it is good practice to treat an English translation with such respect as well.

In Arabic, the Qur'an is just *al-Qur'an*. Sometimes it also will be referred to as *al-Mushaf* (the Book), *al-Furqan* (the Criterion), *al-Huda* (the Guidance), or *al-Tanzil* (that which was Sent Down). To stress its importance, the Qur'an sometimes is referred to as *al-Qur'an al-Karim* (the Gracious Qur'an) or in Pakistan as *Qur'an-e-Pak* (The Pure Qur'an) or *al-Qur'an al-Sharif* (The Noble Qur'an). When translating the Qur'an into English, the Qur'an sometimes has been called the Holy Qur'an, borrowing from the Holy Bible.

Old and worn-out copies of the Qur'an must be disposed of with respect. Normally this is done through burial in a respectful place or at sea, or by fire according to some schools. Strictly this applies to any piece of paper or anything else on which a verse of the Qur'an in Arabic has been written. In some Muslim countries, special disposal bins are made available so that such pieces of paper can be collected and disposed of with respect. When a fast-food chain sponsored the FIFA World Cup and by mistake used the flag of Saudi Arabia, which contains a line from the Qur'an, on its take-out bag, these were recalled and pulped so that the words of the Qur'an would not end up in the gutter or in garbage can bins. Any ornament, piece of jewelery, or wall plaque on which Qur'anic verses have been written should be disposed of with respect.

In a Muslim house, a copy of the Qur'an will be treated with respect. This varies with culture, but it often will be wrapped in a special cloth or kept in a worthy box and then placed on a high shelf in a principal room. No other book should share that shelf, and nothing should be higher than the shelf on which the Qur'an rests. Some Muslims will place a copy of the Qur'an under their head at night. Muslims often show respect for the Qur'an before and after reading from it by touching it to their forehead or reverencing it with a kiss. While being read, it will be held in the hands or placed on a wooden throne or a cushion. If it is to be carried in public, again this will be done with respect, under the arm or in a bag, so that it is not abused. Space will be made on a crowded bus for someone carrying a copy of the Qur'an. If it is dropped accidentally, it will be picked up immediately, reverenced (perhaps with a kiss), and replaced with honor. In some cultures it is customary to make a donation to charity as a recompense for being so careless.

Every Muslim has some verses of the Qur'an in their memory for recitation during prayers. In every generation and culture, some will make the effort to memorize the whole Qur'an under the guidance of a teacher. Someone who has completed this memorization will be shown respect with the title *hafiz* (fem. *hafizah*) as they "carry the Qur'an in their heart." Traditionally this was one of the ways in which blind people could make a living in pre-book societies. They memorized the Qur'an and then recited it whenever Muslims gathered. Special styles for the recitation of the Qur'an (*tajwid*) have been developed, and these are the speciality of a *Qari* (reciter), who will be retained for major public and family recitations. To aid this process of recitation, the Qur'an has been divided into thirty parts, called *juz* or *sipara*; during the nights of Ramadan, one *sipara* is recited each night so that the whole Qur'an is recited in the course of the month.

Over the centuries, traditions have built up of wearing portions of the Qur'an written on pieces of parchment and placed in a leather pouch (*tawiz*) for protection. Certain verses are recited each night before sleeping, before going on a journey, and so on. Those who are

Egyptian mausoleum dome interior. Photo: Marc Ostlie-Olson.

learned in such things can prescribe certain verses to be recited for healing, like a mantra. In some cultures, such verses can be written in saffron water on paper. The paper is then soaked in water so that the writing is washed off and the water then drunk as a way of bringing the words of the Qur'an into oneself. Verses of the Qur'an are used in exorcism to drive out unwelcome spirits. As the Qur'an is literally the Word of God, it has ways of causing an effect on human beings other than just by being read.

Sunni Islam does not allow figurative drawing or painting of animate objects, so the art of calligraphy has been highly developed; in this way the words of the Qur'an can be dignified in their actual writing. There are several different scripts used in such calligraphy, the earliest being the Kufic script, developed in the Iraqi city of Kufa. This script and other forms of calligraphy often are used in mosque decoration and on ceramic tiles, which beautify the homes and public places of Muslims. No pictures of human beings or animals are permitted in mosques. Only rarely have there been human representations in Islamic art, such as in Persian miniatures, in which even Muhammad was depicted occasionally but then often with the details of his face omitted. This has led to geometrical art and Arabesque becoming highly developed art forms among Muslims.

In Arabic-speaking societies, the relationship to the words of the Qur'an is more immediate for the ordinary believer. Most would be able to understand almost every word of the Qur'an as it is read or recited. Only about fifteen percent of Muslims worldwide are native Arabic-speakers. For those who do not understand the language in this way, the Qur'an is memorized in Arabic phonetically so that it can be recited, even though the precise meaning of the language is not understood. This has led to various mystical trends of developing through the words of the Qur'an a relationship with God that goes beyond the level of a linguistic understanding of the Arabic language, beyond the intellectual content, thus leading the believer into a spiritual communion with God. In this way, the Qur'an is similar to an icon that acts as a window into the transcendent world. Many such non-Arabic-speaking Muslims will have memorized Qur'anic verses, exclamations, and prayers in Arabic that are recited. The meanings will be known, even if the precise structure of the language is not comprehended. For Christians, such an experience will be known in various liturgical languages, such as Latin was for Roman Catholics, and Coptic and classical Greek remain for Arabic-speaking Coptic

Christians and Greek Orthodox Christians who speak modern Greek. Some Christian groups, such as the Taizé Community and Roman Catholic monks, retain the use of Latin in chants to take the believer beyond the immediacy of everyday language into a deeper level of spiritual communion.

A *dikka* in the Sultan Barquq Mosque in Cairo, Egypt. Photo: Sally Messner.

4

An Overview of Islamic History

Expansion of the Islamic Empire after the death of Muhammad – intellectual encounters in Damascus and Baghdad – Cairo as a center of Islamic learning – Islam comes to Spain – many intellectual advances by Muslims – the Golden Age of Islamic Spain – Greek thought returns to Europe – the Christian Reconquista in Spain – Jewish–Muslim relations – Israel/Palestine in the twentieth century – the Crusades – Saladdin and Francis of Assisi – expansion of Islam in the non-Arab world – modern period

It is not possible within the limits of this one chapter to give a detailed account of 1,400 years of Muslim history. Certain episodes will be taken that are particularly relevant to a Western audience. For the sake of clarity, modern names will be used for regions or countries that may not have existed at the time in question.

Overview

The Islamic Empire grew rapidly after the death of Muhammad and remained largely united for the first two centuries. Local dynasties arose, the most important of which were the Abbasids, who ruled from Baghdad (750–1258) and later over a much smaller area from Cairo (1261–1517), the Umayyads in Spain (756–1031), and the Fatimids in Egypt (909–1171). The Abbasids were overthrown in Baghdad in 1258 by the invasion of the Mongols, who have the distinction of being converted to Islam by the conquered peoples. This was the age of the second major expansion of Islam in Asia and Africa. In the last five hundred years, empires were more geographically limited, with the most important being that of the Ottomans based in Turkey and at times ruling much of the Middle East (1280–1924), the Mughals in India (1526–1858), the Safavids in Iran (1501–1765), and the Alawids in Morocco and West Africa (1631 onward). During the age of the European empires, only Turkey and Yemen were not colonized.

Expansion of the Islamic Empire

By the time Muhammad died in 632, most of the clans of the lower Arabian peninsula had come under the influence of the Muslim community centered at Madina. Some of the tribes had become Muslims, and the others, especially the Christians and Jews, had signed treaties with Muhammad to secure their peaceful coexistence. The Qur'an had made it clear that Jews and Christians were *Ahl al-Kitab*, People of the Book (or People of the Earlier Revelations) (Q. 3:3, 5:66). As such they were to be allowed freedom of religious practice.

There was something about Muhammad's charismatic personality and his gifts of leadership and wisdom that united tribes that traditionally had been enemies. Soon after his death, some of the Bedouin clans who had been under the influence of Muhammad and Madina began to break loose and go their own way. The first two Caliphs, Abu Bakr (d. 634) and Umar (d. 644), used the Muslim army to bring the former tribes back under control and to expand the Islamic Empire into the present Gulf States, Yemen and Hadramaut. This breaking loose was known as the *ridda*, or apostasy. Under the religio-political system of Islam, to rebel against the authorities or break a treaty was also to ignore the law of God; thus treason and apostasy were closely linked. The Muslim army soon brought things back under control, and the idol-worshipping Arabs were now forced to give up the practice and follow the Islamic way of life.

The first Caliph, Abu Bakr, who ruled from 632 to 634, drew up the rules of engagement for the Muslim army based on Qur'anic verses and the practice of Muhammad (Q. 2:205, 4:89-90, 5:33-34, 60:8). Force was not to be used unless it was necessary; negotiation was to be preferred. All non-combatants—women, children, the sick and elderly, and explicitly soldiers who threw down their arms in surrender—were to be spared attack and were not to be intimidated. It was forbidden to deprive the enemy of basic human needs, so water courses were not to be poisoned, crops in the fields and food in barns were not to be destroyed, and trees were not to be felled, as they provided food and shelter. All "houses in which the name of God is mentioned and those that dwell therein," normally taken to refer to churches and synagogues and religious figures such as monks, hermits, priests, and rabbis, were to be protected, provided that they did not actively promote rebellion against the Islamic authorities.

The first expansion of the Islamic Empire was one of the most rapid in human history as we know it in the West. By 637, Palestine and Iraq had come under Islamic rule, followed by Egypt and Syria by 641.

This represented the entire Arab peninsula and beyond. Their fellow Arabs, who earlier had been largely under Byzantine (Greek) rule, were not unhappy to welcome the Muslim armies from the south. Better to be ruled by fellow Arabs than by foreigners!

The first non-Arab country to come under the Islamic Empire was Iran in 650. Here the status of the People of the Book was extended to the Zoroastrians, who were identified by some as the Sabeans or Magians, as mentioned in the Qur'an (Q. 2:62, 22:17), although, as often happens, the practice did not always live up to the ideal. Parts of north India came under Islamic rule from 712, with the city of Multan in the Punjab (now Pakistan) falling to the army in 773. The Islamic Empire spread up into Central Asia (where it encountered Buddhist practice), through modern Turkistan, Uzbekistan, and Afghanistan by around 750. To the West, the Muslim armies had passed right along the coast of North Africa, through Libya, Tunisia, and Algeria, and into Morocco by 714.

This first rapid expansion of the Islamic Empire often has given rise to misconceptions that Islam spread at the point of the sword. It is important to see this as the expansion of the empire but not necessarily conversion to the faith of Islam. The overwhelming majority of those coming under Islamic rule at this time were the People of the Book, who enjoyed freedom of religious practice and remained Jews, Christians, or, in Iran, Zoroastrians. It took generations and centuries before a majority of the inhabitants of the Arab lands had become Muslims. In Egypt, Coptic Christians remained a majority for many centuries.

While the People of the Book were allowed freedom of religious practice in the empire, their status was clearly subordinate. They could use their existing places of worship but were not free to build new ones. They were not free to seek converts from other faiths. They had to show respect for all Muslims and under certain rulers had to wear distinctive clothing so that they could be identified. They were exempted from military service, as this was a function of the Islamic religio-political system, but instead had to pay a special tax, called the *jizya*. The Muslim army was bound to protect them like all other inhabitants, indeed the name given to them, *dhimmis*, means "the protected people." They were not allowed to have a say in the governance of the empire, nor did they get a share of booty or money from the treasury.

The importance of Jerusalem already has been noted. When the Muslim armies reached the city, the Caliph Umar himself came forward to negotiate the hand-over to the empire. He was taken on a

Fig. 9. The initial expansion of the Islamic Empire

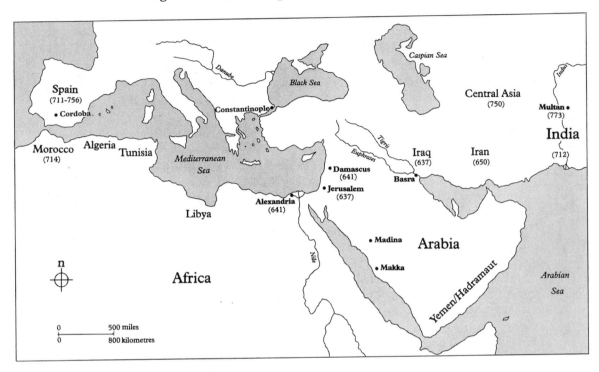

tour of the historic city by the Christian Patriarch, who concluded by taking him to the Church of the Holy Sepulchre. Out of respect for the importance of this place for Christians, Umar declined to offer his formal prayers there in case someone later would claim it as a mosque on the basis that the Caliph had prayed there. Instead he went a little way from the church on to some waste ground and offered his prayers there. During the reign of Caliph Abd al-Malik ibn Marwan (r.685–705), the al-Aqsa Mosque and the nearby Dome of the Rock were built on the Temple Mount, which under Christian rule had become a desolate area. The Dome of the Rock was decorated by Byzantine Christian craftsmen.

The Dome of the Rock in Jerusalem.
Photo: Robert O. Smith.

When the Muslim armies came up from the Arabian peninsula, they were not used to administering a huge empire. They did what all conquerors do in those circumstances; they retained the existing administrators and set new guidelines for the way that administration was conducted. Madina was too far out from the center of affairs to remain the capital of the empire, and a more developed city life was to be found in Damascus, so the Umayyads made that their capital from 661 to 750. Damascus had been an administrative center of the Byzantine Empire, so the administrators there were Christians who knew Greek, Syriac, and Arabic. It was in Damascus that the first systematic encounters between Islam and Greek thought took place, although there had been some stirrings in Basra.

Theology might be described as the process of speaking about one's faith with accuracy, in terms taken from another thought world, so that the people of that tradition can understand precisely what one means. For Islam, the first theology was done in Damascus and was called *ilm al-kalam*. The bearers of Greek thought were Christians, so they questioned their new masters and through a process of talking things through (dialogue) contributed to the development of Islamic religious thought. Soon the wheel turned, and the Muslim scholars began to question the Christians on what precisely they believed. This led to some interesting encounters in which the scholars of the two faiths helped one another refine their respective doctrines. One of the Greek-trained administrators, who was also a theologian, was John of Damascus (d. 750). He grew up in Damascus under the Islamic Empire and followed his father into administration. He became the first Christian theologian to attempt to write theologically about Islam, which he regarded as a Christian heresy, that is, "Christianity gone wrong."

Intellectual and scientific advances

We are all familiar with the great intellectual life of ancient Greece and Rome. We associate the names of Plato, Aristotle, Euclid, Pythagoras, Galen, Ptolemy, and others with that rich heritage. In the fourth century, the Roman Empire embraced Christianity as its official religion through conversion of the Emperor Constantine. By this time in fact the Western Roman Empire already was beginning to shrink so that in the middle of the fifth century, the center of the Roman Empire shifted to the east and took as its capital the ancient city of Byzantium, later to be renamed Constantinople and today known as Istanbul. At the time of the rise of Islam, the Roman Empire actually was centered in Byzantium and had its stronghold around the Eastern Mediterranean, through modern Turkey and Greece, through the coastal Arab lands, and into North Africa. This was now known rightly as the Byzantine Empire, or the Eastern Roman Empire. One chapter of the Qur'an is called *al-Rum*, the Romans, and refers to this Byzantine Empire (Q. 30). It was revealed in 615 at the time that the Persian Empire captured Jerusalem (Q. 30:1-6), which was retaken by the Byzantine Romans in 628. With this shift to the east came a decline in the old Western Roman Empire so that much of northern Europe entered what normally is called the Dark Ages. They were so called because the ancient wisdom of Greece and Rome largely was lost in the West but retained in the East in the Greek language.

Damascus in Syria was part of that Byzantine Empire before the rise of the Islamic Empire. Already here the process of translation had begun in which the ancient wisdom was translated from Greek into Syriac. With the coming of the Islamic Empire, this process was continued in Damascus, with translation now going from Greek and Syriac into Arabic, the scholarly language of the Islamic Empire. Syriac, a Semitic language quite close to Arabic and Hebrew, was a useful intermediate language in this translation program. The process was enhanced greatly when a new Islamic dynasty arose with the coming of the Abbasids in 750. The Caliph al-Mansur (d. 775) established Baghdad as the seat of the Abbasid Islamic Empire in 762, where it remained until 1258, when it was sacked by the Mongols.

With the expansion of the Islamic Empire, great wealth was available to the Abbasid Caliphate. Part of this wealth was used to establish the Bayt al-Hikma, or House of Wisdom, in Baghdad by the Caliph al-Ma'mun (d. 833) in 832. This was first a place of translation, where the ancient wisdom was translated from Greek and Syriac into Arabic.

Al-Azhar Mosque.
Cairo, Egypt.
Photo: Sally Messner.

Once this process was underway, it led to a flowering of philosophical, scientific, and medical thought, which took Greek thinking several steps forward. The Bayt al-Hikma provided all the facilities necessary for translation and the copying of manuscripts, hugely assisted by the importation of paper production into the area by the end of the eighth century. Scholars who had the ancient wisdom were attracted to Baghdad by the facilities and the patronage of the Caliphs, who ensured that there were salaries available to provide for the scholars who did the work. Many of those who came to Baghdad were Christians and Jews, who then sat with Arabic-speaking Muslim scholars to ensure that the work was as accurate as possible.

Arabic now became the language of scholarship, and once the manuscripts were prepared and translated, they could be copied and sent out around the Islamic Empire for scholars to use. One place this scholarship flourished was in Cairo under the Isma'ili Fatimid dynasty, which ruled from its base in Cairo from 909 to 1171. This was a period of massive development of Islamic art and architecture. It was at this time that the great mosque and university of al-Azhar was founded in 978. This was the first university to be created in European and Arab history. There had been great teachers and centers of learning before this, of course, but what distinguished the idea of a university was that many different disciplines were taught alongside one another in the same institution. The foundation of al-Azhar thus came some 250 years before the first of the great universities of northern Europe in Paris (1215), Oxford (1220), and Bologna (1220). With the coming of the Ayyubid dynasty in Cairo (1169–1250), al-Azhar became a center of Sunni learning and remains to this day perhaps the greatest single center of Sunni scholarship in the world.

When the Muslim armies arrived in Morocco in the late seventh century, there was a question of which direction they now should turn. The governor of northern Morocco at that time, a general called Tariq, took his army across what we now call the Straits of Gibraltar and landed in Spain in 711. He gave his name to the mountain on which they landed, *Jabal-i-Tariq*, which later was Westernized into Gibraltar. The Muslim army now marched northward, until by 756 all but a few pockets of the northwest Iberian Peninsula were under Islamic rule. In 732, a small raiding party crossed the Pyrenees and was defeated at Poitiers by Charles Martel.

The Golden Age of Islamic Spain is reckoned from 756 to 1031. A new capital was established at Cordoba, and one of the glories of Islamic architecture in Spain, the Great Mosque of Cordoba, was begun in 786. This developed into a center of learning, considered one of the greatest in the Islamic world and boasting a library of some 400,000 works. It was in Cordoba that the future Pope Sylvester II (r.999–1003) studied. He imported some of the Aristotelean logic and mathematics he had learned there into the Christian scholarly world. In this period the first Alhambra Fort in Granada was built, although the present buildings that make up the Alhambra Palace date mainly from the fourteenth century.

The Golden Age of Islamic Spain, or *al-Andulus* as it was called in Arabic, was a time of great advances in many areas of scholarship. Great developments were made in Aristotelian philosophy associated with Ibn Rushd (d. 1198), or Averroës as he was known in Latin. Neoplatonic thought became important in Spain, developed from the Greek works of Plotinus (d. 270) by such leading Muslim thinkers as al-Farabi (d. 950) and Ibn Sina (d. 1037), who, although he spent most of his life in Persia, was so influential in the West that later he was better known by his Latin name, Avicenna.

Similarly, Ibn Sina developed the Greek medical works of Galen to such an extent that his medical writings were in use throughout Europe until the dawn of the modern period of medicine. Other great medical advancements of this period include the discovery of the pulmonary circulation of the blood by Ibn al-Nafis (1210–1298), and the use of anaesthetics and the structure of the eye by Ibn al-Haytham (965–1039), known in Latin as Alhazen, the father of optics and the inventor of a rudimentary camera and binoculars.

In mathematics, the concept of zero as the meeting point of positive and negative numbers dates from this period. Our present numerals were developed by the Arabs from original Indian work and brought to Europe in the twelfth century. The Abbasids in Baghdad were well-positioned to benefit from Indian thought to the south. Algebra was developed by Muhammad Abu Musa al-Khwarizmi (d. *c*.850) to deal with the complexities of Islamic laws of inheritance. Trigonometry, developed by Abu'l-Wafa al-Busajami (940–998), was refined to ensure that the buildings of Muslim architects would stand.

The first observatories were developed in Spain so that the heavenly bodies could be observed and their movements plotted. This led to maps of the night skies and the development of the astrolabe, an instrument that allowed sailors to locate their position on earth when out of sight of land. Without these developments, it would not have been possible for European explorers such as Christopher Columbus to sail on their voyages of discovery. Al-Biruni (973–1048), working in Afghanistan, calculated the distance from the earth to many stars and planets and also the circumference of the earth. Ibn Fadlan (d. 921) traveled north to Russia and worked on the location of the North Pole. Abu Ma'shar (d. 886) made great strides in astronomy and astrology. His work was influential in many lands and was translated into Latin at Toledo, where he was known by his Latin name, Albumasar.

In Islamic Spain the power rested with the Muslim government, which ruled according to the principles of Islamic law. The majority of the people remained Christian, with a significant Jewish minority. As the People of the Book, these two faiths were given freedom of religious practice and generally were given the rights accorded to them freely to live their lives provided, that they did not attempt to threaten the Muslim government. This was a good example of the *dhimmi* or protected people status. They were able to access education, and for the scholarly classes, this was indeed a Golden Age.

Jewish, Christian, and Muslim scholars worked side by side to bring about the development to which reference already has been made. Arabic was the language of scholarship, and scholars worked within Aristotelian or Neoplatonic philosophical systems. These two points are of crucial importance. In Damascus and Baghdad in the eighth and ninth centuries, and again in Spain, it was possible for the learned from these three religions to engage in discussion in a common language and without any misunderstanding of the terms they used. This is not to say that they agreed with one another in terms of theology but that they *understood* what the other was trying to say. All too often, the scholars of these three religions have failed to understand one another because they did not clarify exactly what the other meant by the terms that were used. This can only be done when there is a common philosophical system.

If we take three examples, this will become clear. The great Muslim philosopher Ibn Rushd (d. 1198) was an Aristotelian working in Arabic. The greatest Jewish systematic theologian of the medieval period, Moses Maimonides (d. 1204), also worked in Spain, wrote in Arabic and Hebrew, and was an Aristotelian. One generation later, the greatest Christian philosophical theologian who built the system of philosophical theology that led to the whole Scholastic period, Thomas Aquinas (d. 1274), was also an Aristotelian, but he worked in Latin. It is almost possible to imagine the three of them engaged in the highest theological discussion, in which there would be no shadow of misunderstanding. The question is, how did Aquinas acquire his Latin versions of Aristotle?

There were basically two routes through which the ancient knowledge of Greek thought and the later developments in all the disciplines pioneered in Arabic came to northern Europe. One of these was through Sicily, but the most important was through Islamic Spain. Perhaps the most influential Christian figure in northern Europe at that time was the Abbot of the great Benedictine monastery of Cluny in France. This was the motherhouse for a chain of a thousand monasteries that spread throughout northern and western Europe. In the monasteries monks enjoyed the leisure for academic work, and so monasteries became centers of education.

One of the Abbots of Cluny was Peter the Venerable (d. 1156). There was a Cluniac monastery in Toledo in Spain, and it was here that another translation bureau was established. This was inspired by Peter the Venerable and the Archbishop of Toledo, who was particularly interested in scientific thought. In Toledo, Jewish, Christian, and Muslim scholars who knew Arabic worked with Christians who knew Latin to make translations and copies of the ancient wisdom available for distribution through the monasteries and the new universities of northern Europe. This was the first time the Qur'an was translated into a European language, and Peter himself wrote a refutation of Islamic teachings, the *Liber contra sectam sive haeresim Saracenorum*. Fueled by these translations in the academic language of northern Europe, the Christian scholarly revival associated with Thomas Aquinas and others could begin. This was the period of the founding of the Dominican Order, the members of which went on to be influential in establishing the first universities in Christian Europe.

Not only on the level of academic theology was there a meeting in Spain between the Abrahamic faiths. Spain at this time was an important center for the Jewish mystical tradition of the Kabbalah. Muslim mystical or sufi life was rich, as might be typified in the life and work of Ibn Arabi (d. 1240), born in Murcia before going on to Turkey and later Damascus and regarded as one of the greatest sufi masters of all time. There was certainly at least one sufi order, or *tariqa*, in Spain that initiated Jews and Christians as well as Muslims into its membership. This mystical tradition had its influence on the Spanish Christian mystic St. John of the Cross (1542–1591) and can be seen in the *Divine Comedy* of Dante (1265–1321).

From 1031 the united Islamic Empire in Spain began to break up. There then followed four centuries of gradual decline as the Christian *reconquista* took Spain for the Christian nobility. This process was not complete until 1492. The history of this period has dark shadows from a Christian perspective. There were forced conversions of Spanish Jews and Muslims to Christianity. Many remained Jewish or Muslim in their hearts but outwardly accepted baptism as being preferable to expulsion or death. This was the age of Ferdinand and Isabella and the

Spanish Inquisition (1479–1808), when those who had converted only outwardly were tortured and killed in an effort to make that conversion inwardly applicable too. Many Jews and Muslims were forced to leave Spain, for example in the Great Expulsion of 1609–1610, when an estimated 350,000 were exiled. They settled throughout North Africa and around the Eastern Mediterranean in Muslim lands.

It is important to see the way in which these Jewish communities were taken in and given a new start in other parts of the Islamic Empire. Too often we get the false idea that Jewish–Muslim relations have always been as tense as they are today. This is not the case. Jews were given *dhimmi* status in many parts of the Islamic Empire when they were persecuted by Christians in Europe. It is only the situation of Palestine in the twentieth century that has brought about the present deep tensions. When Jews started to go to Palestine in the late nineteenth century, escaping persecution in northern Europe, they were welcomed and settled by the Palestinians, both Muslims and Christians. Tensions arose when the numbers of Jewish settlers became too large. Even so, it was not until the founding of the State of Israel in 1948, with the expulsion of Palestinians and the wars that followed, that the present hatred between Jewish Zionists and especially Arab Muslims (and Christians) developed.

The Crusades

While Islamic Spain was in a state of relative harmony, Christians and Muslims were at battle in the Holy Land during the Crusades. Much of the history of this period has been one-sided from both perspectives. European Christians learned one version of history, and Arab Muslims and Christians learned another. The legacy of the Crusades has created a deep scar on Christian-Muslim relations for the past nine hundred years. Not until 1999 was a scholarly history of the Crusades from the Islamic perspective, based on Arabic documents, published in English (Carole Hillenbrand, *The Crusades: Islamic Perspectives*, Edinburgh University Press, 1999).

Three factors were at play in the build-up to the Crusades. The Great Schism between Western and Eastern Christianity finally had come about in 1054. The pope in Rome therefore could use an appeal from Eastern Christians in the Holy Land as a way of reasserting his claim to a universal patriarchate. Muslim Arabs had been threatening the European mainland through the conquests of Mediterranean islands such as Malta and Sicily. These acted as bases for raiding parties on the coast of Italy. Europe was divided between many Christian ruling families and systems, so the Crusades were one way of bringing them all together under the patronage of the pope. Some younger sons of European nobles saw this as a way of gaining fresh territory for themselves.

The First Crusade was called by Pope Urban II in 1095. He called on the Christian nobility and peasants of Europe to "hasten to exterminate this vile race," to be done in the name of God as a kind of penitential pilgrimage. Additionally, the pope at that time thought he had the power to grant people admission to heaven through the forgiveness of their sins. He promised the reward of heaven to all who set out on a Crusade to retake the holy places. Those who survived the Crusades were promised remission of their sins when eventually they did die. He did not hesitate to include in his call those who had been robbers and involved in battles between different Christian factions. Here was a common enemy against whom all could unite.

Groups of Christians began to make their way overland to Palestine. They had to avoid Spain and so traveled around the Mediterranean to the east. As they journeyed across northern Europe, they massacred Jewish communities that they found in their path, for example in Speyer, Worms, Mainz, and Cologne. They finally arrived in Jerusalem on 15 July 1099. The chroniclers of the time told of Muslim bodies "almost as high as the houses." Men, women, and children were put to the sword. Jews took refuge in the Great Synagogue of Jerusalem, where they were burned alive. Horses hardly could make their way through the streets of Jerusalem because of the blood and gore, which came up to their knees. After ransacking the city for treasure, the Crusaders departed, leaving a lasting legacy of Western Christian carnage among Eastern Christians, Muslims, and Jews alike.

The First Crusade was not the end of the story. Further Crusades were called in 1147, 1189, 1202, 1217, 1248, and 1269. It was not until the final fall of Acre in 1291 that the tyranny ended. It cannot be accepted that the Crusades were the action of some Christian nobles who got out of hand. Not only were they called by the popes, but they were preached as a religious duty by leading churchmen such as Peter the Hermit in Germany and Bernard of Clairvaux, the reformer of monasticism and founder of the White Monks, or Cistercians, in France. They introduced a spirit of militant Christianity that led to calls in 1252 by Pope Innocent IV for the use of torture and execution against heretics. This spirit was later rife in Europe after the Reformation, when wars of religion tore Europe apart.

Two brighter elements of this saga are worthy of note. When Salah al-Din (d. 1193), or Saladdin, defeated the Crusaders in the Battle of Hattin in 1187 and retook Jerusalem, the chronicles observe the way in which he respected the Christian and Jewish holy places and did not harm women or children. At the time of the latter Crusades, Francis of Assisi (d. 1226) was a young man growing up with a very different Christian spirit. He took a party of his Brothers to camp between the armies of the Crusaders and Muslims at Damietta in 1219. He was not able to negotiate a peaceful settlement, but the experience had a lasting influence on him. When he came to write his Rule of Life for the Franciscans, he included a chapter on those Brothers who went to live alongside Muslims. They were to do so in a spirit of humility and service seeking to assist those most in need. Under no circumstances were they to insult things that Muslims hold holy, in particular not the Qur'an or Muhammad. They were to remain silent. Their lives were to be of such virtue that by so living they would prompt questions from their neighbors: Why are you doing this? When thus questioned, they were to respond truthfully, guided by a spirit of gentleness, wisdom, and charity. Following in the spirit of Francis was Raymond Lull (c.1233–c.1315), who devoted himself to the study of Arabic and philosophy. He pioneered the study of oriental languages in European universities and worked out schemes to convert Muslims and Jews based on philosophical argumentation.

The legacy of the Crusades lasts to the present age. It has not been forgotten in the Arab world and was evoked, for example, by the Christian militia in the Lebanese Civil War. Muslims worldwide know of this episode in Christian–Muslim encounter. Whenever the term "crusade" is used by Christians, whether it be in military conflicts in the Arab world or by Christian evangelists worldwide, this particular memory is enkindled.

The expansion of Islam to the non-Arab world

The great military conquests of the Arabs have not been repeated in Islamic history. Today only about fifteen percent of Muslims worldwide are Arabs. How then did Islam spread to other peoples around the world? Two particular methods are worthy of notice. Muslims were engaged in trade down the eastern coast of Africa, along the Great Silk Road that led to China, and throughout the islands that make up modern Indonesia. As these traders followed their profession, they established trading posts along the way so that their goods could be sold and other goods purchased to be collected when the traders returned. In many cases these trading posts were made up of members of a Muslim extended family. Over centuries, the lives of these families had such an effect on their neighbors that people began converting to Islam to live as they did. In Indonesia today, there are perhaps two hundred million Muslims, and even in China Muslims make up some five percent of the population of fifty million. Those who followed the inner or mystical dimensions of Islam traveled to take the message to new peoples and invite them to embrace Islam. In this way Islam spread throughout West Africa and in the East to Malaysia.

Modern period

The last of the great Islamic empires was that of the Ottomans, who rose to power in 1281 and came to rule much of the Middle East during the height of their power in the sixteenth century. From 1453, they had their capital at Istanbul (formerly Byzantium and Constantinople). At the time of the 1914–1918 War, they sided with the Germans and subsequently lost their Arab lands to the French and British. This brought about the rise of Mustafa Kemal Ataturk (d. 1938), who responded to the shame at the loss of the empire by disbanding the Caliphate in 1924 and forcibly secularizing Turkey from then on.

One of the strengths of Turkey is that it never was colonized by the European powers. Not so for much of the Muslim world, which was ruled by Britain, France, Holland, and Russia, especially in the eighteenth to twentieth centuries. Great natural riches were taken from the Muslim lands, and the colonial powers benefited from trade. This led to the rise of Europe and fueled the Industrial Revolution. The result in many Muslim countries is a sense of emptiness, a lack of self-respect, an unawareness of their histories, and a sense of resentment against their colonial masters. Part of this decline also affected their intellectual life and the lack of development of Islamic thought. Only the leisured classes have time to spare for intellectual activity. Islamic thought tended to stagnate, with eyes always cast backward to better times. Among the great intellectual revivalists of the colonial period were men like Ahmad Sirhindi (d. 1624) and Shah Waliullah (d. 1762) in India; Jamal al-Din al-Afghani (d. 1897), who taught Islamic unity in Iran, Egypt, India, and Turkey; Abd al-Kader (d. 1883) in Algeria; Ibn Abd al-Wahhab (d. 1792) in Arabia; and Muhammad Abduh (d. 1905) in Egypt. They sought to awaken Muslims to their heritage and revive intellectual thought in Islamic studies.

In the twentieth century the struggle for independence from colonialism and the reinvigoration of Islamic learning led to reform movements in Egypt, such as the *Ikhwan al-Muslimin*, or the Muslim Brotherhood, with which the names of Hasan al-Banna (d. 1949) and Sayyid Qutb (d. 1966) are associated. They sought to reinterpret Islam on the basis of a pure understanding of the Qur'an and Hadith, and thus to gain political power for a reformed Islamic State. Their efforts were paralleled in India and later in Pakistan by Maududi (d. 1978), who sought to transform the young Pakistan into what he called a "theo-democracy." In Turkey, Said Nursi (d. 1960) founded the Nurculuk Movement as a spiritual force against secularism. The legacy of the colonial period has a considerable effect up to the present, as will be touched on at greater length in the last chapter. The twentieth century saw Muslims lose territories in the Balkans, Central Asia, Kashmir, Palestine, and parts of Greece and China.

The Mohammed Ali Mosque in Cairo, Egypt.
Photo: © 2006 Megan J. Thorvilson

5

The Central Beliefs of Islam

Basic creed – God – God is beyond all our concepts – analogy – the Beautiful Names of God – Muslim names – God guides and judges – Angels – *jinn* – the *Shaytan* (Satan): Iblis – Prophets – Books – the power and foreknowledge of God – free will – predestination – human accountability – death – awareness in the grave – the Last Days – return of Jesus – victory of good over evil – general resurrection – judgment – heaven and hell

The Qur'an contains many statements of the principal beliefs of Islam, such as Q. 2:177: "To believe in God, and the Last Day, and the Angels, and the Book, and the Messengers." This has led to scholars drawing up many creeds or statements of belief down through the ages. Often these have been subtly worded, and new clauses have been added to counter perceived misunderstandings. Here we will take one of the simplest of these creeds, often called Iman al-Mufassal: I believe in God, in his Angels, in his Revealed Books, in all his Prophets, in the Day of Judgment, in that everything, both good and evil, comes from him, and in the Life Hereafter. Let us look at these beliefs in some detail.

God

At the heart of the Muslim belief in God is the principle of *tawhid*, or absolute oneness. God is unlike any created thing. God is unique and human beings are unable to talk adequately about God. At best, our language merely points in the right direction but it never can grasp the reality of God. God is above all our concepts and language. Technically we say that God is ineffable, beyond our knowing, or that God is transcategorial, beyond all our categories. As God is one, God cannot be divided or share divinity with any created being. God has no partners. The greatest sin in Islam, the one sin that will not be forgiven (Q. 4:48), is to give partners to God. This is called *shirk*. Belief in the oneness of God is not just an intellectual thing; it also requires action. Human beings were created for the sole purpose of worshipping God (Q. 51:56); what else is life for but to love and serve

God, who is Truth and who alone is worthy of our worship? Love, obedience, and worship go together in the Islamic tradition. To love God is to obey God. To obey God is to worship God. Nothing must be allowed to come between the worshipper and submission to the only being worthy of our love and worship, namely God.

The Qur'an contains many descriptions of God and the ways that God acts. We are told that God sits on a throne (Q. 2:255); mention is made of God's hands (Q. 3:73, 36:71), God's eyes (Q. 11:37), and God's face (Q. 2:115). There are frequent references to God seeing, speaking, and hearing. Some scholars have taken these to be metaphorical references, and others have said that, whatever they mean, they do not mean that God has hands, eyes, face, etc. as human beings have them but nevertheless they are real. There is always a resistance to use human terms, anthropomorphisms, about God. God is beyond such allusions.

Whenever we speak about God, we have to use the language of analogy. This means that our language is the best we can use to speak of God but without penetrating to the reality of God. Let us take two examples. If I say "my foot comes at the end of my leg" and "I go to the foot of the mountain," I am using the term "foot" in two different ways. In the first case, this is a description and in the second an analogy. Mountains do not have feet as I do, but my use of this term gives me an insight without being literal. To take this one stage further, if I wanted to give someone born blind an idea of the color scarlet, I could say that it is "like a fanfare of trumpets." Clearly this is not a literal description, but one can see that it conveys something of the idea to a person who cannot have the category of the color scarlet.

If we search the Qur'an, it is possible to draw from it certain philosophical concepts to speak about God. God is the quintessence of perfection. God is all-knowing, all-powerful (Q. 6:59, 34:22). God is transcendent or totally other. God is beyond all time and space. There was never a time before God existed (Q. 7:7), and we cannot say that God is or is not somewhere (Q. 2:115). God is beyond all that. The danger of this emphasis is that God remains distant from the human being, unapproachable. The Qur'an counters this by saying that "We [God] are nearer to him [human] than his jugular vein" (Q. 50:16). Now, my jugular vein is part of me; through it my life blood courses; without it I would cease to be alive. This speaks profoundly then also of the closeness or *immanence* of God (Q. 2:186).

How can we speak about God or catch any glimpses of what God is like? The scholars of Islam have searched the Qur'an and Hadith to find all the names by which God is called. They give a list of characteristics or qualities of God. These are not technically attributes (*sifat*) of God (that is another discussion), but they tell us something of the way God acts in terms that give us some insight, but without being able to speak of God in God's very self because that is unknowable. There are ninety-nine names by which God is called in the Qur'an and Hadith (Q. 7:180, 17:110, 20:7, 59:23-24). We do not have the space to list them all, and anyway in translation they give us only rough approximations of the Arabic name. However, God is called: the Most Great, the Just, the Almighty, the Source of Goodness, the All-Seeing, the All-Forgiving, the Guide, the Wise, the Truth, the Most Generous, the Creator, the Protector, the Light, the Compassionate, the Source of Peace, the Loving, the Unique, the Friend, and so on.

The Ninety-Nine Beautiful Names are used in Muslim piety. Many times one will see a Muslim with a string of beads called a *tasbih*, *misbah*, or *subha*. This consists of ninety-nine beads and can be used to recite the Beautiful Names. By so doing, one is not only proclaiming the praises of God but also meditating on these characteristics. Within sufi circles, there is a phrase "to be colored with the colors of God." This means, as far as lies within the human capacity, to allow oneself to be formed by these divine qualities. This is a necessary part of becoming more completely the Regent of God on earth. Under the guidance of a sufi teacher, a *shaykh* or *shaykha* (fem.), the student might be given a particular name on which to meditate by many repetitions each day. This might be a quality that the teacher sees to be lacking in this individual. Someone lacking in patience might be given the Name *Al-Sabur* (the Patient One) to repeat a thousand times each day to develop the quality of patience. The *tasbih* is also used for repeating phrases in praise of God. A typical exercise would be to repeat thirty-three times each: *Allahu Akbar* (God is the greatest), *Subhan Allah* (all glory be to God), and *al-Hamdu li 'llah* (all praise/thanks be to God).

For Christians it is worth noting that Muslim tradition does not refer to God as "father" as does the biblical tradition (Isa. 9:6, 64:8; Ps. 68:5; Jer. 31:9). This is because of the potential confusion of running into father-son terminology. The Qur'an says that "God is not begotten, nor does God beget" (Q. 112:3, 19:35, 23:91), meaning that God does not have children, as, for example, the ancient Greeks thought. "Far exalted is He above having a son" (Q. 4:171).

Muslim men often are named by adding the prefix Abd, or Servant, to one of the Beautiful Names. So it is common to find men called Abd al-Rahman (Servant of the Most Merciful), Abd al-Samad (Servant of the Eternal), Abd al-Wahhab (Servant of the Bestower), Abd al-Malik

(Servant of the Sovereign Lord), Abd al-Latif (Servant of the Subtle One), and so on. Muslim women often are named with reference to one of these Names, such as Salma (from Peace), Nurallah (Light of God), Azizah (from Almighty), Karimah (from Most Generous), and so on. In this way, there is a parallel to the old English tradition of naming girls Grace, Hope, Charity, Patience, and so on. Many men have Muhammad as part of their name out of respect for the Prophet, and both sexes can be called after great Muslims of the past such as Ali, Hasan, Abu Bakr, Fatima, Khadija, and Zaynab. The names of earlier Prophets, such as Adam, Ibrahim (Abraham), Musa (Moses), and 'Isa (Jesus) are used often. Women frequently are called after biblical figures, such as Maryam (Mary), Sara (Sarah), and Rahil (Rachael). The name thus gives the person something on which to reflect and a quality or person to be imitated in life.

God is the creator and sustainer of all life; without God's continual engagement with creation all would cease to exist. God is the guide who has revealed to human beings the way life should be lived in accordance with the divine commands (Q. 92:12). God alone is the ultimate judge, who will call all human beings to account (Q. 88:26). As one might imagine, there have been many theological discussions and disputes about exactly how God acts. One of the earliest disputes regarded what to do with someone who becomes a Muslim and then commits a major sin. Some said that he or she should be expelled from the community, others that they should be executed, but the majority eventually said that God alone can judge the intentions of the heart of any human being and so judgment should be reserved to God (Q. 88:21-26), although crimes against the code of law are subject to the courts and their punishments.

Angels

If God is to guide human beings, messengers are needed to convey that guidance to the earth without any possibility of corruption on the way. This is one task of the angels. In Islamic understanding, they are spirit beings "created of light" and therefore have subtle bodies, which means that they can take on different forms, appear, and disappear and do not eat, drink, or reproduce (Q. 19:64-65, 35:1). They do not have free will and so are always absolutely *muslim*. They are told to do a thing by God and do it without question and without the capacity to decide that they know better (Q. 66:6). In this way, they are like automatons or robots; they do exactly what they are programed to do. This makes them ideal as pure messengers from the transcendent world to our created world.

The number of angels and their identities are unknown. Certain angels are identified in the Qur'an and in Islamic tradition: Jibril, the carrier of messages; Mika'il, who guards places of worship; Izra'il, the bringer of death; Israfil, who will sound the trumpet to mark the Day of Resurrection; and Munkar and Nakir, who visit the dead in their graves to conduct the initial interrogation. At the end of every formal prayer, a greeting is given to include the surrounding angels.

The Qur'an tells us that every human being is accompanied through life by two recording angels (Q. 6:61, 50:17-18). One is charged with recording every good deed, and the other records every bad deed. At the final judgment, these records will be produced and everyone judged according to their deeds (Q. 17:13-15).

The question may already have arisen in Christian minds about Satan or Lucifer, the "fallen angel." In the Islamic system, there is no possibility of an angel rebelling against God, and therefore the Satan figure, or *Shaytan*, is not understood as an angel but rather a *jinn* (Q. 7:12-18). The *jinn* are a third form of sentient life alongside humans and angels. They are created from fire, as opposed to the angels from light and humans from clay. They normally are invisible and inhabit a universe parallel to our own, although some particularly pious people claim to see *jinn* and to speak to them. The *jinn* possess some free will and thus will be judged by God. Some are obedient to the divine will and thus are *muslim*, but others have chosen to rebel against God and thus have the potential to be the *Shaytan*.

The Qur'an speaks of an assembly of the souls in Paradise before human beings were sent to the earth (Q. 2:30-34, 15:28-42, 38:71-85). At this assembly, God taught the names of all created things to Adam as the first human being, and thus humans have the power and potential to be the Regents of God upon the earth. God then ordered all angels and *jinn* to bow down before Adam to acknowledge his superior status and knowledge. The angels, having no free will, immediately obeyed. Among the *jinn*, one called Iblis disputed with God, saying that he was superior to Adam because he was created from fire rather than clay. He refused to obey God's command, so Iblis was cast down to the earth, where he spends his time tempting human beings into rebellion. Ultimately, of course, God is God, and good will triumph over evil. God told Iblis that he would have no power over those who are full of *taqwa*, God-consciousness (Q. 15:40-43), but those who neglect the guidance of God are prone to be forgetful and enter into sin (Q. 20:115). There are many references to Iblis in the

Qur'an (Q. 2:34, 7:11-18, 15:28-31, 17:61-65, 18:50, 20:116-123, and 38:71-85).

Some *jinn* then are good, others are bad. They constantly surround human beings and play an important part in popular Islam. They can be dangerous for innocent people to deal with or to take as spirit guides, as they can lead people into evil ways and destruction. They can possess people, and the pious and learned drive them out through exorcism. In traditional societies, many bad things are blamed on the *jinn*, and *jinn* are used to explain what appears to be beyond explanation. Not surprisingly, some people are quick to describe people they do not like or who oppose them as "being possessed by a bad *jinn*." This sometimes is used to explain childlessness, neurosis, mental illness, strong characters, epilepsy, and so on.

Prophets

Much has been said already about Prophets. Here it is necessary to say only that an unknown number have been sent by God to all peoples from the beginning of time. By definition, all are sinless through the protection of God in the form of knowledge. They exemplify the *muslim* way of life and lead others on the straight path. Muslims are required to believe in all Prophets without distinction, but for Muhammad we have the most accurate and extensive data of his life and teaching.

Books

Similarly, God has been sending guidance in the form of revealed Books since the beginning of time. Precisely how many and what they were is unknown. Only the Books referred to in the Qur'an can be known for sure. All these revealed scriptures were in essence the same, as all taught the *muslim* way of life. When Muslims ruled in large parts of India, they took the Vedas, the scriptures of the Hindus, as being the remnants of the Book that was sent to them, and so the Hindus at that time were accorded protected status as People of the Book. The criterion for judgment on all earlier Books is the Qur'an, as it is preserved intact from the time of revelation until the present.

The power and foreknowledge of God

One of the tricky issues all monotheistic religions must resolve is how to make the human being responsible for his or her acts while maintaining the absolute power of God. Let us explore this through some questions. If I am an absolutely free agent, how then can we say that God is all-powerful, because I have my own portion of power for myself? If I am not free in what I do, but my destiny is absolutely laid out for me by God, then how can I be held accountable for my actions? Is not God to blame for what I do, and not me? How can we say that God is just if God punishes me for things God made me do? If God knows everything before it happens, why didn't God stop that person from doing something terrible before she did it? If God knew that person was going to do all those wicked things, why did God create him, or why did God not take his life when he was young? If God both knew the wicked things someone would do and wrote that into the person's destiny, does that not make God evil and wicked? These are seriously deep waters!

These issues have been discussed by Muslim scholars down through the ages. Some took one position and others another. Some held that human beings had complete free will and so deserved whatever happened to them. This led to their saying that God is just and must act justly. To show mercy to one person was to treat another with injustice because each earned his or her rewards or punishments. How can this be understood when God is considered to be all-merciful? Another group said that everything was predestined so that God is all-powerful and the human being acts out the part that was written for him or her by God. The extreme end of this position would be to say that God compels human actions, but the majority regarded this as going too far.

When people think of God predetermining the life of a human being, there is often a pulling back from the idea. We often underestimate the love and mercy of God. A baby who naturally relies on the loving kindness of a mother does not pull back at the idea that this is not a free act. Once we accept that God is wise, compassionate, and merciful, we abandon ourselves to the divine will, freely accepting that God knows what is best for us, even though it may not appear that way at the time. If we let God determine our lives, then we may be sure that God does not will the loss of one of God's servants. Modern people have a high sense of their own importance! But instead of putting center stage the free autonomy of the human being, Islam focuses on God, whose nature is to call, guide, and be merciful toward human beings. God's choices are always for the good, and the only thing that can prevent that good reaching us is our rebellion.

Islam does not have a doctrine of election, which would say that a portion of human beings are predestined for salvation and another for damnation. All human beings are capable of living an ethical life by following the *shari'a* that has been laid out for them. Every human being who becomes truly the servant of God in all things can rely upon the mercy of God on the Day of Judgment. This life is not all there is; there is also the life hereafter, for which this life is only a testing ground and preparation. It is within this mind-set that Islam speaks of people being predetermined by God.

Certain things must be held together. God is all-powerful and cannot be forced to allow something to happen; therefore the power behind every action, both good and bad, comes from God. We would have to say that God wills it, but that is not the same as saying that it pleases God or it is the way God wanted that power to be used. Time for another example. If I lend my car to my son for the night, provided I have made sure that the car is mechanically sound, that my son has been trained properly to drive it, and that I have given him all the necessary guidance to ensure he drives safely, how then can I be held responsible when my son drives too fast around a bend, loses control, and crashes the car? And yet one can say that by buying the car, maintaining it, teaching my son to drive, giving him guidance, and lending him the car, I willed that he should be driving it that night. It was not, however, according to my wish or my good pleasure that he should crash the car—if he had abandoned himself to my will, he would have been safe. He was responsible for the accident, and one could call it an act of rebellion or disobedience to my wishes. In this way we can see that human beings are given the responsibility by God to use God's power even in disobedience to God's clear instructions and even though God hates the evil that comes from human actions.

When I sent my son out that night, I did not know what would happen. I am limited by time and cannot see the future. The difference is that God is not limited by time, and so there is no future with God. God knows every action that I will perform before I was born—the good and the bad. In this way we can say that God has foreknowledge of every act. Why then did God not prevent my son from speeding? If God had done so, then my son would have been deprived of his freedom to act, which is an essential characteristic of being human. If God interferes in that way, human beings are no more than robots or the playthings of God. The Qur'an tells us that God did not create human beings for sport but to love and worship God, that is, to obey God (Q. 44:38). But God wants the freely given obedience of a free being, that is, human dignity. It is a consequence of free will that I can rebel against the commands of God, even to the point of ultimate rebellion, and thus end up in hell.

If we look at this philosophically for a moment, we could talk about primary and secondary causality. God is the primary cause of all actions—*that* the car is driven along the road—as God cannot be forced to do something against God's will. All power is with God. But in terms of secondary causality—*how* the car is driven along the road—that is the individual human being's responsibility. Human beings are given the power of secondary causality.

One of the great Sunni scholars, al-Ash'ari (d. 935), developed a doctrine of attribution. In his theory, all power lies with God, and God wills everything that happens (primary causality); God knows everything outside of time (God has foreknowledge), but, just before a human being does an act, the responsibility for how that act is performed (secondary causality) is attributed to him or her, and so she or he is responsible for it and not God. Thus the human being can be held accountable at the final judgment for the way life has been lived.

There is an element of fatalism here. If everything is predestined then I have no control over my fate, so why should I bother? With too much fatalism in the system there is no moral tension between good and evil. I just do whatever I do. This would prevent me from struggling to be the obedient Servant of God on earth and would mean that I have no incentive to learn God's will, to become God-conscious, and so to act in a godly way. This struggle to do right and to worship God through obedience is an essential part of God's plan for human beings. If I relax this moral tension, then I begin to slip backward away from God. The Qur'an tells us that the human being is naturally forgetful (Q. 39:8). We live in a dynamic universe—it is ever-changing. Once again, life is like being on a moving walkway but going against the direction of travel. To retain my position, I have to keep going forward. To stand still is to be taken backward. This means that I must maintain the moral tension of doing right and avoiding evil all the time.

Muslims are taught to begin every action with the words *Bism' Allah al-Rahman al-Rahim*, or "In the name of God, the Merciful, the Compassionate." These words come at the beginning of every chapter of the Qur'an, except Sura 9. Although God is *al-Adl* (the Just), God has taken upon himself the law of mercy, and so the mercy of God outweighs God's wrath, as we will see when we look at the final judgment in a moment. God has promised in the Qur'an never to allow someone to be tempted beyond his or her means to overcome evil and do what is right (Q. 2:286, 6:152). Remember that the *Shaytan* was told he would have no power over someone who was full of *taqwa* (God-consciousness). The person who truly dedicates every act "In the name of God" has the assurance of the power of God to live a godly life and avoid sin.

Death

Death is inevitable according to Islam (Q. 28:88). Every created being is created in time and space, and so their earthly existence must come to an end. This life is a test that prepares us for death, which is the point of transition to *akhira*, or the afterlife. During the various ups and downs of life, human beings are taught to cultivate the twin pillars of *taqwa* (God-consciousness) and *sabr* (patience). One of the great women mystics of Islam, Rabi'a al-Adawiyya (d. 801), coined a famous saying that human beings should not worship God through fear of hell or in the hope of heaven but purely out of love for God.

Life after death begins as soon as someone is placed in the grave. The records of a person's life, kept by the recording angels, are closed at this time. There is nothing more that the dead person can do to affect his or her fate. Life in the grave, or in *barzakh*, is understood in Islam as a period of timeless awareness during which one awaits the resurrection. Some Muslims believe they can perform pious acts in the name of the person who has died and thus assist them during their time in *barzakh*. As soon as the mourners have filled in the grave and left, the angels Munkar and Nakir appear. They conduct an initial interrogation, asking the dead person who is their Lord, what religion they followed, and who their Prophet was. This leads to a foretaste of the joys of heaven or the torments of hell. If the former, then the grave is held to expand, to become light and airy, and to be filled with the sweet scents of heaven. If the latter, then the grave contracts, becomes dark and cold, and is filled with the stench of hell. This state of *barzakh* is hard to describe accurately. On the one hand it is real and is to be feared or awaited; on the other hand, Muslims know that if one digs up a dead body some time later, the process of decay will have taken place.

Our human language and knowledge break down beyond death. One way of glimpsing this is to recall the *mi'raj*, or Night Journey, of

Muhammad. You will recall that Muhammad was taken from Makka to Jerusalem and from there ascended to heaven, where he had an audience with God. All this took place in an instant. Yet the tradition tells us that on the way to Jerusalem, Muhammad passed the grave of Moses and saw Moses there in prayer. When he arrived in Jerusalem, Muhammad was greeted by all the earlier Prophets, including Moses, and he led them in prayer. After his initial audience with God, Muhammad met Moses in heaven and conversed with him. That is three meetings with Moses in three very different contexts, all in a single instant. In this way we see that what happens after death can be both "real" and beyond our earthly comprehension.

The Last Days and the final judgment

The Last Days will be the period of time before the end of the world. How long they will last is not known. At the start of the Last Days, *al-Mahdi*, or the Rightly Guided One, will appear. He will begin a rule of justice on the earth. For the Shi'a, *al-Mahdi* is associated with the return of the Twelfth Imam, who is currently in occultation. Muslim history has seen many who falsely claimed to be the Mahdi. It was a way of rallying Muslims to their cause. One example is the Mahdi of Sudan (d. 1885), who fought the British for independence.

For the Sunnis, after the coming of *al-Mahdi*, 'Isa (Jesus) will return to the earth and lead the great battle of good versus evil. The forces of evil at this time will be led by *al-Dajjal*, literally the "Charlatan," or "Great Impostor." He becomes known in tradition as a form of the Antichrist, who epitomizes evil and rebellion against the will of God. Jesus will lead all true believers in this battle and will be victorious over *al-Dajjal* and all evil. Jesus then will rule the world for a period of time in complete obedience to the will of God, that is, in the state of *islam*. At the end of this time, Jesus will die and will be buried alongside Muhammad in Madina, where his grave awaits him. This will be the signal for the end of time.

At the end of time, all who are then alive will die. Then will come the sign for the general resurrection. The Angel Israfil on this day will sound the trumpet to signal the resurrection. All will rise from their graves and be clothed in "new bodies" that lie beyond our earthly comprehension, as a butterfly must be for a caterpillar (Q. 56:60-61). Then all will be held to account for their actions (Q. 23:99-100). Each will stand alone and naked before God as Judge (Q. 35:18). "Alone" here means that no one will be held responsible for the sins of another; blame cannot be transferred to anyone else (Q. 82:19). Naked means there will be no place to hide anything; all will be known by God and must be acknowledged. The Books of Life, the records kept by the Recording Angels, will be produced, and each will be weighed in the balance of God's justice (Q. 17:13-14). While God is just, God is also merciful, and the mercy of God outweighs God's wrath. This is exemplified by the tradition that on the last day every good deed weighs ten times more than every bad deed.

The Prophets also will line up before God, and they too will be questioned. The Qur'an says explicitly that Jesus will be asked if he taught his followers to take him and his mother as gods beneath God (Q. 5:119). He will of course answer that he did not. Some scholars hold that God will grant permission to each of the Prophets on this day to intercede on behalf of their followers. So, for example, Muhammad will intercede only for Muslims. This will be an action of the mercy of God and not something to which the Prophets have a right independent of God's mercy. Once each person is weighed in the balance, he or she will be sent to heaven or hell. There is no third option.

Heaven and hell

The Qur'an tells us that the nature of heaven and hell is beyond our earthly capacity to understand (Q. 32:17). Heaven is most often referred to in the Qur'an as *al-Jannah*, literally "the Garden" or "Gardens." The Qur'an uses images of heaven that are physical: joy and peace, gardens with running water, food without labor, and mates of the opposite sex. Some scholars have interpreted these more metaphorically, in line with a Hadith that speaks of heaven as a state no human eye ever has seen nor human ear heard.

Hell has many descriptions and terms in the Qur'an. The most commonly used is *al-Nar*, literally "the Fire." It is also referred to as *al-Hawiya*, the Abyss; *al-Hutama*, literally "that which shatters"; *Jahannam*, literally "the Depths"; *al-Jahim*, "the place for idolaters"; *Laza*, literally "the Great Furnace"; *Sa'ir*, "the Blazing Inferno"; and *Saqar*, "the Scorching Fire." The common theme here is of unimaginable torment and loss. The question was asked by some: Is hell eternal? Some scholars have argued on the basis of Q. 11:107-108 that some might be sent there only "for a time" to be purged from their sins, after which the mercy of God will overwhelm them and they will be admitted to heaven. However, the Qur'an states explicitly that the sin of *shirk*, that is, to associate created beings with God, to say that God shares divinity with any created thing, never will be forgiven (Q. 4:48).

Dome over the mausoleum of the Mamluke Sultan Qaytbay in Cairo, Egypt. Photo: Marc Ostlie-Olson.

6

The Principal Practices of Islam

Islam stands on five pillars or principal practices – *shahada*: there is one God – conversion to Islam – conversion: marriage – conversion: intellectual inquiry, the sufi way, seeking a home – informal prayer – prayer of the heart – *salat*: formal prayer – regular rhythm – call to prayer – direction for prayer – preparation: washing (*wudu*) – preparation: intention (*niyya*) – a unit of prayer (*rak'a*) – the *imam* at congregational prayer – women and *salat*: in the mosque and at home – Friday congregational prayers – *zakat*: purification of wealth – setting up charitable trusts (*waqf*) – economic exploitation forbidden (*riba*) – the circulation of wealth (*infaq*) – *zakat* calculation and payment – *sawm*: the fast during the month of Ramadan – the lunar calendar – moon sighting – practicalities of fasting – a review of life – the Night of Power – exemptions – children – 'Id al-Fitr

For a human being to be *muslim* is as natural as a bird on the wing or a fish in the sea. The natural state of all human beings is to be in perfect harmony with God and with all of creation. We all were born in this state. However, our world is constantly changing, and if we do not strive to live a *muslim* life, we will drift off in forgetfulness of God's ways. We need the ritual practices of religion to keep us focused, to remind us of the guidance we have been given, and to train us in upright living.

It is said that Islam is like a building standing on five foundations, or pillars—the five principal practices of Islam. While they are good and necessary in themselves, their ultimate aim is to train those who practice them so that they will be ever-mindful of living a godly life. These practices are a training program to build *taqwa*, God-consciousness, within the Muslim so that she or he may be led into the perfect state of *islam* and thus be both happy in this life and rewarded with Paradise in the hereafter.

The five pillars are:

- *Shahada*: to profess and practice the principal belief of Islam
- *Salat*: to perform ritual prayer five times daily
- *Zakat*: to purify one's wealth by providing money to those in need
- *Sawm*: to fast during the month of Ramadan
- *Hajj*: to make the pilgrimage to Makka once in a lifetime, if health and wealth permit (see chapter 2).

Fig. 10. The Five Pillars of Islam

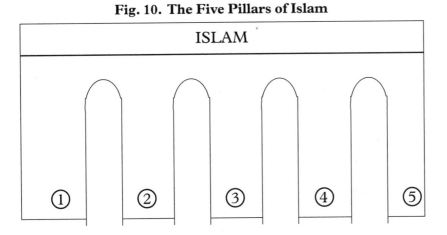

1. *Shahada*: to profess and practice the principal belief of Islam
2. *Salat*: to perform ritual prayer five times daily
3. *Zakat*: to purify one's wealth by providing money to those in need
4. *Sawm*: to fast during the month of Ramadan
5. *Hajj*: to make the pilgrimage to Makka once in a lifetime, if health and wealth permit

Shahada: To profess and practice the principal belief of Islam

The *shahada* states: "I bear witness that there is no god (that is, nothing worthy of worship) save God; Muhammad is the Messenger of God." This is the principal statement of belief for a Muslim, and every Muslim repeats it several times a day. It often is found written on the wall of a mosque and frequently is written in beautiful calligraphy and displayed in public places and in Muslim homes. It serves as a constant reminder that a Muslim cannot allow anything to get in the way of the loving worship of God alone.

Fig. 11. The Pillars and Foundations of Shi'a Islam

In the Shi'a system, things are drawn rather differently. Here, Islam stands on ten pillars, which themselves rest on five foundations. In this system, each individual believer is responsible for coming to their own conviction in faith, based on reason, for the five foundations of Islam. Only then can one build on this foundation the ten principal practices of Islam. These practices are discussed in various places in these chapters. There is much common ground with the Sunnis, but the last two pillars are specific to the Shi'a. They focus on the attitude of the believer toward the Family of Muhammad (Ahl al-Bayt), comprising Muhammad, Fatima, and all Twelve Imams (Q. 42:23)

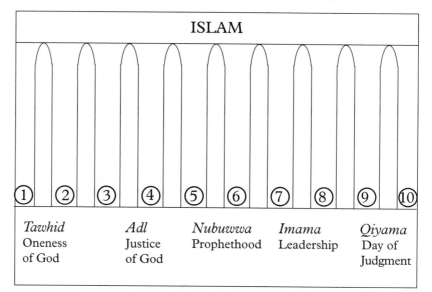

1. **Salat**: the five daily ritual prayers
2. **Sawm**: to fast during the month of Ramadan
3. **Hajj**: to make the pilgrimage to Makka
4. **Zakat**: the payment due to the poor and those in need
5. **Khums**: twenty percent of surplus wealth administered by the scholars for the welfare of the community (Q. 8:41)
6. **Jihad**: to stuggle and strive in the way of God (Q. 2:190)
7. **Amr bil Maruf**: commanding the good (Q. 3:104)
8. **Nahy anil Munkar**: forbidding evil (Q. 3:104)
9. **Tawalla**: to love and respect the Ahl al-Bayt
10. **Tabarra**: to turn away from those unjust to the Ahl al-Bayt

The *shahada* is in two parts that are inseparably linked. The first part is an abstract statement to say that nothing else is worthy of worship save God. The second part gives a concrete content to this statement. How do we know about God and that it is God alone that we worship? Through the guidance sent by God to the Messenger Muhammad. This gives a definite content to the abstract saying. One does not stand without the other. This is the core statement of belief going back to Adam and Eve. In the time of Moses or Jesus it would have read: "There is no god save God; Moses (or Jesus) is a Messenger of God." Each Messenger in turn has received a revelation that gives content to the ultimate belief.

The last and protected revelation was given in the Qur'an, from which we know that God is one, unique, indivisible, and unlike any created being. God does not share divinity with any created being, so nothing can be associated with God. To associate anything with God is *shirk*, that is, "to give God partners." God alone is worthy of worship, without any intermediary between the human being and God. The *shahada* does not rule out only idols, idols in the sense of human inventions that people worship instead of or alongside God. It also rules out the modern idols of power, wealth, prestige, high birth, racial superiority, nationalism, and so on. Nothing can be allowed to distract from the love and worship of God alone.

As we live in a dynamic, changing world, we cannot perform the *shahada* just once and then forget about it. Each day, each minute must be put to the worship of God alone. Muslims constantly are required to reexamine their lives to ensure that they have not allowed any distraction that might divert them from absolute obedience to God; that is what worship means. It is like being married. One might make the commitment to marriage on one's wedding day, but that needs to be renewed constantly if the marriage is to be kept alive and dynamic. Once one acknowledges the reality of God and that all else is vain, then things come into their rightful place.

Conversion to Islam

It is through professing the *shahada* that someone becomes a convert to Islam. Since being *muslim* is our natural state, and we all were born in this original state, some people prefer to speak of someone "reverting" to Islam, rather than converting. For someone to become consciously a Muslim, they have only to make the *shahada*, knowing and understanding what they are doing, in front of witnesses. Even if someone were washed up alone on a desert island and came to this realization, they could profess the *shahada* to God and then live a Muslim life. He or she would be accepted as a Muslim from then on.

In some Christian churches, it is common to undergo a lengthy period of instruction and testing before one is admitted to baptism. This is not the case in Islam. Provided one is sufficiently informed to know what one is doing, one can become a Muslim immediately. To be a Muslim is the natural birthright of every human being; how then can anyone say "wait a bit" before making this decision? To become a Muslim is like claiming the right to breathe oxygen. To be convinced that God alone is God and Muhammad is God's Messenger is sufficient to take up one's natural condition of following that guidance. From this moment on, the new Muslim should aim to implement that guidance in every aspect of life. Naturally there will be a lifetime of learning more about that guidance and committing oneself more and more to complete obedience to the way God wants us to live, but it starts straight away once one is convinced. Beginning the process of bringing our natural state to the perfection of being fully human should not be delayed.

This is an appropriate moment to consider the trend in the West of conversion to Islam. There appear to be four general contexts in which people in the West are converting to Islam: marriage; through intellectual inquiry; on the mystical path; in search of friendship, dignity, and support.

In the Sunni tradition, a Muslim man is permitted to marry a Muslim woman or a woman from among the People of the Book (Q. 2:221; 5.5). A Muslim woman must marry a Muslim man. In most schools of Shi'a Islam, both partners in a permanent marriage must be Muslims, but some Ayatollahs will permit men who follow their teaching to take Christian wives. In all cases, Islam is the natural birthright of a child, and so all children must be brought up as Muslims.

Let us take first the case of a Muslim woman who falls in love with a non-Muslim man. They are faced with only three possibilities. He can explore Islam and come to the decision to convert, and then they can marry. They can decide to break off their friendship on the basis that there is no future and that continuing would bring them both more hurt. The woman might decide to marry the man outside the bounds of Islamic law. Such a decision most probably would have massive consequences in terms of her future relationship with her family and the Muslim community. This would be considered a major sin, a direct rebellion against a clear command of God in the Qur'an. Some Muslim women feel in their conscience that they should do this and continue to follow the Islamic way of life, but this would require considerable personal strength of character and either a very "understanding" family or an ability to live estranged from the family and community. According to Islamic law, if a Muslim woman were to marry in such circumstances and then later decide that she wished to be reconciled with God and the community, she would need to divorce her "husband," who would not be recognized as such by Islamic law. Not surprisingly, there is considerable pressure on the man in such circumstances to consider converting to Islam in order to marry and retain his wife's connection to her family and the Muslim community.

Such issues concerning the selection of a marriage partner and the raising of children are common in Christianity, Judaism, and other religions too. A Roman Catholic is required to seek permission from the church to marry a Christian from another tradition. A more stringent permission is required to marry a non-believer or someone from another religion. The Catholic partner is expected to do everything possible to ensure that children are brought up as Roman Catholics. An initiated Sikh can marry only another initiated Sikh, and Hindus are expected to marry within their castes. Within Orthodox Judaism, a Jew must marry another Jew, as Judaism is passed down through the woman to her children. For a Jewish man to marry outside the community is a major tragedy, as it effectively puts an end to that Jewish line of descent. While a Jewish woman who marries outside the community technically has Jewish children, where is the Jewish family life that will support and nurture those children in their faith? Some Orthodox Jews in this situation will affiliate with the Progressive movement within Judaism, which holds that Jewishness passes down through either partner and which will support families in which only one partner is a Jew.

In the case of a Sunni Muslim man, he is permitted to take a Jewish or Christian wife, and she is free to continue to follow her religion, although the children will be brought up as Muslims. This is according to Sunni law, but that may not agree with what the man's family thinks! Often Muslim men in such circumstances are put under considerable pressure from their families to suggest that the woman convert to Islam before the marriage takes place. This would be absolutely necessary for most Shi'a Muslims.

Even if married life begins with the woman remaining a Christian, that is not necessarily the end of the question. Some women convert to Islam later on, after they experience the warmth and support of living within their husband's extended family. Some convert when children come along in order to present a united family context to their children. Some are made to consider these issues again when their children grow old enough to ask their mothers the awkward questions that make them rethink their positions. It is never easy to live in a nuclear or extended family in which the family cannot pray together and in which two codes of life are followed.

Some men and women consider conversion to Islam through their intellectual inquiry into the Qur'an and the guidance that it gives for human life. Islam prides itself on being a rational, balanced, common-sense vision of reality and way of life, and this attracts some people who just find that this is the natural way that makes sense for them. Islam is also possessed of a great body of scholarship down through the ages, and some people find their way to Islam through intensive study of the tradition. The Islamic code of life gives clear guidance on every aspect of human living, and some people are attracted to this clarity in a Western context where other faiths, like Western Christianity, may have become too nuanced or lacking in the clear-cut answers they seek.

For centuries, a steady flow of Western people have been attracted to Islam through the inner path of sufi mysticism. Here they find a code of mystical training and experience that leads them into a deeper communion with God. This is particularly noticeable in our own times when many in the West are searching for a meaning to the deeper spiritual questions of their existence. They find a rich body of sufi teaching, practice, and writing that fulfills their inner search for meaning. Some who come to Islam in this way take an active part in community affairs, while others prefer to make this spiritual ascent as part of a smaller group without necessarily having much to do with the organized community of Muslims.

There are people in our society who feel they lack community support and friendship, and this they find through their association with Muslims of their acquaintance. This applies particularly to people who have gone astray, like people in prison or suffering from substance abuse, for whom the obvious formal structure of Islamic practice can give a secure framework for their lives.

The Islamic code of life gives great dignity and equality to women (see chapter 7), and this appeals to some Western women who feel that they are exploited by contemporary society. Other groups who have experienced exploitation, for example African Americans, have found in Islam a code of equality and dignity that has restored their self-esteem and enabled them to overcome prejudice in the West. Some people feel disgust at what has happened in Western society and so turn to Islam out of a search for a purer way of life.

Islam, like Christianity, is a missionary faith that seeks new members. It would be strange to feel that one has the God-given secret of a balanced and fulfilled way of life on earth that will lead to Paradise through obedience to the ethical will of God, yet not want to share it with others. This is particularly so in Islam, which sees itself as the natural state of every human being and thus part of the human birthright. It always has been part of the Islamic tradition to invite others to consider following the straight path of Islam; this is technically called *da'wa*, and someone who engages in this way is called a *da'i*. This can take the form of producing books and videotapes to promulgate the message of Islam, and some people will approach friends and acquaintances directly to extend the invitation to them.

Turkish prayer rug. Photo: © Minneapolis Institute of the Arts.

Salat: To perform ritual prayer five times daily

Prayer in Islam can be seen in three broad divisions: *salat*, or formal, liturgical prayer; *du'a*, the informal prayer of supplication or "speaking to God"; and *dhikr*, the training of the heart constantly to remember God and thus ascend to a state of *taqwa*. Before moving on to look at *salat*, we will consider the other two forms.

The classical Western Christian definition of prayer is that it concerned the raising of the mind and heart to God. *Du'a* is the raising of the mind to God in supplication, praise, thanksgiving, and seeking forgiveness. It is part of the personal relationship of the Muslim with God as Creator, Sustainer, Lord, Friend, Guide, and All-Merciful. The Muslim is trained to punctuate the day with prayer, and *du'a* have been written to accompany every act from waking in the morning to going to sleep at night (Q. 33:41-42). *Du'a* might be made before eating, before beginning work, on beginning a journey, before visiting the toilet, before making love, and so on. In this way, every element of the day is offered to God in prayer, and God's guidance is sought so that it might be brought to a godly conclusion. Immediately on becoming aware of a sin, one is to make a *du'a* to seek the forgiveness of God. Such *du'a* can be in any language and can use the believer's own words or prayers crafted by earlier generations. Particular attention is given to the *du'a* found in the Qur'an and the Hadith. Books of *du'a* may be found in many languages, and those written by particular Friends of God (*wali*, pl. *awliya*) are widely used. The most common and simple form of a *du'a* is to commence any action by commending it to God with the *Basmala* (*Bism' Allah al-Rahman al-Rahim*, In the Name of God, the Merciful, the Compassionate).

Muslims are trained to raise their hearts to God through the practice of *dhikr*, or the remembrance of God. This is to train the heart as the seat of all wisdom and knowledge to live constantly in a state of *taqwa* or God-consciousness. Even when the mind and hands are occupied in other work, the heart still can be engaged in the remembrance of God. God is constantly aware of all that we do, and no secrets are hidden from God, who is an invisible witness to every human activity (Q. 58:7). Muslims are trained to remember that they live constantly in the presence of God: even though they do not see God, God sees them (*ihsan*). God is closer to each human being than the jugular vein (Q. 50:16). Through *dhikr*, the Muslim develops a sense of thankfulness to God (*shukr*) in every aspect, for example by repeating the phrase *Al-hamdu li 'llah* (All praise/thanks be to God). The whole of life is a blessing (*baraka*) from God. Through *dhikr* the Muslim is reconciled to accepting the will of God in all things, for all is according to the divine will (Q. 6:17). No one knows the hour of one's death, when the Books of Life will be closed, and so the remembrance of God should be constant.

Such training in *dhikr* may take the simple form of repeating many times phrases like *Subhan Allah* (All glory be to God), *Al-hamdu li 'llah* (All praise/thanks be to God), *Allahu Akbar* (God is most great), and many more. At first these are repeated with the lips, then the breathing is attuned to carry the prayer deeper, and then bodily movements might be added. Such practices are highly developed within sufi circles (*tariqa*), where members are taken deeper and deeper on the inner journey under the guidance of a spiritual teacher (*shaykh*, fem. *shaykha*).

Turning now to *salat* itself, a Muslim is required to offer the formal *salat* five times each day in obedience to the command of God. The Qur'an is clear in the requirement of the regular rhythm of *salat*, and the frequency was decreed when Muhammad had an audience with God during his *mi'raj*, or night journey. The times are worked out according to the passage of the sun so that they punctuate the whole day. Everyone can see the sun and tell when it rises, sets, etc. This means that such a method of timing makes all human beings equal; no one needs someone else to tell them when to pray.

The five times are:

- *Salat al-Fajr* before sunrise
- *Salat al-Zuhr* a little after the sun has passed its zenith
- *Salat al-'Asr* in the late afternoon when the shadows lengthen

- *Salat al-Maghrib* directly after sunset
- *Salat al-'Isha* at nighttime.

In this way it can be seen that never more than a few hours pass before the Muslim is called to leave off work and turn to God in prayer. In all cases except *Salat al-Maghrib* there is a "window" of time during which the prayer can be offered. The only times at which *salat* is forbidden are the three times associated with the worship of the sun, namely at sunrise, when the sun is at its zenith (not always precisely at midday away from the Equator), and at sunset. The precise timings of each prayer vary with the different schools of Islam. The working day can be ordered around these times for prayer, which should be offered separately if possible, though they can be combined if the need arises. Within the Shi'a school of Islam, it is customary for convenience to combine prayers into three groups each day, although praying the five separately is recommended.

The sun rises and sets at different times each day and at different times depending on where one is in the world. This means that a prayer timetable must be worked out for each location, and many mosques print such a timetable on a monthly basis for the guidance of local Muslims.

As regular *salat* is commanded by God and the creator knows what is best for the creature, offering the regular *salat* is itself beneficial in obedience to God's command. It brings the Muslim back into the correct relationship with God, a relationship of total submission to God and recognition of one's need for guidance and forgiveness. Verses from the Qur'an are recited at each time of prayer, so that the guidance is heard and noted afresh, and so that any sins that might have been committed since the last time of prayer can be acknowledged and brought before God for forgiveness. If the Muslim has the correct *niyya* or intention, then one can rely on the all-merciful nature of God and be assured of forgiveness. *Salat* is spoken of as though it is a river of mercy flowing from God in which the Muslim is immersed and purified five times each day. Thus regular *salat* is an instruction and purification that brings the believer into that relationship of *taqwa*, or God-consciousness. If this state of *taqwa* is realized at the climax of each *salat*, it can be maintained until the next *salat* by use of *du'a* and *dhikr*.

In order to summon the community to prayer at the correct times, Muhammad established in Madina the practice of having someone stand on a high place and call out in a loud voice. This person became known as the *Muezzin* (or *Mu'adhdhin*, as it sometimes is written).

Fig. 12. "A *taqwascope*"

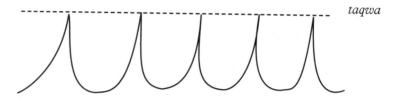

The five peaks represent the five regular prayers (*salat*). The "troughs" can occur when one engages in the normal affairs of life and becomes forgetful of God. These can be "flattened out" by remembering God through *du'a* and *dhikr*.

The aim is to remain in a constant state of *taqwa* through the practice of *salat*, *du'a*, and *dhikr*.

With the building of mosques, a tall tower or minaret was incorporated for the purpose of making this call heard throughout the neighborhood. Gradually the custom was introduced of placing a minaret on every side of the mosque on which there were houses. Today this has been replaced in many countries by the use of directional loudspeakers, which can be positioned so that the call can be heard everywhere. In a Muslim city, the call to prayer is begun from the minaret of the principal mosque and then flows out as though in waves to permeate the whole city. This can be an enchanting and beautiful effect. Even those who choose not to obey the call to prayer are reminded that this is a duty incumbent on all Muslims.

The call to prayer is given before each *salat*, whether from a minaret or just within the mosque itself. In some Western towns and cities, the use of loudspeakers that might disturb the neighborhood becomes controversial. When permission is granted by the civil authorities, it is often after consultations with those within earshot of the minaret. Often conditions are imposed as to the frequency of such a broadcast (how many times each day), the duration of each call (in Muslim cities it is often prolonged by the use of certain melodies), the parameters of time (not before/after a certain time each day), and the level of sound (like any other public noise, such as a burglar alarm).

The call to prayer, or *adhan*, varies a little between different schools of Islam, but it is called in Arabic, and in the Sunni schools typically runs as follows (each line repeated twice):

Allahu akbar	God is most great
Ashhadu an la ilaha illa allah	I bear witness that there is no god but God
Ashhadu anna muhammadan rasul allah	I bear witness that Muhammad is the Messenger of God
Hayya 'ala al-salat	Hurry to prayer
Hayya 'ala al-falah	Hurry to success
Allahu akbar	God is most great
La ilaha illa allah	There is no god but God

For *Salat al-Fajr* in the early morning, most schools include the line

Al-salat khayrun min al-naum	Prayer is better than sleep

When the *salat* is to take place in a congregation, a further call, in wording much like the *adhan*, known as the *iqama*, is made to signify that the formal *salat* is about to start.

While regular *salat*, a duty placed on each individual Muslim, can be performed alone, there is an increased blessing if one prays together in congregation with others, and so this is recommended. It is a sign of unity, a way of giving mutual support and acknowledging that others have rights over each individual. After prayers, worshippers greet one another and share news and concerns. The custom arose for people to meet in extended families or neighborhood mosques for the daily *salat*. For the principal prayer of the week, the *Salat al-Jum'a*, or Friday Prayer, which takes place shortly after the zenith of the sun on Fridays, everyone gathered in the principal mosque of the town (or quarter in a larger town or city), which became known as the Jum'a Mosque. Twice each year, on the two principal festivals of 'Id al-Fitr and 'Id al-Adha, the whole town would assemble on an open piece of ground so that they could pray as a single community. Ultimately, once each year on the great pilgrimage, or *hajj*, the whole worldwide community (*umma*) would assemble symbolically to remind believers of the oneness of the human family on earth.

Salat does not need to be offered in a mosque, but people can congregate at home or at work or in any clean place. The saying of Muhammad applies: "The whole world is my mosque." A clean place is somewhere that is not made unclean by its use, such as a toilet or abattoir, and that has been physically swept out or washed as necessary. It is quite normal for people to pray in the open air on a clean piece of ground. In order to make a clean place fitting for *salat* to be

Fig. 13. The Ka'ba as the earthly focus for prayer

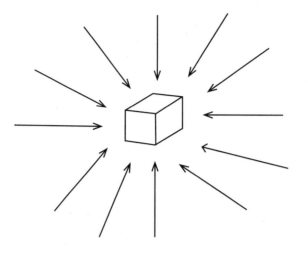

Muslims are turning to offer their *salat* in the direction of the Ka'ba at every second of every day and have been doing so for centuries. Thus they form a single worldwide community united both in time and space.

offered, it became customary to use a prayer mat, which could be unrolled and rolled up again as necessary. Shi'a Muslims have the tradition of placing their forehead on earth or something that grows from it when they prostrate during *salat*; commonly they use a small tablet of clay taken from a holy place, such as Karbala where Imam Husayn was martyred. Mosques are usually carpeted to maintain their cleanliness. Such carpets are often marked out in lines so that worshippers can assemble in rows, shoulder to shoulder. The rows are made up from the front, with each row being completed before the next row is begun. In this way, the united congregation at prayer and the equality of each individual are symbolized; no one has a special place according to their rank or wealth.

Salat is offered always in the direction of the Ka'ba in Makka; this is called the *qibla*, meaning direction. The Ka'ba thus becomes the earthly focus for all *salat*. Wherever Muslims are in the world, they turn toward the Ka'ba five times each day in prayer. It acts like the hub of a wheel with spokes radiating throughout the world. Similarly, because the time of *salat* is regulated according to the passage of the sun, which is always rising and setting somewhere on earth, at every second somewhere Muslims are turning toward the Ka'ba in prayer. Indeed since the early expansion of Islam, one can see that Muslims have been turning toward the Ka'ba constantly without a break for many centuries. Although the Ka'ba is sometimes called the House of God, no one thinks that God is located there; God is far above such things. The Ka'ba is merely the earthly focus for the prayers of the worldwide community, united thus in time and space.

A purpose-built mosque will be orientated in such a way that one wall forms the *qibla* wall and people can line up facing it. This is normally marked by a niche cut into the wall, called a *mihrab*, in which the leader of the congregation at prayer, the *imam*, will stand. Whenever two or more Muslims assemble for *salat*, there always must be someone to lead. In a gathering of men or a mixed congregation, the *imam* will be a man, although in some schools of Islam a woman can lead a gathering of women and children. This is based partly on modesty, as the prayer requires the prostration of the body from a kneeling position so that the forehead is placed on the floor; and partly it stems from the single nature of leadership in which the Prophet and his successors, the Caliphs or Imams, were spiritual, political, judicial, and military leaders. This meant that the one who led the prayers also had to lead the army into battle and so had to be a man.

For Muslims who are traveling, it is common to carry a small compass so that in a strange place the *qibla* can be found. In Muslim countries, this often would be indicated for strangers in places like railway stations or airports. It would be quite common for a traveler to find a *qibla* arrow and a pile of prayer mats at the appropriate end of a railway platform. Of course, as the Qur'an reminds us, "In God there is no East or West" (Q. 2:177), and so someone circling the earth in a space rocket could pray in any direction!

Before beginning the *salat*, one must be both physically and ritually clean. The physical cleaning may take the form of a shower or washing as necessary, and clean clothes should be worn if possible. Ritual cleanliness is achieved through performing the ritual washing, or *wudu*. This requires that the hands, arms, mouth, nose, ears, head, and feet are washed. Different schools of Islam give varying precise instructions. Some require that the feet are washed each time while others say that if socks and shoes have been worn, damp hands simply can be wiped over the socks. This *wudu* can be performed at home or in the mosque, where there will be washrooms.

The ritual washing symbolizes breaking off from the normal routine of affairs to concentrate exclusively on prayer. The parts that are

A man performs *wudu'* before praying.
Photo: Sally Messner.

A *minbar* (right) and a *mihrab* (left) in the 'Amr Ibn al-'As Mosque in Cairo, Egypt. Photo: Sally Messner.

washed are the parts of the body engaged in our working lives. They are also the parts of the body most likely to have been involved in any sin we might have committed since the last *salat*, so in washing these an examination of conscience takes place as the worshipper recalls any sins that need to be brought before God for forgiveness. Washing is also like putting on a spiritual armor to prepare oneself for an encounter with the Lord and Judge. Such regular washing therefore promotes good physical, mental, and spiritual health.

Some schools recommend that a visit to the toilet be made before *wudu* so that there is no build up of waste matter and one is not distracted during prayers. If someone has had contact with a dead body, then a full shower, called *ghusl*, is required. A similar *ghusl* is needed by both partners after sexual activity, or by a woman after childbirth or the completion of her monthly period. As it is not possible for a menstruating woman to retain a state of ritual purity throughout the *salat*, she is exempted from prayers at this time. In preparation for Jum'a Prayers, it is recommended that one has a shower and puts on clean clothes and perfume, as this is like a weekly festival.

A Hadith of the Prophet Muhammad says that "All actions are but by intention," meaning that someone must state or settle on an intention before an act is done. This means that a declaration of intention, or *niyya*, is required before beginning the *salat*. The Muslim stands ready to begin the prayer and declares their intention to perform whichever prayer is about to commence. From this time on, no distractions are permitted; this time is dedicated to God alone.

Each *salat* is made up of a number of cycles of prayer, called *rak'at*. The number of *rak'at* for each *salat* is as follows: two at *fajr*, four at *zuhr*, four at *'asr*, three at *maghrib*, and four at *'isha*. Even here, the practicality of Islam can be seen: the morning prayer is shortest when time might be at a premium, before the day's work begins.

Each *rak'a* comprises recitation of the Qur'an, bodily postures, and prayers, said aloud or silently. The *rak'a* begins when the Muslim raises the hands in a gesture of submission, concentration, and separation from this world; this is accompanied by the words *Allahu akbar* (God is most great). Next comes the recitation of the Qur'an; first the opening chapter, or *Surat al-Fatiha*, and then a selection of verses as each person wishes. In some *salat* that are prayed in congregation, the *imam* will select the verses to be recited and will recite them aloud on behalf of the whole congregation, which must pay careful attention and correct him if he makes a mistake. This is followed by a bow from the waist to acknowledge the guidance of God in the Qur'an. In this position the worshipper says in Arabic: "All glory be to God." This is followed by a moment of silent prayer in the standing position in praise of God. Then the Muslim kneels and goes into the first prostration in which the forehead and palms of the hands are placed on the floor in submission to God. At this point, the prayer changes to a confession and request for forgiveness. Another slight pause is taken sitting back on the feet, which is followed by a second prostration. The Muslim now stands, and this marks the end of one *rak'a* of prayer.

Because *Surat al-Fatiha* is so central to Muslim life, the full text is offered here:

> *In the name of God, the Compassionate, the Merciful.*
> *Praise be to God, the Lord of Creation,*
> *The Compassionate, the Merciful,*
> *Master of the Day of Judgment.*
> *You alone do we worship and to you alone we pray for help.*
> *Guide us to the Straight Path,*
> *The path of those whom you have favored,*
> *Not of those who have incurred your wrath,*
> *Nor of those who have gone astray.*

At the end of the set number of *rak'at* at each *salat*, the Muslim remains sitting back on the heels and recites the *shahada*, then invokes God's blessings upon Muhammad and his family as well as Abraham and his family. The conclusion comes when each turns in unison to the right and to the left and gives the greeting *al-Salamu 'alaykum* (Peace be with you). This is directed at all other worshippers present, the angels that constantly surround us, and by extension to all humankind and the whole of creation. These prayers may be followed by *du'a*, made either individually or by the *imam* on behalf of the whole assembly.

The *salat* is always made in Arabic and follows precisely this set formula. The only thing that changes is the selection of verses from the Qur'an that are recited. At least three verses must be recited in each *rak'a* in addition to the first *sura*. If time permits, each *rak'a* can be lengthened by the inclusion of as much recitation of the Qur'an as one chooses. The verses from the Qur'an must be recited from memory and not read from a book. This means that every Muslim is required to have memorized some Qur'an verses in order to be able to pray. The more one has in one's memory, the wider the selection that can be made. Even those who do not understand Arabic will have memorized the prayers of *salat* and some verses of the Qur'an. New Muslims are encouraged to attend congregational prayer, when the *imam* recites on behalf of all.

A *mihrab*.
Photo: Sally Messner.

In addition to these obligatory (*fard*) prayers, it also is common to find people praying more optional *rak'at* following the example of Muhammad; in general these are known as the *sunna* prayers. If someone has missed an earlier *salat*, it is possible to make amends by catching up. If one has limited mobility such that bowing and prostrating are not possible, one makes the movements to whatever extent one can manage. It is common to find a few chairs in a mosque for those who need to sit throughout; they then make their prostration by bowing from a sitting position. Even someone confined to bed or unable to move their limbs can make the prostration by as little as a movement of an eyelid if necessary.

The *imam* is a key person in all congregational *salat*. He sets the pattern and rhythm of the prayers. Everyone moves according to his instruction and example. When worshippers hear a particular line of prayer, they know that it is time to move into the next position. There is no ordained priesthood in Islam. Anyone can act as *imam*, provided they are pious and have the necessary knowledge to perform the prayer properly and recite the Qur'an. In any gathering, someone will be selected based on these two criteria of piety and wisdom. In the formal setting of a mosque, it is common for someone to be appointed by the mosque committee to lead the prayers; this ensures that they are conducted properly and avoids any questions about who should lead. In some cases, this person might be retained as a paid official, in which case he might also be responsible for conducting the funeral prayers, officiating at weddings, and teaching children and new converts to Islam. It is normal that such a man would have made a systematic study of the Qur'an and Islamic tradition so that he can guide the whole community worthily.

Women are free to attend mosques for prayers as they wish, though in practice some small mosques in converted buildings do not have facilities to accommodate female worshippers. There should be a separate women's entrance and washing facilities. When they do attend, women pray with the men in the same congregation but are physically separated. They follow the lead of the *imam* but may be in a gallery or their own room connected by a loudspeaker or in rows behind the men. Such separation is common in many religions, such as Orthodox Judaism or Eastern Christianity. It is for modesty and proper order rather than to suggest a subordinate position for women, which Islamic law does not permit. Separating the sexes in this way prevents any distraction by those who might be tempted to look at women during the prayers. Everyone is required to give their full attention to prayer by keeping their eyes fixed ahead on the floor at the spot where the forehead will come to rest in prostration. As people pray in tight ranks, touching at the shoulder, it is too easy to be distracted by the close physical proximity of someone from the opposite sex.

One of the duties laid upon a mother is to establish the routine of *salat* within the home. This makes the home a place of blessing and sets an example for younger children, who will be present at home to see their mother and the other women of the household forming a congregation for the regular *salat*. Children thus want to join in at home from an early age and are encouraged to do so as soon as they begin to realize what is happening. As they get older, they are instructed in the form of *wudu* and *salat* so they can participate correctly. It is common for boys, and sometimes young girls, to accompany their fathers to the mosque. As children grow older, they are encouraged to pray regularly the five daily prayers. This becomes a requirement for them once they reach puberty, but many form the habit well before this time.

The *Salat al-Jum'a*, or Friday Prayer, is compulsory for all Muslim men to attend, if at all possible. Women are free to attend but are not under the same obligation; it is recognized in traditional societies that this would place an undue burden on them in addition to their duties looking after children and the elderly. Women who do not attend the mosque for *Salat al-Jum'a* are required to pray the usual *Salat al-Zuhr* at home. The Friday Prayer consists of only two *rak'at*, with the other two being replaced by the two-part *khutba*, or address. This is given by someone of learning, perhaps the resident *imam*; in some big mosques a special "preacher" will be retained for this purpose called the *imam khatib*. The person giving the *khutba* stands on a raised platform, normally with a minimum of three steps, called the *minbar*. This is placed at the front of the mosque, normally to the right of the *mihrab* in which the *imam* will stand to lead the prayers. The *khutba* is in two parts, at least one of which is given in Arabic. The other, or an additional address, might be given in the language most common among the congregation assembled. In Britain this sometimes means that the *imam khatib* will deliver an address first in Urdu, then in English, and then the final formal part of the *khutba* in Arabic. The *khutba* normally will include a recitation from the Qur'an and then might range far and wide over any aspects of life that are affecting the congregation at that particular time. Friday is not a day of rest in Muslim societies, and so people disperse after the prayers to continue their normal business.

Carpet rows in a mosque. Photo: Sally Messner.

Zakat: To purify one's wealth by providing money to those in need

The Qur'an frequently links establishing the regular cycle of *salat* and paying the *zakat* (Q. 2:43). *Zakat* is an annual portion of one's wealth that no longer belongs to the individual concerned but must be distributed to those in need. It is all part of an economic and social welfare system and needs to be placed in this context to be understood fully. The idea of *zakat* stems from the understanding that God is the creator of everything, and so what we appear to own is really only entrusted to us to be used according to the good pleasure of God. The way we handle creation is part of *'ibada*, or the worship of God. If we handle this correctly, it will allow human beings to be more centered on *taqwa*, or God-consciousness. A correct relationship with the created world is part of the responsibility and dignity of every human being as the *khalifa*, or Regent of God upon earth.

The underlying principle of *zakat* is *sadaqa*, best translated as, "bearing one another's burdens." All humankind is one family, and thus if someone is in any kind of need, it becomes the concern of all. *Sadaqa* is a basic humanitarian principle, without any distinction between different groups of human beings. Islam is not against personal wealth provided that it is earned in upright (*halal*) ways, invested without exploitation of others, and used according to the principle of *sadaqa*. Generosity is encouraged in Islam (Q. 2:195), since it softens the heart to allow a greater spirit of *taqwa* both in the giver and in the recipient (Q. 2:264-265). As in all things, God knows the inner intention of each person and sees the true nature behind such acts (Q. 2:270).

This principle of *sadaqa* can be seen at work in the creation of welfare provisions within Muslim societies. Those who had surplus wealth established a charitable trust, or *waqf* to provide for the poor, widows, orphans, and the disabled, to educate people, to establish libraries, to house the homeless, and to provide health care for the sick. When someone dies, their ability to do good dies with them, except for those who have established a *waqf*, in which case people will continue to bless their name in future generations. Hospitality is a hallmark of Islamic societies, in which it is unthinkable to visit someone and not share food and drink with them. Travelers in a strange place traditionally headed for the local mosque, where they would be found and taken care of by the worshippers when next they came to pray. At least they would be given lodging in the mosque, and food would be brought from someone's home. Often they would be taken home and accommodated there.

All forms of economic exploitation are forbidden in Islam. This is part of the concept of *riba*, which is usually translated as usury, or giving and taking interest on a loan. In traditional societies, someone only looked for a loan when they were in need, for example if someone was sick and needed medical care. The principle of *sadaqa* would require Muslims with surplus money to give or lend it to someone in need without seeking any interest. To seek to make a profit out of someone in need would be a form of exploitation. Similarly, it is exploitation to wait to buy perishable goods until their price has been reduced to clear them, and it would be an exploitation against the principle of *sadaqa* to hoard goods until there is a shortage with the opportunity to inflate prices.

Even when someone is looking for a loan for business purposes, Islam forbids that this should be lent at interest. The normal practice of advancing a loan secured against someone's assets privileges capital against the human endeavours of the person who borrows the money. If the business does not prosper in spite of the best efforts of the borrower, the lender can then recover their loan from the business or personal assets of the borrower. In an Islamic system, a profit can be made only if the lender is exposed proportionally to the same risks as the borrower. This means that capital is injected into a business on the basis of shared equity. If the business prospers, the lender receives back the capital and a share of the profits generated, but if the business fails, then the lender too must bear a proportional share of the losses. This tends to make for much more responsible lending. Similarly, lending at interest is held to be inflationary, as the producer must sell their goods at an inflated price in order to meet the interest payments on the loan.

In a modern Western economic system, it is difficult to escape from the grip of an interest-based economy. Problems have been faced by developing countries, which have sought international loans to develop their infrastructure and economy. Such loans normally are based on interest repayments. How is such a country to develop without taking such loans? This has caused some scholars to seek to establish whether in such circumstances the good consequences of a loan outweigh the problem of interest.

On a personal level, almost all Western banks work on an interest-based model. If one deposits money, the bank uses this to lend to others at interest. If the individual does not take the interest due from their deposit, this makes the bank even richer. If one takes the interest and gives it away to charity, it still has been made through the exploitation of others. The same would be true of a credit card. Even if one pays off the balance every month so as not to pay interest, the company exists through charging interest to others. It is almost impossible to escape from the system of interest in the West.

In a home-owning society, very few people can afford to buy a house outright without taking a mortgage. The alternative to owning a home is to rent one. Often this means paying more per month in rent than would be paid to repay a mortgage. When the mortgage is repaid, at least one owns the house, but in a rental system there is never a return on the money paid out. One has only made the landlord richer, and without control over the repair and maintenance of the house. This raises the question of who is being subjected to the greater exploitation.

This has led some Muslim scholars in the West to suggest that a limited repayment mortgage may be necessary as the lesser of two evils. Typically, their advice is to seek the smallest mortgage possible to buy an adequate but modest home, to repay the loan as quickly as possible, and to take such a mortgage only for essential accommodation, that is, not for a vacation home or a yacht. In practice the principle of *sadaqa* plays a part here too, where a Muslim will inquire of their family and friends to see how many could make a modest interest-free loan to assist the purchaser and thus reduce the amount borrowed on a mortgage. People know that next year someone else may come looking for a similar loan, and thus burdens are borne as equitably as possible. Some financial institutions have developed shared-equity schemes for house purchase, in which the individual buys the house in partnership with the institution and progressively buys a greater share of the equity each year while renting the remainder from the institution.

It is quite permissible in Islam to make provisions for the future, whether for retirement, for the education of children, for health needs, for property repair, and so on. How is such money to be saved outside of an interest-based economy? Many Muslims have turned to ethically-screened investments for such needs. A basic principle in Islam is that if something is forbidden for a Muslim to do, it also is forbidden for a Muslim to profit from that same action. Take alcohol as an example. Consuming alcohol is forbidden in Islam, so it also is forbidden to own shares in a brewery and thus to make a profit from what is forbidden. Similarly, it is forbidden to trade in alcohol, so one should not sell alcohol in a restaurant or have shares in a distribution company. To take control of the way in which money is invested requires a considerable amount of effort on the part of the Muslim in society; by making this effort Muslims are constantly aware of the guidance of God in such matters, and so this promotes a sense of *taqwa*. Various ethically screened investment trusts have been established in the West to allow Muslims and others to save money in a *halal* way.

An important economic principle is that of *infaq*, or the circulation of wealth. Money must not be hoarded but must be put to work for the good of the whole society. This applies only to those who have wealth in addition to their basic needs and only after they have made provision for their family's future. Such people are guided by a Hadith of Muhammad that spoke of surplus money being put to work on the principles of *sadaqa* and *infaq*. This might mean that a wealthy Muslim is in a position to give start-up grants to others who want to establish a business so that they can support their families and thus become economically active themselves. Let us say that a group of carpenters were in need of funds to provide a cooperative workshop so that they could become economically self-sufficient. A wealthy Muslim could provide this money as a gift without any thought of a return for herself or himself but in the knowledge that he or she is obeying the guidance of God and thus would be rewarded in this life or the next, as God knows best.

It is within this context that we can understand the duty of paying *zakat*. *Zakat* is calculated as a percentage of the money left over after the basic running costs of the family have been met. Such surplus money, in excess of an agreed minimum (*nisab*), must have been held for a lunar year. This is calculated at two and a half percent a year. *Zakat* is also payable on livestock, gold and silver, trading merchandise, crops, and minerals. The calculations for each vary and need not concern us here. *Zakat* is calculated annually, so if one has a vacation home or a collection of gold jewelery in the bank, then the same asset will be liable for *zakat* every year. Each adult Muslim is individually responsible for calculating their *zakat*. Once this is done, it is like a legal charge on one's assets and technically does not belong to that person anymore. That person's duty is to see that it is distributed according to the principles of *zakat*. One meaning of the word *zakat* is "purification," and so it is as though the remainder of one's wealth is purified for one's own use once the *zakat* has been paid.

The Qur'an lays down certain purposes that may benefit from *zakat* (Q. 9:60):

- to bring relief to the poor and needy;
- to allow slaves to buy their freedom, or to ransom prisoners of war;
- to relieve the burdens of debtors;
- to assist those who want to become Muslims but who would suffer financial hardship if they did;

- to help travelers who are stranded;
- to spread the message of Islam;
- to support those who administer the *zakat* funds.

Here again, the balanced common-sense approach of Islam can be seen. If people are to administer the *zakat* funds on a voluntary basis, then their families might suffer through their not having sufficient time to earn an adequate living. In such circumstances, the temptation to support their own families from the *zakat* funds would be too great. To remedy this, the administrators are paid adequately, and then any malpractice is punished, since there should be no extenuating circumstances.

In an Islamic state, the collection and distribution of *zakat* would be undertaken by a government agency. In the absence of an Islamic state, it is the duty of each individual Muslim to ensure that the funds reach the appropriate recipients. Some people in the West support family members or friends in need in their countries of origin. Other Muslims pay their *zakat* to a recognized charity, which will ensure that it is used correctly.

Among Shi'a Muslims, the same basic economic principles apply, but *zakat* is understood rather differently. In addition, they have the system of *khums*, in which twenty percent of certain kinds of surplus wealth must be given to the scholars who administer it in the name of the Hidden Imam. It then is used for a wider spectrum of society-building causes than those listed under *zakat*.

The practice of *qurbani* has been noted already in relation to animals sacrificed on 'Id al-Adha. Here one third of the sacrificed meat must be distributed to the poor and another third to neighbors. In Western countries, it has become common to pay for an animal to be sacrificed as *qurbani* in a poor country, where the whole of the animal will be used by those in need. A similar practice based on the principle of *sadaqa* takes place at the end of Ramadan, when each household pays *Zakat al-Fitr* before celebrating the festival at the end of the fasting month. This is calculated as the price of one meal for each member of the household. This money is distributed to the poor so that also they will have the means to participate in the festival.

Sawm: To fast during the month of Ramadan

By now it should be clear that observing the twin pillars of *salat* and *zakat* requires considerable self-control and discipline. One way to build up this self-discipline is through *sawm*, that is, fasting during Ramadan, the ninth month of the Muslim calendar.

Fig. 14. The "lunar-solar bicycle"

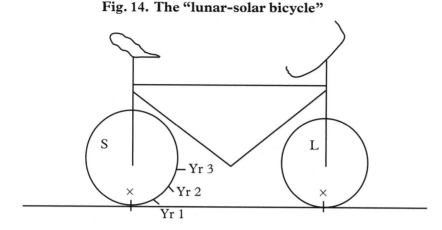

The lunar year (smaller wheel) is approximately eleven days shorter than the solar year (larger wheel). If the bicycle is pushed forward one rotation of the lunar wheel, an event (marked by ×) will appear to fall eleven days earlier according to the solar year; and so progressively each year. Thus Ramadan, or any other event in the lunar calendar, moves through the seasons, appearing eleven days earlier each solar year.

Islam took over the names of the months from the pre-Islamic Arab calendar, but the Qur'an made it clear that the moon is to be the measure of time (Q. 10:5). This ended the practice of putting in "leap months," like the Jewish calendar, to keep the months coordinated with the seasons. Thus the Islamic calendar follows an unadjusted lunar system, which means that each year is approximately eleven days shorter than a solar year. This means that everything timed according to the Islamic calendar appears to move forward by approximately eleven days each year when judged by the solar calendar. Thus Ramadan moves through the seasons of the year and returns to approximately the same time in the solar calendar once in every thirty-three solar years. This is especially important for Ramadan, which involves a fast during the daylight hours. When this falls in winter, the days are shorter and cooler, but when it falls in summer, the days are both longer and hotter.

Each month begins on the night that the new moon is sighted and lasts for twenty-nine or thirty days, depending on when the next new moon is seen. According to Islamic law, it is compulsory to have certain people looking for the appearance of the new moon, but in some countries today astronomical tables are used as an aid in deciding the change of the months. This means that the precise start and finish of Ramadan can vary from one community to another depending on which method they use and whose sighting they follow; in European skies it often is not possible to see the new moon itself due to cloud cover. Some communities in Europe contact Morocco, as the nearest Muslim country, for news of the new moon; others telephone the country from which their family originally came; others go by the sighting in Makka; still other groups takes the astronomical data to determine when the new moon would have been born and seen if the clouds had not blocked it from sight.

The fast during Ramadan requires that all adult Muslims refrain from eating, drinking, and engaging in sexual relations from before sunrise in the morning until after sunset at night. These rules are interpreted strictly, and even those who are not regular in praying each of their daily *salat* will make a special effort to observe the fast during Ramadan.

The fast is commanded by the Qur'an (Q. 2:183-187); it is "for God," and it is for the benefit of human beings to observe it. Eating, drinking, and sexual relations are in no way considered bad by Islam. They are natural and necessary parts of human life, but they are some of the strongest instincts we as human beings have. Islam teaches that if Muslims can control these instincts during Ramadan, then they will learn self-discipline during the rest of the year in all aspects of life. Fasting is not allowed to become torture; it is forbidden to fast if it would endanger life, and it is not permitted to extend the fast beyond sunset. It reminds people that everything they take for granted is a gift from the providence of God and builds up strength to face testing times when they come. It is a sign of solidarity with the poor, who often are hungry and thirsty not through choice but on account of their poverty.

The fast during Ramadan is a community event. All Muslims should be fasting at the same time. This builds up a sense of unity and community support. One member of the family will awaken another to make sure they rise in time to eat and drink something before the fast begins. Young people might gather around their mother for support during the later hours of the fast so that they can help one another to endure. Often, in Muslim societies, the pattern of the day is altered so that people rise for work early and then rest during the afternoon. Shops will stay open late at night. This is a reminder that every habit is subject to alteration at the command of God.

Sawm is not a negative experience but one to which Muslims look forward throughout the year. It is a time of spiritual renewal when old quarrels are forgiven and a review of life takes place. Muslims examine their lives to see how well they are following the guidance of God in every aspect. There is the "fasting of the hands," when one considers how one earns a living and spends one's money. There is the "fasting of the tongue," when one considers how truthful one has been and whether one has engaged in gossip. Has one looked at things that one ought not to, or listened to things that ought not to be heard? And so on.

Here we see that *sawm*, much like the other pillars, is a training program in *taqwa* in which the Muslim grows in God-consciousness and seeks to live a life in total harmony with God, within oneself and with the community of humanity. This involves an element of seeking the forgiveness of God and making new resolutions for the future. Ramadan is a particularly sacred month because it was toward the end of this month in 610 that the Qur'an first was sent down as guidance for all humanity. This night is called *Laylat al-Qadr* (the Night of Power/Destiny) and was one of the odd-numbered nights at the end of the month. Many remember this on the twenty-seventh night, but the date is not certain, so others observe special prayers on the last few odd-numbered nights in the month. This night is reckoned to be better than a thousand months because God sends the angels to earth to hear prayers that are offered and to deliver messages (Q. 97:3-5). Many will spend the whole of the Night of Power in prayer until dawn.

One of the spiritual practices observed by Sunni Muslims during this month is to listen to the whole of the Qur'an being recited. This is done at night during special *tarawih* prayers, with one-thirtieth of the Qur'an being recited each night. This often takes place in a mosque or in the courtyard of someone's home. A skilled reciter (*qari*) will be retained for the purpose, and food often will be prepared for those who come to pray.

Following the balanced pattern of Islam, some people are exempt from fasting. Those who are too old or too young are exempt, though the elderly often keep up the practice of fasting well into old age. Those who undertake journeys are exempt if fasting would cause serious suffering. Women do not fast during the days of their monthly period, during pregnancy, and while breast-feeding, but they make up the missed days later in the year. The sick and insane do not fast. Those whose exemption is temporary, like travelers or the sick, make up for missed days at some other time. The elderly who can afford it make a donation of food to the poor to compensate for not fasting.

The whole of the family routine is changed during Ramadan, and young children often want to be part of the fast. They are not obliged to fast until they reach puberty, but many seek their parents' permission to begin fasting earlier. They might begin when they are young by keeping a fast from breakfast to lunchtime when they are not at school. Later they may fast all day at weekends. By eight or nine years of age, many keep the last ten days of fasting completely with the adults.

These last ten days are the climax of the fast, and coincide with the Night of Power. Some Muslims will seek to spend these in solitude (*i'tikaf*) in a mosque. This time will be spent in prayer and in meditating on the guidance of the Qur'an.

Sawm is not a sad or somber time. When the fast is broken at sunset, a light communal meal (*iftar*) is taken. It was Muhammad's to break his fast with water and dates or figs, so this is a common practice. Friends will be invited for *iftar*, and, after *salat al-maghrib* is offered, a larger meal will be shared by all present. Often people gather in mosques or at their workplaces to make *iftar* together. This must be done at precisely the appointed time, and so those following a normal working day may need some time off to eat, drink, and pray. People who are away from home often will carry a bottle of water and some food for this purpose.

The practice of fasting is not restricted to the month of Ramadan alone. Many Muslims observe additional voluntary fasts at other times during the year. Shi'a Muslims especially will fast for some days during the month of Muharram to remember the martyrdom of Husayn, the grandson of Muhammad and the third Imam in the Shi'a tradition. Some Muslims fast one or more days each month, although moderation is recommended. It was the practice of Muhammad, according to his wife A'isha, to fast for three days each month. Fasting is also recommended for unmarried men and women, to help control sexual urges until such time as they have a *halal* outlet in marriage.

The day after the sighting of the next new moon is kept as a festival, 'Id al-Fitr (the festival of Fast-breaking); on this day fasting is forbidden. Before this can be celebrated, each household must pay the *zakat al-fitr*, as previously noted. The festival begins with breakfast after sunrise to show that the rules of *sawm* no longer apply. Everyone takes a shower and puts on new clean clothes. The whole community assembles during the morning for a special *salat*, which includes two *rak'at*, special prayers, and a *khutba*. This will be followed by a festive meal and much visiting of friends and relatives. Often people visit the graves of dead members of their family and pray there in solidarity with those who have died. Presents are given, and sports and games are usual. As the date is determined by the sighting of the new moon, it is not always possible to predict it exactly in advance. As noted already, different Muslim communities in the West follow different practices in determining this sighting, and so the 'Id might be celebrated on different days. Muslims seek a day off from work or school for 'Id al-Fitr. A solution to this problem is to grant two days off to coincide with the two days on which the festival is most likely to occur.

Muslim farmers near the village of Minya, Egypt. Photo: Marc Ostlie-Olson.

7

A Muslim Life

Birth – contraception – abortion – in vitro fertilization – naming – circumcision – education – memorization of the Qur'an – adolescence – sports – music – alcohol – gambling – universities – job selection – marriage – partner selection – marriage ceremonies – polygamy – exclusivity of marriage – divorce – adultery – remarriage – child custody – family life – the extended family – women's rights and duties – the four "perfect women" – inheritance – food laws – slaughter of animals – alcohol – food additives – eating with right hand – mealtime etiquette – sickness – transplants – suicide – egg/sperm donation – homosexuality – death – as death approaches – preparation of the body – autopsy – burial – funeral prayers – graves – mourning

Family customs and traditions vary around the world from one culture and school of thought to another. Here we trace a typical Muslim life and encounter some of these practices.

Birth

The birth of a child is cause for great rejoicing in a Muslim family. Having a child is itself an act of faith in the providence of God. In pre-Islamic Arabia, it was the custom, if too many girls were born, to bury a baby girl alive as a way of limiting the population. This was explicitly forbidden by the Qur'an, which instead counseled reliance on the providence of God (Q. 16:57-59, 81:8-9). As soon as the baby is washed and clothed, the father or another senior man from the family or the *imam* whispers the call to prayer (*adhan*) into the child's right ear and the call for the prayer to begin (*iqama*) in the left ear. This is a sign that the child is born a Muslim and will in time take on the way of life required by Islam. Some Muslims follow the example of Muhammad, putting a small portion of pre-chewed date into the child's mouth as its first nourishment outside the womb. Prayers are offered for the health of the child, and people come bearing gifts.

Having a child is a great responsibility, and parents are encouraged to invoke God before making love, so that they may be blessed with a conception. Children are a natural part of married life and so should not be excluded from a couple's plans. Contraception is permitted to space pregnancies out or when the couple decide that their family is complete. This normally would be after at least two children, often at least one of either sex, so that the human community continues. In some parts of the world, as many as one-third of all children die before maturity. This means that couples tend to have several to ensure that some survive. In most countries people do not have pensions or provisions for their old age. They rely on their children to look after them. Because girls generally leave home to live with their husbands, boys are needed to secure a couple's old age. All this tends toward larger families, and so this becomes the norm. In recent years, some discussion has taken place concerning abortion. A new individual is created at conception, and so abortion is strongly discouraged. Some Muslims follow the classical understanding that the human soul is implanted about forty days after conception and so permit an early abortion if necessary. If there are grave circumstances, such as the mother's life being in danger if the pregnancy continues, many Muslims will permit an abortion even after the fortieth day. However, abortion is never something to be entered into lightly.

Similarly, recent developments in in vitro fertilization have been considered by Muslim jurists. Most are agreed that this is permissible provided that both sperm and egg come from the married couple. Donation of sperm or egg outside the bond of marriage is not permitted in most schools of thought, since it would break the sanctity of marriage and deprive the child of the knowledge of his or her birth parents.

Normally, the child is named within the first ten days after birth. Many names are derived from one of the Beautiful Names of God recorded in the Qur'an and the Hadith. In the case of boys, these are prefixed with Abd, meaning "the Servant of...." Abd al-Rahman, "the Servant of the Merciful," would be a common example. The names of Prophets recorded in the Qur'an are also common for boys. Girls often have a name derived from one of the Beautiful Names, or a member of the Prophet's family, or one of the virtues in life. Biblical names are quite common, especially Adam, Ibrahim (Abraham), Musa (Moses), 'Isa (Jesus), and Maryam (Mary). It is common for boys to be given the name Muhammad as an additional name.

Naming does not end there. Often, children are named in relation to a parent with the addition of *ibn*, son of, or *bint*, daughter of. So a boy might be called Muhammad Abd al-Rahman ibn Umar (son of his father Umar), or a girl Salma bint Ahmad (daughter of her father Ahmad). This addition is called the *nasab*. Later, when the child in turn has the honor of becoming a parent, an additional name might be given with reference to a child by adding *Abu*, father of, or *Umm*, mother of. So Muhammad Abd al-Rahman ibn Umar might be known also as Abu Yusuf (the father of Yusuf), or Salma bint Ahmad might be known as Umm Zaynab (the mother of Zaynab). This addition is called a *kunya*. Further, some people acquire a nickname, called a *laqab*, that might be derived from their place of birth (al-Ghazali, from Ghazala), a profession (al-Hallaj, the wool carder), having studied at a great institution (al-Azhari, one who has studied at al-Azhar), or maybe even through some distinctive feature or achievement.

Another feature of the naming is the rite of shaving the child's head. The hair is collected and weighed against silver or gold, the money value of which is then given in charity. Many Muslims also follow the tradition of sacrificing one or two animals on this day, called *'aqiqa*, and feeding all who come to the naming ceremony.

Forty days after the birth, when the mother has recovered fully from childbirth, she takes a full bath (*ghusl*) and once again takes up the duties of *salat* and fasting.

It was the *sunna*, or customary practice of the Prophet Ibrahim and other Prophets, to circumcise boys by removing the foreskin of their penis. This practice is followed universally in Islam, where it is known as *khitan*. It is not mentioned in the Qur'an but is clear in the Hadith of Muhammad. The age at which this is done varies considerably in different regions of the Islamic world. In the West, it is becoming common practice to do this in the first few weeks or months of life, if the boy's health permits. Here it usually is done by a doctor, under sterile conditions, and with anaesthetic. In certain more traditional societies, it commonly occurs later during childhood, perhaps around the age of seven, or even later, when it becomes a pre-puberty rite of passage to adulthood. Whenever it takes place, it is often accompanied by a celebration meal with many guests. Adult converts to Islam are often circumcised, although not all schools of Islam consider this essential. It is required, however, if the man is going on the *hajj*; this emphasizes the Abrahamic origins of the rites and the continuity of Islam with the earlier revelations.

The practice of female circumcision, known as *khafd* in classical Arabic, or female genital mutilation (FGM) as it has come to be called in the West especially by those who oppose it, is known in some Muslim societies. It is not restricted to Muslims but is practiced also in some Christian societies and in some African traditional religions. It stems from an ancient practice in the time of the Pharaohs in Egypt. There is a Hadith of Muhammad that refers to it by saying, "Do not cut severely, as that is better for a woman and more desirable to a husband." All schools of thought agree that it is not essential in Islamic law; some say it is recommended and others that it is permitted. In many Muslim societies it is completely unknown. It traditionally was found in Egypt, the Sudan, among some Arabs, in sub-Saharan Africa, and in Indonesia. Some governments, like that of Egypt, have declared it illegal. The actual operation varies in severity, the most modest being to nick or reduce the girl's clitoris.

Education and childhood

It is the natural birthright of a child to be brought up to know and practice Islam. How could a child be deprived of something so natural, the best way of life? As soon as children begin to talk, they will be taught to say the *basmala* ("In the Name of God, the Merciful, the Compassionate") and other pious phrases. They are schooled in Islamic manners, such as respect for parents and elders and eating with the right hand. Children learn by imitation, so parents are careful to give the right example of Islamic conduct to their children. When they are able to speak, children are taught at an early age to memorize verses from the Qur'an.

Afghan school children with their teacher. Photo: Linda Wiehl.

Traditionally, many children learn the alphabet and reading from the pages of the Qur'an. It became the central medium for educating the young. Children were taught to sound out the words and thus imbibe the Qur'an even before they could read with understanding. This practice is common even in non-Arabic-speaking countries, where the phonetic reading of the Qur'an is part of every child's education. This leads to learning by heart so that verses are there in the memory as the child begins to pray. Children in the West who attend state-funded schools by day normally attend a mosque or Islamic school (*madrasa*) in the evenings or on weekends. Here they learn more of the Qur'an, how to perform the ritual practices of Islam, and gradually Islamic religious education, history, and etiquette. Boys and girls have equal access to education, but this normally is delivered in single-sex classes. The teacher is much more than a guide to discovering knowledge; she or he is also expected to teach by example and become a positive role model to the students. Education is considered to be "of the whole person," and so the intellectual, moral, and spiritual are integrated.

A group of the Companions of Muhammad took upon themselves the memorization of the whole of the Qur'an so that it would be preserved and passed on to later generations. This practice has continued ever since, with significant numbers of Muslims in every generation and society memorizing the entire Qur'an. Such people are called *hafiz* (masculine) or *hafizah* (feminine). They "carry the Qur'an in their hearts" and thus are given respect in all Muslim societies. The process of memorization normally begins in childhood and takes several years. One *hafiz* teaches another, and so methods of memorization and repetition have been developed to make the process easier and more secure. Once learned, the *hafiz* must practice recitation regularly so that the facility is not lost. A *hafiz* can be called upon to recite at any Muslim gathering, and they are in high demand during Ramadan. The science of Qur'an recitation is called *tajwid*. There are several styles, which vary in the way that sounds are emphasized, lengthened, and so on. This stylized form of recitation is the aural equivalent of the written art of calligraphy.

Growing into adulthood

The onset of puberty marks the time when young Muslims take on their own adult responsibility for the ritual practices and the life that they will live in obedience to God. From now on they are answerable to God for following the path laid out in the Qur'an and Sunna. Parents do not give up their position as role models, but now they become encouragers and guides. Even if they mixed together as younger children, the sexes now are segregated for sleeping, study, and recreation. Boys and girls are trained in modesty and self-control. It is at this time that many girls begin to cover their heads, if they have not been accustomed to doing so already. Any form of sexual practice outside marriage is forbidden in Islam, and so teenagers do not go out together or attend social events except in the company of adult family members. Early marriage has been traditional in Islamic societies to provide an appropriate outlet for natural sexual energies.

Sports play an important part in developing a healthy body, but care is taken to ensure that the rules of modesty are observed. No Muslim should appear naked in front of anyone but their marriage partner, and so communal showers and changing rooms are a problem. Muslims would look for individual changing cubicles and showers so that modesty might be observed. Mixed sports are not permitted, and in many societies watching members of the opposite sex engaged in sports is discouraged. Modest dress, which does not reveal the contours of the body, is required in Islam for both sexes. This usually means that men and boys should be covered from the navel to the knees, and women and girls should wear long sleeves and be covered from their necks to their ankles. Baggy tracksuits are common sportswear for males and females, and bodysuits have been developed for (single-sex) swimming.

Music is another issue with young people. Muslim opinions on music differ, but all are aware of the potential for music to lead to a loss of self-control and possible immorality. Some Muslims consider all forms of music forbidden; others permit certain forms of unaccompanied singing; still others permit the use of a *daff*, or drum like a tambourine (without the cymbals). In some sufi circles, the flute or lute is permitted. Less strict rules about musical instruments apply in some Muslim societies, but others will regard such practices as unacceptable. One form of melodious singing common in the Indian subcontinent and elsewhere is the *nasheed*, or song in praise of the Prophet Muhammad.

The Qur'an is clear in the prohibition of alcohol (Q. 5:90). Alcohol promotes a loss of self-control and can lead to immorality. This prohibition is extended to any form of narcotic or other drug that alters the mental state (unless prescribed by a doctor). Similarly, all forms of gambling are prohibited. This includes betting, card games, dice, games of chance, lotteries, and raffles. Muslims must earn their money by lawful means and not through gambling.

Growing up in contemporary Western society is not easy for people of many different faiths. Muslims share the concerns of other parents about the influences that press upon all young people. They want to raise their teenagers within the clear guidance provided by the Qur'an and dislike many of the contemporary messages carried by films, television, videos, magazines, advertising, and song lyrics. Single-sex schools are in high demand, and it is common for young people, girls especially, to be escorted to and from school. There is a high value placed upon education, but Muslims would not want this divorced from a clear moral framework. University education is also highly prized, with many Muslim students continuing to live at home and commute to their studies each day. Often groups of young Muslim women stick together for traveling and study so that they can provide companionship and support.

When it comes to seeking a job or profession, the guidance of Islam continues. Work that would involve something prohibited, like dealing in alcohol, gambling, or exploiting others, is forbidden. A job that could lead to immorality is discouraged. Jobs that enable the person to break off at appropriate times for prayer are encouraged. Professions that allow people in need to be helped according to the principle of *sadaqa*, such as a doctor, teacher, or lawyer, are encouraged.

For women especially, it is important to ensure a sufficient number of female teachers and doctors for the next generation of girls and women.

Marriage

There is a saying in Islam that "marriage is half your religion," meaning that it is a training ground in *taqwa* and a way of fulfilling one's full potential as the Regent and Loving Servant of God upon earth. This means that being celibate is not an option and is discouraged, as it leaves the single person without a legitimate outlet for their sexuality. However, if someone is unable to bear the financial burden of marriage, or if for some reason a person remains unmarried, then this is to be accepted without becoming an excuse for sexual license. There have been mystics and scholars in the Islamic tradition who have so devoted themselves to the study of the Islamic sciences that they have not married. These exceptional circumstances are tolerated.

It is part of the responsibility of a parent to ensure that their children are assisted in finding appropriate and compatible marriage partners. Marriage is never just the concern of two people but a relationship between two families. It is unusual for a Muslim to seek a marriage partner without reference to their family, and most unusual for someone to marry against the wishes of their family, as it was in Europe until recent decades. In the last resort, however, the two people concerned have the final decision about entering into marriage, although in most schools of Islam a woman who marries for the first time should seek the active support of her father or guardian.

In many societies around the world—not only Muslim societies— it is common for the families to seek a marriage partner and make the arrangements. There is a clear difference between a marriage arranged by the two families, in which the couple have the final decision, and a forced marriage, in which one or both partners are denied their rights under Islamic law; it is important to emphasize that such a forced marriage is illegal in Islam. It is related in the tradition that a woman came to Muhammad to complain that her father had married her to her cousin without her consent. The Prophet annulled the marriage. The woman, free to declare her own choice, now married her cousin. The episode reinforces the necessity of the free consent of both partners for a valid marriage.

With the mass migration of Muslims to the West, sociological developments are changing the process of finding a marriage partner. Often now, the two young people concerned are put in contact through friends or meet during their studies or through work. In such cases, the families often are called in to assist the couple in making sure that they are making the right decision. Matrimonial agencies have sprung up, and advertisements appear in the Muslim press to assist those who might be living away from their families. Some professional people attend supervised introduction events in which they might meet potential partners and then go on to seek an introduction of the two families involved.

The prohibited degrees of marriage are spelled out clearly in the Qur'an (Q. 4:23) but do not include marriage to first cousins. Indeed, cousin marriage has the approval of the practice of Muhammad, who married his daughter Fatima to his cousin Ali. Such marriages are common among Arabs, not just those who are Muslims. All parents want the best for their son or daughter when it comes to marriage, and the child of a relative is likely to be a "known quantity." Parents have seen the way in which their relatives raise their children, and such a marriage tends to bind the family together. It also means that there are plenty of willing counselors within the family to help the couple through difficult times. Concern has been expressed about the potential for progressive genetic weakening when successive generations marry too closely within the extended family. A *sayyid* (also commonly spelled *syed*), or *sharif*, is someone who can trace their ancestry back to Muhammad himself; in some Muslim societies it is common for such a person to seek a marriage partner of similar ancestry so that the lineage is strengthened and continued. Color, ethnicity, and caste should play no role in seeking a Muslim marriage partner, and marriages that cross these boundaries are common within Muslim societies.

There is a Hadith of Muhammad that says the most important consideration in seeking a marriage partner is the way in which the person follows the guidance of Islam. A pious person is to be preferred to rank, beauty, or wealth. The modern Western idea of romantic love as the basis for marriage is not shared by many Muslims, who believe that love will grow between them during the years of marriage when both parties are observant in following the guidance of Islam and have mutual honor, respect, and commitment.

Marriage itself is based on a legal contract, which is drawn up by the two parties, normally with the active involvement of their families. Various schools of Islamic law differ in fine detail, but generally it is permitted to put mutually agreed clauses into this contract concerning, for example, consultation with the first wife before the husband considers seeking a second wife, or what might happen in the case of divorce. Such a contract forms the basis of the marriage ceremony or *nikah*. The marriage may take place in a mosque but often happens in the home or in a hall in which a reception can also be held. It often takes place in the presence of a Muslim official, but this is not necessary. Two witnesses are required to hear the verbal consent of each partner to the marriage; this then is certified by signing the written contract. The partners to the marriage do not have to be physically present to hear the other's consent, but the same two witnesses are required if it is only a verbal contract. The man gives his consent first; then the woman is assured of this prior to giving her consent. In Western countries where it is usual for marriages to be registered under the law of the land, this either takes place separately from the *nikah*, or, in some larger mosques, an official is recognized by the civil law to do both ceremonies at the same time.

An integral part of Muslim marriage is the *mahr*, or dowry, that is given to the bride by her husband. This is mutually agreed on before the marriage and may take the form of money, goods, or a service, such as the man agreeing to teach his wife Arabic. The *mahr* becomes the legal property of the wife, who may dispose of it as she wills. Generally it is non-returnable except under certain conditions of divorce. Even if the marriage breaks up before it is consummated, the wife is entitled to retain half of the *mahr*. The practice in some cultures of demanding huge dowries from the bride's family has no place in Islam.

Within the Ja'fari School of Shi'a Islam, it is possible for two adults to enter into a time-limited contract for a temporary marriage, or *mut'a*. Sometimes the woman receives a fee under such arrangements but no *mahr*. As these marriages are for a fixed time, there is no need for divorce. Such marriages, which are not common, are seen as a legitimate way of containing sexual desires when for some reason a permanent marriage is not possible at present. Sometimes couples use a temporary marriage as a way to get to know each other in a *halal* way before entering a permanent contract. They might also be used by couples who cannot yet afford to marry. These temporary marriages are not permitted by Sunni schools of Islam.

In pre-Islamic Arabia, unlimited polygamy was practiced. This was restricted by the Qur'an, which permitted a Muslim man to marry up to four wives at any one time provided he could treat them all equitably (Q. 4:3). Later in the same *sura*, it is noted that "You will not be able to be equitable between your wives, be you ever so eager" (Q. 4:129). These verses are interpreted variously in different Muslim societies. Some Muslims distinguish in such marriages between financial equity, which is easier to practice, as opposed to emotional equity, which is much harder. Some Muslims hold that there is a clear Qur'anic preference for monogamy, while others strive for equity knowing how diffcult it is to achieve. Often this varies with different regions of the world, polygamy being more common in sub-Saharan Africa than in the Indian subcontinent, for example.

Certain circumstances that make limited polygamy the preferred option are cited. If the first wife is unable to have children, then marrying a second wife is seen as better than divorce, as a woman who is known to have been divorced under such circumstances is unlikely to find another husband and thus will be without the honor and protection of married status. When many men were killed in battle, there might be a surplus of women who would be denied the human fulfillment of marriage and children were polygamy not practiced. This was the case in Europe after the 1914–1918 War, when many women had to remain single. Such an unequal loss of male life has been seen in our own times in the wars in Bosnia, Chechnya, Iran, and Iraq. When women are abandoned by their husbands or widowed, then becoming a second wife gives them security. These considerations applied more in traditional societies than in the modern West. It is rare to find second wives today in Western countries. To marry a second wife would not be bigamy under civil law unless one attempted to register that marriage. Muslims in Western societies often respond to criticism of the Qur'anic permission for polygamy by pointing to the now common liaisons between men and women that do not give the same degree of legal status as a second marriage does under Islamic law. Finally, it is important to note that in Islam polygamy is only permitted, never prescribed. The overwhelming majority of Muslim marriages today around the world are monogamous.

Needless to say, marriages within Muslim societies are surrounded by many traditions of feasting, parties, songs, and dancing. In many traditional societies, such merry-making takes on a host of local folklore and usually is conducted by the men and women in separate locations or in two parts of the same venue. It is customary for the two extended families and many guests to attend, to eat together, and to give gifts to the couple. In some traditional societies, the new wife moves into her husband's family home, but this custom is breaking down in the West. In other societies, the newly married couple will set up home near to their families but in a separate house.

Marriage is an exclusive sexual bond within Islam, and sexuality is not to be exercised outside of it. Men and women are equally bound to observe modesty and self-control in terms of dress, behavior, and in their hearts. The husband is responsible for meeting the costs of providing for his wife and family, even if she has her own income or wealth. She must guard her husband's honor and not gossip about his business affairs. Both must observe proper Islamic decorum in dress so that they do not attract unwanted attention from other men and women. Only the husband or wife is permitted to see the intimate parts of the other's body, and women are required to cover their *'awra*, which might be translated as their "attractive charms" or "allurements." This term is understood variously by different schools within Islam and in different societies, but generally it is held to be the entire body except for the face, hands, and feet. All is a precious jewel that must be covered as a sign of respect. Collectively, this modest clothing is referred to as *hijab*. The clothing for both men and women should be sufficiently loose-fitting that the contours of the body are not revealed. This becomes especially relevant in the West, where degrees of public nudity are tolerated and where women's bodies especially are abused through advertising. To dress Islamically in this context becomes a "statement" or part of struggling in the cause of God.

Divorce

If troubles arise within a marriage, it is not left only to the couple to attempt to resolve their problems. The Qur'an counsels swift arbitration in the hope of reconciliation (Q. 4:35). A senior member of each of the two families is appointed to arbitrate and seek ways to keep the marriage intact. If this requires some practical assistance, then it is up to the families to seek remedies. If it requires a change in attitude or behavior within the marriage, then the arbiters try to work toward this. In many cases, such family involvement prevents the need for divorce.

If a reconciliation is ultimately impossible, then divorce is permitted in Islam (Q. 2:227-237). There is a Hadith of the Prophet that divorce is the most detestable of permitted things. There is much said in Islamic law about the fine details of divorce, but the main point is that, if one or both parties to the marriage decide that they no longer can live with the other, then they may divorce without having to prove due grounds in public.

Traditionally, the man has the advantage of initiating the procedure and can simply repudiate his wife; this process is called *talaq*. The husband declares formally "I divorce you," and then must wait for one full menstrual cycle before a repetition. After the second declaration of "I divorce you," another monthly period of waiting must be observed. After this, a third declaration of "I divorce you" is final and binding. During the two waiting periods, attempts at reconciliation are recommended. If the couple returns to marital relations during these waiting periods, then this is taken to be an act of reconciliation, and the declaration is nullified. Once the third and final declaration of divorce has been made, the woman must wait a further monthly cycle before she is free to marry a new husband. The idea of the three months in total waiting period (*'idda*) ensures that the woman is not pregnant from her marriage.

The husband does not have to state the grounds on which he wants to divorce his wife, although it is recommended that he does so. After the third and final repudiation, the couple is not permitted to remarry unless the former wife first has married another man and then been divorced from him. There are cases when such a second marriage was "staged" but not consummated so that it could proceed immediately to a divorce (Q. 33:49).

Some schools of Islam will permit that the three repudiations are made at the same time. This is not recommended, as it does not allow for reconciliation, but it is valid. This triple *talaq* must be followed by a three-month waiting period before the woman can marry again. The presence in all cases of the waiting period, or *'idda*, stresses the need in Islamic law for the parentage of a child to be known clearly.

Several Muslim countries now have introduced legal procedures for divorce cases to be heard in a civil court. In such cases, the traditional forms of *talaq* are no longer recognized by the state as valid. A wife who wishes to initiate divorce proceedings must apply to a Shari'a court (Q 4.128). In modern practice, this procedure is facilitated greatly if conditions such as the wife's right to seek a divorce in certain circumstances are written into the initial marriage contract. A Shari'a court is able to grant a woman a divorce even against her husband's wishes, if the marriage has broken down irretrievably. The waiting period must be observed before the woman is able to marry again. Under certain conditions it may be required by Islamic law that the wife return part of her *mahr* if she initiates the divorce.

Adultery is a most serious sin in Islam, as it destroys not only the marital bond but also attacks a fundamental element of the stability of society. The Qur'an lays down a special procedure for divorce under such circumstances (Q. 24:6-9). If a man accuses his wife of being pregnant by another man, he can make a solemn oath four times that she has committed adultery. These are followed by a fifth oath to the same effect in which he invokes the curse of God upon himself if he is lying. The woman may deny the charge by a similar series of four oaths, followed by a fifth in which she invokes God's curse upon herself if she is lying. After this double procedure, the divorce is final, but the woman is not liable to punishment for adultery nor the man for making a false accusation. It then is left to God to decide the matter in the light of the mutually exclusive oaths.

A woman who has been divorced is both permitted and encouraged to marry again. The Prophet Muhammad himself married divorced women as an example that no stigma should be attached to this. In practice, some men are disinclined to marry a divorced woman.

If a woman is pregnant at the time of a divorce or is breast-feeding a child, she is entitled to the support of her husband until the child is born and raised. As long as she looks after the children of their marriage, then their father must support them (Q. 65:4-7). Islamic law generally says that children should remain with their mother, provided that she is suitable, until they are at least two years old, and in most schools much longer. Eventually the time comes when either the children are old enough to be able to choose between their parents or custody reverts by preference to the father. This sometimes can lead to problems in the West when a woman is divorced according to civil law and given custody of the children. If she then takes the children on a visit to a country that is influenced by Islamic law in these matters, the former husband could apply for custody of his children under that legislation and it could be granted, especially if the children are older or if he can claim that the mother is unsuitable.

If a couple are married according to civil law, then they must seek a civil divorce if they wish to be free to remarry civilly. A potential conflict can arise if the civil courts grant custody of the children, maintenance for the wife, or the division of matrimonial goods in a way that runs counter to the practices of Islamic law. This would have to be resolved by mutual consent or by further recourse to the civil courts.

Family life

The extended family, rather than the individual nuclear family, is the basic unit of Muslim societies. When a couple marries, they take on the responsibilities of the other in relation to their extended families. This means that a wife has responsibilities in her husband's family as a daughter-in-law, and a husband has responsibilities in his wife's family as a son-in-law. In this way, the extended family is strengthened and expanded. This traditional way of living can bring problems in a Western context, especially with refugees who have had to leave their extended families behind.

An emphasis on community is central in Islam. Muslims are encouraged to pray together to strengthen this sense of community. Many forms of charitable work have a community dimension, such as welfare trusts and caring for mosques. Extended families are bound together into the local community, but this is always broadened to include the worldwide community of believers, the *umma*. In this way, all Muslims feel a sense of kinship with other Muslims worldwide, especially when they are suffering, be it through human actions such as war or persecution, or through natural disasters such as famine, earthquake, or flooding. This is the practical application of the idea of the universal human family symbolized on the Plain of Arafat during the *Hajj*.

Within the extended family, elderly parents and relatives are looked after. Children become part of the responsibility of everyone, so that a mother with a newborn child should find plenty of support in looking after her older children while she recovers from giving birth. Grandparents and uncles are on hand to take children to school, and grandmothers and aunts provide natural childcare for working mothers. Family members with disabilities can be looked after, and help is on hand at times of sickness, bereavement, and personal or work concerns. A unit of an extended family will have others to turn to in financial difficulties, and there are always great family gatherings for any celebration.

Within the family, different rules for social mixing apply. A Muslim man or woman normally would not be alone in the company of a member of the opposite sex outside the family circle. Within the family, those too closely related to marry are called *mahram*; they would include parents, grandparents, brothers, sisters, aunts, uncles, nephews, and nieces. Within such close blood ties, people can mix freely. Within traditional Muslim societies, a Muslim woman would seek the company of a *mahram* if she had to travel outside the house. A man who is not a *mahram* would not expect to enter a friend's house if the husband were not present, unless one of the wife's adult *mahrams* were present. Even if the man knew both partners in the marriage well, so that there would be no suspicion of impropriety by the husband, such a visit would be inappropriate, as neighbors might gossip and the good name of the wife might be at risk.

An adult woman has many rights within Islam that were granted by the Qur'an and Hadith of Muhammad but for which Western women have had to fight in the twentieth century. Both men and women have an equal responsibility to follow the Islamic way of life (Q. 33:35). A Muslim woman is allowed to own property in her own right and dispose of it without reference to her husband. She normally keeps her own

name after marriage. She is permitted to make her own will to dispose
of her goods after death. She is entitled to education at all levels equal
to that of a man. She is entitled to sexual fulfillment. She has the right
to engage in any profession or business. She should be consulted in
public affairs, following the example of Muhammad, who habitually
sought the opinion of some of the Muslim women before making a
decision. She has the right to keep and control her own earnings, it
being the duty of the husband to meet all domestic expenditure, house
his family, and educate his children (Q. 4:34). There are no grounds
for her to be a domestic drudge, it being technically the husband's
duty to see that hot food is laid before his wife. The only duty laid
upon a wife is to be open to bear children, should God so bless the
couple, and to nurse them when they are young, although even here a
wet nurse can be retained. These are of course the ideals as provided
by Islamic law, but the realities in Muslim families around the world
do not always follow these prescriptions.

Reference often is made to the verse in the Qur'an that appears to
allow a husband to beat his wife (Q. 4:34). The context here is one
of *nushuz*, a violation of duties on the part of the religious wife. This
verse of the Qur'an lays down four steps to be taken, which may be
seen as a correction and limitation of pre-Islamic practices. First, the
man should speak to his wife. If this fails, he should then refuse to
sleep with her. Only if this fails to change her ways is he allowed a
kind of symbolic humiliation by striking her with his *miswak*, a piece
of wood smaller than a pencil, the tip of which is used for brushing the
teeth. Even this is considered inadvisable in some schools of Islam,
and any form of cruelty, including verbal abuse, is unanimously forbidden. Should all this fail, then the couple should seek arbitration
within the family.

Women are important models of faith for Muslim men and women.
The wives of Muhammad are referred to in the Qur'an as the "Mothers
of the Believers" (Q. 33:6). Islamic tradition speaks of four "perfect
women." These include Khadija, the first wife of Muhammad, and
their daughter, Fatima. The third is Mary, the mother of Jesus, who
is a model of chastity, faith, and devotion (Q. 66:12). The fourth is
'Asiyah, the wife of Pharaoh, who saved the life of the infant Moses
(Q. 28:9). Pharaoh typifies arrogance and wickedness. 'Asiyah had
her life focused on God, shunned wrongdoing, and sought the life
of heaven (Q. 66:11). She was, of course, the follower of no known
Prophet. Thus her example is particularly important, as she demonstrates that the natural condition of human beings is to be *muslim*
and to live a life of *taqwa* even if we are separated from the earlier

guidance sent by God. In such circumstances, our natural *muslim* nature can flourish through reason and reflection, and 'Asiyah is the perfect example of this.

The laws in Islam governing inheritance are extremely complex, and the details need not concern us here. Generally speaking, two-thirds of someone's estate is divided according to set patterns laid out by the different schools of law. The remaining third may be disposed of freely by the individual according to the terms of their will.

Food is an important part of any family's life. The Qur'an lays down four types of food that are forbidden, or *haram*, for Muslims (Q. 2:173). These are carrion, meaning any animal that dies through natural causes, illness, accident, or improper methods of slaughter; blood, meaning any liquid blood or food made from blood; pork, which includes any food made from the flesh of a pig; and any food over which any name other than God's has been pronounced, for example, food that has been sacrificed to idols. Some schools of Islam will allow that, if there is no evidence that the name of anything other than God has been pronounced over food, but there is doubt that the food was dedicated in the name of God, then it can be rendered fit for Muslims to eat by speaking the *basmala* over it. Working on this basis, Muslim scholars generally are agreed that animals that eat other animals, such as predatory birds and land creatures, are *haram*. Such a classification variously prohibits dogs, crocodiles, foxes, ravens, and so on. For most Muslims, the sea is considered to be pure, and so all sea and freshwater creatures are permitted, or halal, for food. In some Muslim schools, shellfish and fish without scales and fins are *haram*.

Why, it might be asked, is the pig singled out for special *haram* status? The first and clearest reason is that this is stated expressly in the Qur'an and therefore is part of God's guidance (Q. 2:173). Other indicators might be that pigs are notoriously omnivorous about what they eat, being known in the Arab lands to eat even dead human bodies. It is known that their flesh becomes unsafe to eat very quickly in any hot climate, and they sometimes carry within their bodies worms that can be transferred to human beings. Finally, the cry of a pig being slaughtered is very reminiscent of the cry of a human baby.

An animal that is halal while alive, like a sheep, must be slaughtered in the appropriate way in order to make it halal to eat. Such animals must be well tended while they are alive and given food, water, and space while they are waiting to be killed. No animal is permitted to see or hear the suffering of another, so even in an abattoir, arrangements must be made to separate the animal being slaughtered from those next in line. Before it is killed, the name of God must be spoken over it, to thank God for its life and to acknowledge that it is a creature of God (Q. 6:118-121). The animal must be killed as quickly and painlessly as possible, thus causing minimal suffering. The blood must be allowed to drain from the animal (in Semitic thought the life of any creature is contained in the blood). This means that a skilled person must take a razor-sharp knife and cut the throat of the animal so that the artery, vein, and windpipe are severed in a single stroke. This cuts off the blood supply to the brain meaning that the animal does not suffer, even though muscular contractions might mean that it writhes and blood is pumped from it. Every life is a sacred gift from God; no animal should be killed in excess of what is needed for food (hunting or shooting for sport is forbidden in Islam).

This method of slaughter has much in common with the Jewish kosher practice and with the way in which Christians slaughtered their animals until very recently. There is considerable concern among Muslims and Jews about modern methods used in abattoirs in the West. In such slaughterhouses it is common for animals to see others suffer, for them to be pre-stunned by electric charges that in some cases kill the animal, and for there to be reduced pumping out of the blood due to pre-stunning. Methods of slaughter that do not entail the release of blood, such as electrocution in the case of poultry or a captive bolt in larger animals, are not acceptable for Muslims. In the case of seafood, most Muslim schools accept them as *halal* no matter how they are killed, provided that they were alive when they leave the water.

All vegetables are halal for Muslims with no particular rules about their preparation. Some Muslims are vegetarians. This is tolerated as long as it is a matter of personal choice and the vegetarian does not say that eating meat is wrong. To say such a thing would be to contradict the Qur'an, which is unacceptable (Q. 5:87-88).

Alcohol in all its forms is forbidden under Islamic law whether for drinking or for use in cooking. Even in medicines, an alcoholic base should be avoided if at all possible. Many Muslims have become concerned about much of the processed food available in the West since certain additives are derived from *haram* sources such as improperly slaughtered animals, pig products, insects, and so on. When giving a food gift to Muslim friends or providing refreshments for a meeting, it is important to check that all ingredients are halal and to make available the ingredient lists from packaging, so that Muslim guests can check for themselves. Processed foods containing additives and preservatives are best avoided. Caution should be exercised with any baked product that might contain lard or animal suet as shortening. Sweets can contain gelatin from *haram* sources.

In many societies around the world, not only Muslim ones, it is customary to eat using the hands. There are records in the Hadith of Muhammad following the Arab custom by so doing, but also occasionally using a knife when eating meat. Spoons and sometimes forks are used commonly in Muslim societies. It is customary to take only the right hand to the mouth and to use it alone for eating. This is because hygiene requirements in traditional societies reserved the left hand for lavatory uses. A spoon or fork normally would be held in the right hand, which also would be used when serving from the dish. This preference of the right hand is widespread in all aspects of life. Money is given and received with the right hand, right hands are shaken in greeting, goods are extended and taken with it, and so on. To offer or take something with the left hand can be considered offensive.

Eating customs vary from one Muslim culture to another. Some people tend to eat in silence; others share from a common dish. In some places, men will eat in one place, and women will eat with children in another. Sometimes women serve the men first and eat only when the men have finished. All these are local customs and not ordained by Islamic principles. Often a visitor to a Muslim household will be served first with some of the senior men. In such cases a woman visitor might expect to be seated with the men until regular visits bring sufficient familiarity with the women of the household for her to be taken immediately to their quarters.

Sickness is a factor in the lives of most people. Muslim doctors have always been committed to bringing people back to health and were pioneers in the medical field, especially in the eighth to thirteenth centuries, when many of the foundations for pre-modern medicine were laid. The healing properties of Qur'an verses and prayer already have been noted. Certain plant extracts and animal products, like honey, were commended by Muhammad for their health-giving properties (Q. 16:69). Sickness must be borne with patience (*sabr*), but modern medicine has been embraced as part of God's unfolding wonder in creation.

Death is part of being human, but life is to be preserved if possible. This principle is seen in the case of someone suffering from thirst or hunger. If a Muslim's life is in danger and if there is no halal food available, something that is clearly *haram*, such as pork or alcohol, may be consumed to keep the person alive (Q. 5:3). The Muslim may continue to take in as much as is necessary to keep them alive, until the crisis passes. There is an indication here of the lengths to which Muslims may go to preserve someone's life. Transplanting an organ from a dead person or a blood transfusion is permissible. It is not permitted, however, to mutilate one's body, so taking one kidney from a living person to implant it in someone else would not be acceptable, generally speaking. Nevertheless, some schools will allow this as a last resort, although it is discouraged strongly. Because God is the creator, our lives are not ours to end when we wish, so suicide is forbidden in the Qur'an (Q. 4:29). People contemplating suicide are counseled to trust that the providence of God will provide all that is necessary for life. Some Muslims do commit suicide when circumstances or illness have deprived them of a sound perspective to make a balanced judgment; such are commended to the mercy of God.

The importance of the sanctity of marriage and the need to know the parentage of any child already has been stressed. Egg or sperm donation would not be permitted in most schools of thought, as this technically would break the bond of marriage and mean that any ensuing child was unsure of its parentage. In the same way, the practice of adoption in the West becomes problematic when the anonymity of the birth parents is guaranteed. This makes it an unacceptable practice in Islam. Recent trends in Britain toward giving all adopted children the right to know their birth parents make the process of adoption easier for Muslims to embrace.

Questions have been raised in modern times about the position of homosexuality within Islam. This is of course not a new phenomenon, but it now receives open discussion and publicity. The general Muslim position is to oppose any form of sexual encounter that is not both heterosexual and within marriage. As far as male homosexual acts are concerned, these are forbidden clearly by the Qur'an (Q. 4:16, 7:80-84). Some Muslims accept that a person may have a homosexual disposition, but this is differentiated clearly from homosexual practice. Someone with such a disposition is counseled not to engage in sexual acts and to control their desires by fasting. Suffering does not go unnoticed by God, who will reward those who endure. Many Muslim scholars tend toward the behavioral view of homosexuality: that it is a learned pattern of behavior rather than something genetic. Because of this, they see the modern West's more liberal attitude toward homosexuality as being an encouragement for more people to experiment and develop homosexual tendencies.

Death

As death is an inevitable part of human life, it is something to which the dying person and the relatives should be reconciled rather than resisting it or grieving excessively. When it becomes clear that the time of death is approaching, the dying person should be positioned so that they are facing the *qibla*, that is, toward the Ka'ba in Makka. The *shahada* should be repeated so that the person can hear and dwell on these words, which act as a reminder of the answers needed during the interrogation in the grave by the angels Munkar and Nakir. Passages from the Qur'an are recited, in particular *Sura Ya Sin* (Q. 36). This follows the advice of a Hadith from Muhammad that anyone who recites this *sura* with the correct intention will have their sins forgiven. The *sura* deals at length with death, resurrection, and judgment.

After the death, the body should be prepared for burial as quickly as possible. If the death occurs in the morning, then ideally the burial should be later that day; if the death occurs in the evening, then the burial should be the following day. The understanding is that the dead person is in a sense uneasy until they are buried. Relatives often remain with the body throughout, from death to burial.

A dead body should be given the same respect the person received in their lifetime. Interfering with the body in any way is discouraged. If the law absolutely requires an autopsy, then it should be conducted as quickly as possible and with the minimum interference to the body. In Western countries where deaths must be registered and permission granted for the burial of a body, there is often a longer period of delay than Muslim families would desire. This can be made worse if cemeteries do not open on weekends and graves can be dug only during the workday. Many discussions take place between coroners and Muslim leaders to resolve some of these problems and keep the delay to a minimum.

The dead body is prepared for burial by being washed by people of the same sex as the deceased. The dignity of the dead person is preserved by not exposing the naked body but washing it under a sheet. The body is washed completely, according to a set procedure, and then wrapped in burial cloths. These are simple sheets that should conceal the body. Often the two white unsewn cotton sheets, or *ihram*, worn by the dead man when he made his *Hajj* are used as his burial shroud. No ornamentation is permitted, and no expensive materials should be used in preparing the body. Perfume is customarily used to anoint the body after washing. The shrouded body may be placed in a coffin, but this is not traditional practice. In the case of someone considered a martyr, who died for the sake of Islam, they are not washed or shrouded, nor are prayers said. Such a person is held to have been purified by their martyrdom and thus destined for Paradise (Q. 2:154, 3:169-172, 195). A foetus that died part-way through gestation is given a name and buried in a plain cloth without ceremony.

The Muslim custom always has been to bury a dead person in the place where they died. The person fortunate enough to die in Madina would be buried there in the graveyards near the grave of the Prophet. In recent times, with air transport and mass migration of Muslims around the world, many have requested that they be transported back to their home village and buried there. This necessarily involves a considerable delay and requires the embalming of the body for hygienic purposes. It is also expensive. Some Muslim scholars discourage this practice on account of the delay and concern over the interference of the embalming process and the substances that are used. As time goes on, it becomes more common for Muslims who have migrated to be buried in their new place of residence, where their family can come to visit and tend their graves.

The funeral itself may be conducted at the family home, or more usually, in the grounds of the mosque. Some mosques have been equipped with mortuary facilities so that the body can lie near the prayer hall but not inside it; to take the body inside would be to make that place ritually impure. The funeral prayers, or *salat al-janaza*, generally are led by a senior man from the family or the *imam* from the mosque. The prayers are said standing with the dead body at the front, so there is no bowing or prostration. They consist of recitations from the Qur'an invoking God's blessing on the Prophet, *du'a* that God will be merciful to the deceased, and *du'a* for the family and everyone. Since prior to puberty children are not held accountable for their sins, there is no need for prayers to be offered for their forgiveness. Taking part in a *salat al-janaza* is a duty upon the Muslim community that can be fulfilled by a portion of the community, or *fard kifaya*. Many Muslims try to be present for these prayers invoking God's mercy on the deceased, and often the gatherings are large.

Muslims are by custom buried in the ground, although in cities and rocky places they have been buried in tombs cut out from the stone or constructed with stones. Cremation is not a tradition and is not permitted as an alternative. This does not mean that someone who is lost at sea, burned in a fire, eaten by animals, or disintegrated in an explosion is somehow outside the mercy of God. God can overcome all those things, but by choice Muslims always will choose burial. Graves are used for only one person at a time, although after a period of years both graveyards and stone tombs have been reused in Muslim societies. The grave is dug in such a way that when the body is laid in it, on its right side, the head can be turned to face in the direction of the Ka'ba in Makka. In many societies a niche is dug at the bottom of the grave to receive the body, which then can be covered with wooden sticks or earthen bricks and the grave finally filled in by the mourners. It is normal that only men and boys accompany the body to the burial ground, but in some schools and societies women attend as well.

In some schools of Islam, it is customary to remind the dead person of the oneness of God and the prophethood of Muhammad as the last act before the grave is filled in. These are the first of the responses necessary when the angels come to interrogate the body in the grave. Prayers normally are offered beside the filled grave, and sometimes there is an address and a recitation from the Qur'an. The mourners are often quite slow to leave the graveside, pausing to offer further prayers. The tradition relates that, as soon as they have retreated from the grave, the angels appear to begin the initial interrogation. In some Muslim societies, men will spend the first night near the grave reciting the Qur'an, since it is believed that the first night in the grave is the most difficult. Now begins the waiting period in the grave known as *barzakh* (see chapter 5).

The period and style of mourning after someone's death vary between schools of Islam and cultures around the world. Prayers to ask God to be merciful to the dead person are common, and there are often communal Qur'an recitations and shared meals. The fortieth day after death marks the end of the mourning rites for some Muslims and is commemorated even more widely. A widow is required to remain in mourning for four months and ten days, after which time she resumes normal life and is free to marry again.

The grave often is mounded and a grave marker erected with the person's name and sometimes a verse from the Qur'an. In some cultures and schools of Islam much more elaborate grave stones are erected, even a mausoleum in the case of a prominent person, although such practices are condemned by other Muslim scholars. In most schools, it is common to visit the grave periodically to recite for the deceased person favorite verses from the Qur'an and to invoke God's mercy alongside the grave. In the case of people of outstanding piety and wisdom, such graves may become places for people to visit. Again, some groups within Islam would disapprove of such practices.

8

Living Constantly Remembering God

Shari'a: a complete code of life – not arbitrary but divinely revealed – Qur'an as principal source – attention to the context in which verses of the Qur'an were revealed – commentary on the Qur'an (tafsir) – various schools of tafsir – the lived example of Muhammad (Sunna) – Hadith – classification of Hadith – Hadith collections – intellectual reasoning by analogy (qiyas) – devising new rulings (ijtihad) – classification of actions – schools of law – present day questions –"Islamizing" national laws today – the penal code – jihad – the struggle against the wayward self – legitimate use of force – rules of engagement – indiscriminate killing: weapons of mass destruction, "suicide terrorism" – the sufi path – the ascent of the heart to God – a spiritual chain – importance of the shaykh – tariqa – systematic progression: stations and states – the circle of dhikr – sufi writers – great sufi orders

To live constantly remembering God, the life of *taqwa*, is on the one hand simple: it is living naturally in peace with all and in submission to the will of God. On the other hand, it is complicated because one has to work out what the will of God is and how to follow it in detail. Even if one understands Arabic, and only a small proportion of Muslims do, gaining a detailed understanding of the Qur'an and the teaching of Muhammad is not simple. Others have been doing so for centuries, and one needs to take notice of the complexity and subtlety of what they have written. For most Muslims, living a godly life means that one follows a code of conduct (Shari'a) worked out by others. Even this is not enough as there is a big step from knowing how to live to actually putting it into practice. This is a lifelong struggle (*jihad*). For many Muslims, this outer struggle is based on the journey inward: to get closer to God, to be more obedient to the divine will, or to seek communion with God through the sufi tradition. This chapter attempts to explore this whole area and to show some of the foundations for living a life of constant God-consciousness. Of course, each individual is not alone on this earth, so this requires looking also at *taqwa* in relation to others and to society. There is a Hadith of Muhammad that says, "None of you will have faith until he (she) wishes for his (her) brother (sister) what he (she) would like for himself (herself)." This is the spirit in which we begin this rather complex journey.

Shari'a

Human beings were not created in a vacuum, but with a definite purpose: to worship God (Q. 9:31, 51:56, 98:5). One of the greatest acts of worshipping God is to live according to the guidance that has been given. The term *islam*, as we have seen, means the deep harmony and peace that comes through complete submission to the divine will as revealed in the Qur'an and put into practice by Muhammad. Each human being is responsible not only for her or his own actions but for creating a just social order and tending the whole of creation as the Regent of God (*khalifa*) on earth. In God's justice and mercy, God has sent essentially the same guidance to all humankind through Prophets. Each of these Prophets interpreted through their life and teaching the guidance that they had received. In this way they set a pattern or model of *islamic* living for their followers to imitate. When this pattern is later drawn up as a complete code of life, it is called a *shari'a*.

The word *shari'a* literally means a road or highway, a well-beaten path that leads to a definite place. The path trodden from a village to a river or well to fetch water would be a *shari'a*. The path made by animals that always follow the same track to reach their destination would also be a *shari'a*. Such a path becomes so clearly defined that one can see it in the dark. In technical religious terms, it is a clearly defined way of following the guidance of God that was left as a pattern for *islamic* living by each of the Messengers. Moses (*Musa*) left a *shari'a* for the Jews based on the guidance of God in the Torah (*Taurat*) and the tradition that he established. Although in essence the guidance is always the same, the precise details of that guidance and therefore of the *shari'a* that was based on it may vary. We have seen for example, the many similarities between the Jewish rules for kosher food and the Muslim rules for halal food, but there are differences in the specific details. The same pattern can be seen in the case of Jesus and every other Prophet who was sent with a revelation from God.

Shari'a is never arbitrary law made up by the Prophet or by a vote among the people. It is a divinely ordained way that the Prophet implemented and human beings are to follow in obedience to the will of God. It will make for a happy, just, upright, fulfilled life on earth and has as its ultimate destination the gateway to heaven in the life after death. It applies to every aspect of life and concerns all personal, family, and communal actions. As the Shari'a concerns the basic unchanging human condition, its principles never change, although fresh circumstances often require that those principles be applied anew in each generation and context.

Reading the Qur'an.
Photo: © 2006 Megan
J. Thorvilson.

The Shari'a of Islam is held by Muslims to be the final, most perfect, and universal Shari'a. Its principal sources are first of all the Qur'an as the Word of God and second the Sunna, the lived example of the Prophet Muhammad. The Qur'an is not a manual of laws in which one may look up the correct answer as though looking for a recipe in a cookbook; it is the revealed ethical guidance for human living that needs to be understood and applied to develop laws. The first and best interpreter of the Qur'an was Muhammad. Everything he said and did and the things he approved were the practical application of his being imbued with the Qur'an in his heart. This lived example of Qur'anic guidance was called his Sunna, meaning a pattern of behavior that people should follow. The Sunna of the Prophet as his infallible implementation of the Qur'an becomes the second source of guidance for human living.

During the lifetime of Muhammad, these two sources were enough; new or diffcult questions always could be referred to the Prophet. When that was no longer possible, additional methods based on the Qur'an and the Sunna had to be approved. A well-known Hadith records that Muhammad was sending Mu'adh ibn Jabal (d. 640) to be the judge (*qadi*) in Yemen. Muhammad asked him how he would reach a decision on questions referred to him. His response was to cite the Qur'an and Sunna as his first two guides. "What will you do if you do not find the answer in those two sources?" the Prophet asked. He replied: "Then I shall come to a decision according to my own opinion without hesitation." To this Muhammad responded: "Praise be to Allah who has led the messenger of the Messenger of Allah to an answer that pleases him." In this way, human reasoning was brought into the process. This is not surprising when we remember that reason is also a gift from God. The Qur'an calls on people to use their reason for puzzling out answers by exploring the created world around us. We now explore these sources for the Shari'a in more detail.

Qur'an

The Qur'an is the primary deposit of God's guidance for all human-kind. The Creator knows best how the creation should operate; therefore nothing can contradict the clear guidance contained in the Qur'an. Remember, though, that the Qur'an was revealed over a period of twenty-three years, and so every part of the Qur'an was revealed in a particular context. In order to understand the precise meaning of each individual revelation, we need to know the context or question to which the revelation was the divinely ordained answer. These contexts are important and have been retained in the early histories of Islam, the commentaries, and the Hadith as the *asbab al-nuzul*, the "occasions of revelation." Clarity about Qur'an's guidance involves historiographical study of the life and times of Muhammad and a sociology of those times to see what effect the Qur'anic revelation was intended to have.

The Qur'an rarely says everything there is to say on a particular question at any one time. Scholars interpret every revelation of the Qur'an against its particular context. The goal is to arrive at the "golden principle for human living" contained in the Qur'an as a whole. It is not simply a case of finding one verse that mentions a particular teaching and taking that to be the sum total of an Islamic way of life, or Shari'a.

We could take as an example the Qur'anic guidance on alcohol. The first guidance on this (Q. 4:43) was revealed about three years after the arrival of Muhammad in Madina. It warns people not to come to their prayers in a state of intoxication. It seems that getting drunk was common among Arabs before the rise of Islam. A second verse (Q. 2:219) was revealed soon after. It noted that the ill-effects of alcohol far outweigh any good ones; therefore it is better to avoid it. Finally at the end of Muhammad's life, the final guidance was revealed (Q. 5:90-91) prohibiting all alcohol and gambling as a cause of unrest within society. As the community settled and matured, people were ready to receive the fullness of revelation on this question. From this can be drawn a principle of gradualism, a principle which often is useful in the life of a new convert to Islam. This same principle was accepted by Ibn Taymiyya and used by Lord Headley, one of the leading Muslim converts of early twentieth-century England, to lead new converts gradually into the full observance of Shari'a as it applied to alcohol, regular *salat*, and fasting.

This process of understanding the *intention* of the Qur'an led to the Islamic discipline of *tafsir*, or Qur'anic commentary. The Prophet himself gave an interpretation of the meaning of the Qur'an to his followers, and this was handed down by oral tradition. The first school of *tafsir* was known as *tafsir ma'thur*, or commentary that is handed down. One of the earliest systematic scholars of the Qur'an in this school was al-Tabari (d. 923), also a great historian who recorded much of the early history of the Islamic period. In his massive work of *tafsir*, he preserved a wealth of history and the interpretations handed down in the oral tradition. He reviewed various possible readings of complex verses of the Qur'an, then offered and defended his own interpretation. This became a basis for later scholars, who produced various personal interpretations that sometimes differed from al-Tabari. The point here is that a massive deposit of *tafsir* accumulated over fourteen centuries of which any modern commentator needs to be aware when seeking the meaning of the divine guidance. It should be obvious that the scholar who engages in the process of *tafsir* needs both a thorough knowledge of the Arabic language in its many shades of meaning and the way that it has been used in Arabic literature.

The second major school of *tafsir* to emerge was called *tafsir bi al-ra'y*, or interpretation based on individual rational judgment. This tended to be more philosophical and speculative in its nature and was especially favored by the Mu'tazilite or rationalist school of Islam. The great name associated with this school is al-Zamakhshari (d. 1144), who is widely respected on account of his linguistic and stylistic understanding of the language and meaning of the Qur'an. Even when orthodox Islam reacted against this excessive rationalism, the work of al-Zamakhshari retained an important place in the work of orthodox scholars such as Fakhr al-Din al-Razi (d. 1209) and al-Baydawi (d. *c.*1286), whose own orthodox *tafsir* took full advantage of al-Zamakhshari's method and insights without falling into al-Zamakhshari's excessive rationalism. The commentaries of al-Tabari and al-Baydawi are within modern Sunni Islam among the most widely used and respected from the classical period.

Within Shi'a Islam, the understanding developed that the Imams were infallible and thus were capable of giving a definitive interpretation of the Qur'an and indeed of infallibly deducing new guidance in their own right. Within this school especially, the additional form of allegorical interpretation known as *ta'wil* emerged. The sixth Imam of the Shi'a tradition, Ja'far al-Sadiq (d. 765), is recorded as saying that there are four levels of understanding contained in the Qur'an: the literary (*'ibarah*) for the masses, the allusion (*isharah*) for the scholarly elite, the hidden meaning (*lata'if*) for the Friends of God (*wali:* a

Friend of God or saintly person), and the spiritual truths (*haqa'iq*) for the Prophet and Imams. Similar multi-layered meanings for the verses of the Qur'an are found in sufi *tafsir* among both Sunni and Shi'a mystics.

In conclusion, interpreting the guidance contained in the Qur'an requires extensive knowledge and wisdom. It is not a case simply of looking up an index and reading off simple rules for living a Muslim way of life. This is not to say, however, that only first-class scholars can be Muslims. Reading the Qur'an affects each individual Muslim, even if the meanings are not fully understood.

Sunna

As we have seen, the teaching and example of Muhammad was the model for putting the guidance of the Qur'an into daily life. A famous saying from A'isha (d. 678), the "favorite" wife of Muhammad's later life, says that to see the life of the Prophet was to hear the Qur'an and to hear the Qur'an was to see the life of Muhammad. It is no surprise that those around Muhammad remembered in minute detail elements of his teaching, the way he conducted his life, and the way he approved of or corrected the common practice of the Arabs of his time. These elements were passed around the early Muslim community as the Hadith, or Traditions of Muhammad.

Muhammad made it clear when he was speaking in his own right as the Prophet and when he was conveying the revelation from God in the Qur'an. The two were quite distinct. A third category, a group of sayings called the *hadith qudsi*, were words of God given to Muhammad but were not part of the Qur'an. These also were collected and have a special place in the Islamic tradition.

As the Hadith of Muhammad circulated within the early Muslim community, each *hadith* developed a chain of transmitters, or *isnad*. These chains were a way of demonstrating the authenticity of a Hadith and followed the form "A heard it from B, who heard it from C, who heard the Prophet say...." The final part of each *isnad* had to rest with one of the Companions of the Prophet, who heard it from the Prophet's lips or observed his practice. Great care was taken to preserve every Hadith's *isnad*, which was memorized as a sign of authenticity. Naturally some elements of Muhammad's teaching were reported by different Companions, and so several chains of transmitters might pass on the same saying of the Prophet. Such multiple chains were highly prized as further proof of authenticity. Later in Hadith criticism, care was taken to establish that A actually did or at least could have met B to hear the Hadith transmitted, and that every person contained in a chain of transmitters was of sound character and pious life so that their word could be trusted.

The second part of each Hadith is the actual element of teaching or practice observed; this was called the *matn*, or body of the Hadith. Once the *isnad* of a Hadith was secured, the *matn* could be considered. Obviously, anything contained in a *matn* that contradicted something in the Qur'an was a sign of its inauthenticity. Later, the science of Hadith criticism would look at each authentic Hadith and weigh it against the agreed-upon elements within the Sunna of Muhammad.

The earliest deposit of Hadith material is found in the writings of Malik ibn Anas (712–795), who lived in Madina and was a descendant of one of the Companions of Muhammad. He also was the founder of an Islamic school of law, which will be discussed later. One generation later in Baghdad, another founder of a school of law, Ahmad ibn Hanbal (780–855), was reported to have memorized a million Hadiths and left a collection of them called the *Musnad*, which contains some forty thousand.

Eventually, great collections were gathered and written down, beginning in the ninth century. Most important, these collections were systematic in their arrangement of the material, grouping Hadith around particular topics and classifying them by their authenticity. The two highest classifications used were *sahih*, meaning sound without defects, and *hasan*, meaning good and reliable but not as clearly authenticated as a *sahih*. There are several classifications of less reliable Hadith, the most important being *da'if*, meaning weak, usually due to a break or uncertainty in the chain of transmitters.

Within Sunni Islam, there are six great systematic collections of Hadith that are highly respected, although Hadith appear in many other minor collections and writings. These six are associated with the men who traveled the Muslim world of the time, collecting the Hadith and testing both the chains of transmitters and the bodies of the Hadith in circulation. They are renowned for the care that they took in meticulously sifting out any saying that was not of the highest quality in both regards.

The six major collections of Hadith in Sunni Islam are those of Al-Bukhari (810–870), Muslim (820–875), Abu Dawud (817–888), Al-Tirmidhi (824–2), An-Nasa'i (830–915), and Ibn Majah (824–886). Each contains anywhere from four to nine thousand Hadiths. The timing of these great collections coincides with the industrialization of paper production in the ninth century and with a struggle over the role the scholars (*ulama*) would play in the Muslim community. Al-Shafi'i (d. 820) stressed the importance of the Hadith in the hands of the scholars; political power was stressed by Caliph al-Ma'mun in 833 when he implemented the first theological inquisition in Islam, which lasted through two more Caliphs, until 848.

Among the Shi'a, different chains of transmitters are used, which trace themselves back to Imam Ali or one of his party. The great Shi'a collections, generally compiled about a century later, are associated with al-Kulayni (d. 940), Shaykh Saduq (923–991), and al-Tusi (995–1067). In addition, there is a collection of sayings by Imam Ali himself called the *Nahj al-Balagha*. A Hadith of Muhammad promises a blessing to anyone who memorizes forty Hadith. This led to a tradition of collections of forty Hadith that were then memorized. The best known of these was by al-Nawawi (d. 1277) and normally is known by the name *Arba'in*, in English *The Forty Hadith*.

For the last two hundred years, Western scholars have been turning their interest toward Islam. Many who have studied the Hadith material have been critical of its authenticity as a deposit of the actual sayings of the Prophet. As a body of material, it clearly dates back to the early centuries of Islam, but their criticism tends to be based on Western literary-critical methods. Their work has been overwhelmingly rejected by Muslim and some other Western scholars, and several scholarly works have been written to rebut it. It has, however, had its effect on some modern Muslim scholars who have become more critical of certain Hadith, seeing them as having been generated by Muslims to defend certain positions against those with whom they disagreed.

Intellectual activity

As was seen earlier, there always have been situations in Muslim life that are not dealt with directly by the Qur'an and the Sunna of Muhammad. The case of Mu'adh ibn Jabal has already been cited, with the Prophet's approval of his use of personal judgment. This use of personal judgment, or *ra'y*, was common in the first century of Islam as it spread rapidly into different contexts far removed from Madina. It gradually developed into a systematic form based on the principle of *qiyas*, or analogical reasoning. The aim was to find an already-decided situation analogous to the new situation. By logical extension, the earlier judgment was thus developed to cover the new question. This process was accepted in various forms by most schools of Islam as an acceptable third source of Shari'a, but a ruling derived by *qiyas* alone could not become a source for future rulings. Rulings always needed to be rooted in the Qur'an and the Sunna of Muhammad, thus limiting the potential for subjective errors of reasoning.

The principle of *qiyas* led to a systematic process of striving by legal reasoning, or *ijtihad*, to find an opinion on a new question. Developing such opinions was the province of a suitably qualified scholar, a *mujtahid*. Such scholars had to demonstrate how they arrived at their judgments and were thus subject to the scrutiny and correction of other scholars. It was always acknowledged that no single scholar was going to be right all the time, a fact emphasized by the tradition that there was a blessing for performing *ijtihad* and a further blessing for being seen to be right by the scholarly community, known as the *ulama*, or the learned. Gradually this process led to a body of scholarly opinion, and such independent reasoning gave way to a spirit of imitating what had gone before, known as *taqlid*. Within Shi'a Islam, a senior *mujtahid* or Ayatollah generates a following among the faithful who adhere to his judgments in the spirit of *taqlid*.

The product of this intellectual activity, based firmly on the Qur'an and the Sunna of the Prophet, resulted in a consensus in legal matters. This consensus, or *ijma*, necessarily began as a consensus of the scholars who were equipped to handle the original sources; but by extension the goal was for that consensus to be accepted by the whole Muslim community. This universal consensus is in the spirit of a Hadith of Muhammad that said that the Muslim community would never agree on an error, and so something that had the status of *ijma* was considered to be a solid element of Islamic law on which later generations could build.

In conclusion, the role of scholarship and the way in which this scholarship built up over centuries should receive special notice. Again we see that it is no simple task to apply the guidance of the Qur'an and the Sunna to contemporary questions such as living in a Western political and economic system or dealing with advances in medical science.

Classification of actions

Islamic law came to recognize five categories of actions that can be applied throughout life. This grew from a recognition that, while certain things clearly were either obligatory or forbidden by the

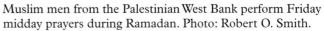

Muslim men from the Palestinian West Bank perform Friday midday prayers during Ramadan. Photo: Robert O. Smith.

Dome and minaret of the Al-Azhar Mosque in Cairo, Egypt. Photo: Sally Messner.

Women pray in a mosque in Mumbai, Bombay, India. Photo: © Peter Adams/zefa/Corbis.

A man reads the Qur'an in the Al-Azhar Mosque in Cairo, Egypt. Photo: © 2006 Megan J. Thorvilson.

Page from the Qur'an in Kufic script, 10th century. Photo: © The Minneapolis Institute of the Arts. Bequest of Mrs. Margaret McMillan Webber in memory of her mother, Katherine Kittredge McMillan

Afghan school children with their teacher. Photo: Linda Wiehl.

Mosque in Al-Jimi, Al-Ain, United Arab Emirates. Photo: Angela Pierce.

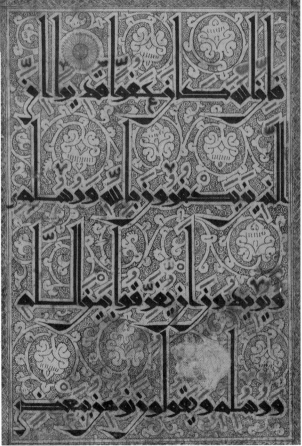

Page from an Iranian copy of the Qur'an, 12th century. Photo: © The Minneapolis Institute of the Arts.

Muhammadiyah Muslim
women leaders in Indonesia.
Photo: Nelly van Doorn-Harder.

A muslim student in the Netherlands.
Photo: © 2006 Anke Leunissen.

The Sultan Agung Mosque
in Medan, Indonesia.
Photo: Paul Harder.

Muslim children in the village of Sheik Yasin, Afghanistan. Photo: Linda Wiehl.

Muslim farmers near the village of Minya, Egypt. Photo: Marc Ostlie-Olson.

Dome over the mausoleum of the Mamluke Sultan Qaytbay in Cairo, Egypt. Photo: Marc Ostlie-Olson.

The Mecca Masjid in Hyderabad, India. Photo: David Coward.

Turkish prayer rug, 17th century.
Photo: © The Minneapolis Institute of the Arts.
Gift of Bartev A. Keljik

An Egyptian dance troupe performs their "whirling dervish" Sufi dance. Photo: Sally Messner.

Interior of the mausoleum and khanqa of Ibn Barquq, in the "City of the Dead" in Cairo, Egypt. Photo: Marc Ostlie-Olson.

Courtyard of the of the 'Amr Ibn al-'As Mosque in Cairo, Egypt. Photo: Sally Messner.

A man performs *wudu'* outside the Suleyman Pasha Mosque in Cairo, Egypt. Photo: Sally Messner.

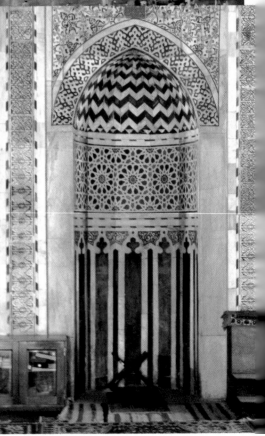

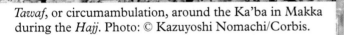

Tawaf, or circumambulation, around the Ka'ba in Makka during the *Hajj*. Photo: © Kazuyoshi Nomachi/Corbis.

A *dikka* in the Sultan Barquq Mosque in Cairo, Egypt.
Photo: Sally Messner.

A *mihrab* in the Suleyman Pasha Mosque in the Citadel. Cairo, Egypt. Photo: Sally Messner.

Qur'an and the Sunna of the Prophet, others were either encouraged or discouraged, and a significant majority of actions are matters of personal choice toward which the sources are indifferent. This led to the following widely accepted classifications.

Those actions that are required of all Muslims were classified as *fard* or *wajib*. Examples of these are the principal religious duties of *salat*, *sawm*, and so on. A further classification was made to distinguish between things that are obligatory for every Muslim, called *fard 'ayn*, like *salat*, and those things, called *fard kifaya*, that are obligatory for the community but which can be discharged by a group of people on behalf of the whole, such as looking for the new moon or taking part in the funeral prayers for a deceased Muslim.

Acts that are recommended for Muslims and carry a reward if performed but which do not involve punishment if omitted are called Sunna or *masnun*. Examples might be giving the greeting *salam alaykum* when one Muslim meets another, additional *rak'at* before and after the compulsory *salat*, and visiting the sick.

The middle category of acts, to which the Shari'a is indifferent, is called *mubah* or *ja'iz*. Neither reward nor punishment is attached to such actions. Examples of this could be styles of dress, types of diet, choice of career, or literary tastes, provided they all fall within the boundaries of the acceptable norms of Shari'a.

Actions that are disapproved of but without specific punishment if committed are called *makruh*. Smoking tobacco is often classified in this way. This is a good example of the way in which an action might be subject to reclassification: as more information becomes available about the health risks of smoking, some scholars want to see it reclassified as forbidden on the basis that one is forbidden to kill or harm oneself.

Any action that is clearly unlawful and which carries a punishment if committed is classified as *haram*. Examples include drinking alcohol, exploitation, and sexual misconduct.

Naturally, there are many levels of sophistication within the various schools of Islamic law, and some acts are classified differently within the three middle categories.

Schools of law

From the beginning of the Islamic period, the centrality of the Qur'an and the Sunna of Muhammad were strong uniting features. At the same time, as Islam spread rapidly during the first century after

Sultan Agung Mosque.
Medan, Indonesia.
Photo: Paul Harder.

Muhammad, considerable variations arose in the way the principal sources were applied in daily living. Islam has never been as monochrome as some people think. There has always been a healthy tension between unity and diversity.

As Islam encountered other traditions in different parts of the Islamic Empire, Muslims continually refined the process of defining ever more precisely the Shari'a. This led to the development of a number of schools of law, or *madhahib* (sing. *madhhab*, meaning path or way to go). The first school of law established was based in Baghdad and is associated with the name of its founder, Abu Hanifa (d. 767). He is credited with much of the development of *qiyas* and *ra'y* as legal principles. His school has spread to become dominant in the Indian Subcontinent, Central Asia, Turkey (formerly the Ottoman Empire), and parts of Egypt.

The name of Malik ibn Anas (712–795) has already been encountered as a collector of Hadith. He founded the Maliki School from his base in Madina. He lived most of his life there and became the Imam of Madina in his time. This gave him a strong sense of the connection to the living tradition of Islamic practice stemming from the Prophet's own time in Madina. Today the Maliki School is to be found in North Africa, parts of Egypt, and parts of West Africa.

Al-Shafi'i (767–820) had the benefit of studying under Malik in Madina and practicing law in Baghdad alongside the Hanafi School. He later settled in Egypt and is credited with developing the principles of systematization of Sunni law that later were widely adopted by all schools in that tradition. In particular he developed the importance of the Hadith of Muhammad as the second source of Shari'a and greatly enhanced the status of *ijma*. This emphasis on consensus as a principle led to the attitude that once something had been agreed on by the community of scholars (*ulama*), there was no further need for discussion. The step from this to the automatic following of earlier teaching (*taqlid*) was a short one. Today the Shafi'i School is dominant in Indonesia, Malaysia, East Africa, parts of Egypt, and in most Arab countries.

The fourth classical Sunni school of law was founded by Ahmad ibn Hanbal (780–855), who already has been noted as a monumental collector of Hadith. This reliance on Qur'an and the Hadith as the principal sources of Shari'a and his bitter battles with more rationalist Muslims gave the characteristic stamp to the Hanbali School. It had a profound influence on one of the great Sunni systematic theologians, Ibn Taymiyya (1263–1328), and more recently on the Wahhabis, the followers of the reformed puritanical movement initiated by Ibn Abd al-Wahhab (1703–1792). The Wahhabi movement aimed to purge Sunni Islam of what it considered to be innovations (*bid'a*), such as a belief in the intercession of the Prophet and the Friends of God and various ritual acts at their graves. Today the Hanbali School, especially in its Wahhabi form, is dominant in Saudi Arabia.

Within Sunni Islam, all four of these schools are regarded as being orthodox, and there is a consensus among them on most of the central aspects of the Shari'a. From the geographical dispersion, it can be observed that the school to which a Sunni Muslim belongs is largely determined by one's place of birth. This would mirror the dominance of Orthodox Christianity in Greece, of Lutheran Christianity in Scandinavia, of Roman Catholic Christianity in Spain, and so on. That is not to imply that people do not change their school on occasion or take the rulings of another school on a particular question, when they find these rulings to be more appropriate than those of the school into which they were born. There were several other Sunni schools of law in earlier centuries, but these have gradually died out for lack of followers and have been absorbed into the four principal schools.

Within Shi'a Islam, one's school of law depends on the branch of Shi'a tradition to which one belongs. The major group, the Ithna 'Asharis, who recognize a line of twelve Imams, follow the Ja'fari School, associated with the name of the sixth Imam, Ja'far al-Sadiq. This school shares the common basis of the Qur'an, augmented by the secondary source of the Hadith of Muhammad according to the Shi'a collections. An important difference from Sunni Islam is that the Imams of the Shi'a tradition are understood to be infallible guides and interpreters of the Qur'an and Sunna. This makes their teachings a further source of guidance for Shi'a Muslims. The Twelfth Imam is in occultation since 941 as the Hidden Imam, but he is still held to guide his people by working through the highest rank of Shi'a scholars, the Ayatollahs. This School has a highly developed place for legal reasoning within its system, and *ijtihad* is still very much alive. It follows from this that the sense of *ijma* is much less developed; ultimate authority rests with the infallible Imam rather than with a consensus of the believers. This gives a "top down" sense of authority within the Shi'a tradition.

Among smaller Shi'a groups, the Zaydis have their own school of law, which is heavily influenced by rationalism. The Ismailis have broken into different groups, such as the Bohras, with their own subgroups, each with its own legal traditions, and the Nizaris, for whom the Aga Khan is the Living Imam and thus the infallible guide of his people. The Nizaris especially follow a *batini*, or hidden esoteric interpretation of the Qur'an, of which the Living Imam is the custodian. This has enabled them to develop a considerably different way of life from that of other Muslim groups.

A further ancient independent school of Muslims is known as the Ibadis, taking their name from Abd Allah ibn Ibad, a leader of the Kharijites in the first century after Muhammad. The distinguishing feature of the Kharijites was their belief that a grave sinner excluded himself or herself from the Muslim community and thus was destined for hell, although over the centuries some have been willing to suspend judgment and leave the final decision to God. The Ibadi School shares much with the Maliki, but their theological development was influenced considerably by rationalism. Today their numbers are small, and they generally are found in Oman, East Africa, and North Africa.

Contemporary situation

Before leaving the question of legal frameworks for following the guidance of Islam, it is important to touch on the contemporary situation. The various schools of law exist, and Muslim scholars need to make a profound study of the principles of jurisprudence, or *usul al-fiqh*, before going on to study the body of knowledge within their particular school. A scholar of Islam is called an *alim* (pl. *ulama*), and one who specializes in the study of Islamic law is called a *faqih*. The science of law in Islam is known as *fiqh*. If an ordinary Muslim is confronted with a question on how to live a Muslim life, the normal procedure is to seek the guidance of a local *alim* or *faqih*. In the West, this sometimes is done over the Internet by sending the question to a recognized helpline, such as those run by the European Council of Fatwas or the International Fiqh Academy in Jeddah. If it is a simple query that has been dealt with by the body of scholars, then an answer can be obtained swiftly.

If the problem is something that needs original research and a "learned opinion," the question must be referred to a *mufti*, who is an *alim* generally recognized by the *ulama* as being of outstanding learning. A *mufti* is capable of using personal judgment to apply the principles of *fiqh* to a new question (*ijtihad*). This personal judgment would be given in the form of a *fatwa*. A *fatwa* is a learned opinion and must be respected as such, but it is not necessarily the last word on the subject. The same question can be presented to another *mufti*, who may bring forward another *fatwa* or may reinforce the earlier opinion.

This is much like seeking a learned opinion from a specialized attorney in Western law. Here it can be seen that all authority is based on knowledge, not from politics or an ordained priesthood. In a Muslim society, there is another legal officer called a *qadi*, or judge, who would sit in a court and dispense justice.

A contemporary Western example of seeking a *fatwa* is the question of the acceptability of organ transplants for Muslims. Clearly this is a new question and has been submitted for guidance to *ulama* working in the West. A *fatwa* was developed and refined through discussion among these *ulama*. Eventually guidance was given that this is an acceptable practice provided that the organ donor is already certified as being dead.

Law in an Islamic state

In the media, the term "Shari'a" often is used to refer only to particular punishments in a Muslim country. By now it is clear that the term means far more than that. Some Muslim-majority countries in the world claim to found their laws on Islamic principles. Others periodically attempt to "Islamize" the laws they inherited after the European colonial period to bring Muslim societies back to the path of Shari'a. Most scholars would agree that, although some countries use the title "Islamic" in their names, no countries today abide fully by the principles of Islamic law.

One aspect of an Islamic state is that it should be shaped by the principle of *sadaqa*, or bearing one another's burdens. A state that allows rampant inequality, exploitation, and corruption cannot be described as Islamic. During the Prophet's time in Madina, some people stole food from others' storerooms during a severe famine. Muhammad suspended the usual punishments for theft at this time because of the extenuating circumstances of some families starving while others had food in storage. It is sad to note that many male-dominated legislations that propose to Islamize their legal systems tend to begin with tighter control of sexual impropriety among women rather than ridding their lands of exploitation, eradicating poverty, and establishing a system based on the whole spectrum of Islam so that extenuating circumstances can be eliminated and people liberated to live a fully human life. Deprived of any extenuating circumstances, such acts would meet the full force of the law.

Attention is often drawn to the penal code of Shari'a. The Qur'an and the Hadith give direction and punishments for a limited number of major public crimes that threaten the authority of law and the stability of society, such as murder, theft, giving false evidence, sexual misconduct, and drinking alcohol. To understand these punishments, one first must note that the Qur'an uses the term *hadd*, meaning limit or boundary. Like the famous "eye for an eye" of the Hebrew Scriptures, such laws sought first to limit excessive punishments for crimes (Q. 2:178). Further, while some scholars interpret the *hadd* as a mandatory punishment, others see it as a maximum or the highest tariff that could be applied, the actual sentence to be decided by the judge. Prisons are a modern form of punishment, whereas in traditional societies the punishment was much more likely to be corporal or sometimes a financial compensation to the victim's family (Q. 4:92-93). A typical *hadd* punishment was corporal in the form of a beating or, for the severest cases of theft, amputation (Q. 5:38). Such beatings were conducted in public so that the humiliation of the guilty person and the example set to the masses were at least as important as the pain endured (Q. 24:2). Thieves with an amputated hand would serve as a public example for the rest of their lives. The awesomeness of such punishments underlined the serious nature of the act and hopefully acted as a deterrent to prevent them from ever being needed.

The use of an awesome punishment to drive home the serious nature of a crime can be seen in the case of adultery (Q. 24:2-4), for which, under certain circumstances, the *hadd* was death according to the Hadith. The idea of stoning to death someone guilty of adultery comes, of course, from the Hebrew Scriptures. In order to pass the death sentence, the judge had to have an extraordinarily high level of evidence. There had to be four adult eyewitnesses who could testify to seeing the actual act of penetration itself or the persistent confession of the guilty person. Naturally the judge would want to know that the confession was the product of a sound mind and had not been obtained under duress. One can ask reasonably what sort of eyewitnesses would stand by and observe such an act of adultery and why some of them had not acted earlier to prevent it happening. A severe beating was prescribed by the *hadd* verses for someone found guilty of giving false evidence in such a case, as they bring the reputation of the accused into question (Q. 24:4). Remember that we have already seen in the case of divorce that if a husband makes a series of oaths stating that his wife has committed adultery and she counterswears in the same fashion that she has not, then the marriage is dissolved, the man cannot be

LIVING CONSTANTLY REMEMBERING GOD   153

convicted of giving false evidence, the woman cannot be convicted of adultery, and the matter is left in the hands of God (Q. 24:6-9).

Before hasty judgments are made about Islam based on the actions of some Muslim people or governments around the world, serious issues must be considered. Millions of people in developing countries know of the West only through television and film. The picture they see is of a rich but morally decadent society corrupted by alcohol, drugs, family breakdown, crime, abuse of sex, and economic exploitation in which many innocent victims suffer without redress. They want to resist any forces that could lead them in the same direction. Some Muslims even question the wisdom of locking up prisoners for decades at a huge expense to law-abiding citizens so that they become "professional criminals," and the mercy of keeping someone on death row for years.

Jihad

To live constantly remembering God is, on the one hand, something very natural. On the other, most people are forgetful and lack the discipline to keep their life, mind, and heart focused on God all the time. This is a constant struggle. Although Islam teaches that every human being is born *muslim*, we have a tendency to forget the guidance of God and drift off into disobedience. To counter this tendency, each Muslim is required to make *jihad*. In this sense *jihad* is a necessary, compulsory duty for every Muslim. This form of *jihad* is known as the "greater *jihad*," or *al-jihad al-akbar*, the constant struggle against the wayward self (Q. 17:19, 29:5-6, 47:31, 76:22).

This sense of struggle against evil and our tendency to forget the command of God to do good by following God's guidance as faithful servants means that every Muslim should be active in the fight against sin. Temptation is to be resisted with all of one's strength. If one does sin, one should repent immediately and seek the mercy of God. Full repentance (*tawba*) means avoiding in the future the circumstances that led to that sin. This might mean avoiding certain employment, or places, or the company of certain people. It might also mean removing oneself from a whole society that leads to sin. *Jihad*, in this case, might involve *hijra*, or moving to a more Islamic environment. This might mean a physical removal to another town or country. It might also mean a psychological withdrawal from corruption: to be in the world but not of it.

Jihad is not limited to the personal life of an individual Muslim. Justice is a key attribute of God and is next to piety in the life of a Muslim (Q. 5:8). A Muslim is required to stand firm on the principle of justice without regard to the status of an unjust person or society. Justice overrules all bonds of family, and one must do justice even if it goes against oneself (Q. 4:135). *Jihad* means to struggle and strive on the path of God to establish goodness and justice and to root out evil and oppression (Q. 4:74-76). The Muslim is not supposed to sit back and allow evil to pollute the world but is required to "command the good and forbid the evil" upon the earth (Q. 3:104,110, 9:71,111-112, 22:41). This is part of being the obedient servant of a just God. As a servant, one does not own one's own life, and so the struggle for justice upon the earth might involve persevering unto death in martyrdom, if God so wills. This helps to explain why some Muslims are prepared to fight against injustice even at the cost of their own lives.

The journey as an obedient servant of God must always begin in the individual Muslim's heart. Unless evil is conquered in the heart, the Muslim is in no position to right the wrongs of the world. Here we can see why the inner struggle is called the "greater *jihad*." This struggle occupies every Muslim all the time and is the quest for *taqwa*, as has been seen earlier. Another form of *jihad* in the Islamic tradition—called *al-jihad al-asghar*, or the "lesser *jihad*"—means the legitimate use of force against those who would "do evil upon the earth" (Q. 2:190-193).

When it comes to the lesser *jihad*, there is first of all the counsel of wise judgment. What exactly can be done? A tradition in Islam says that the Muslim who becomes aware of a certain evil in the world will, if possible, change it through action. In other words, he or she must put it right. If this cannot be done, the Muslim is required to correct it with the tongue, or speak out against it. If this is not possible, then the Muslim at the least must correct it in her or his heart and not allow the evil to take root there.

When action is necessary, Islam is not a pacifist way of life. If there is no alternative and everything else has been tried, the Muslim is permitted and indeed required to fight for the just cause. Such a military *jihad* is subject to strict conditions. Taking up arms is permitted only in defense, to protect the oppressed, or to preserve the Islamic way of life against injustice. In this sense one is "defending the rights of God." A *jihad* is not to be used for territorial gain like an expansionist war, although it did happen this way on some occasions in history. It should be always a defensive war against oppression and ungodliness. There must be a good chance of success, and it must be a collective effort, built on a consensus of the people and declared by a legitimate ruler. Muslims are forbidden to make *jihad* against other Muslims. If another group who proclaim themselves to be Muslims are engaged in oppression and injustice, they must first be declared unbelievers (*kafir*) before *jihad* can be waged against them.

Strict rules for the conduct of *jihad* were laid down in the earliest period of Islam and formalized by the Caliph Abu Bakr (r.632–634). Minimum force is to be used, and this must be directed against opposing combatants. Non-combatants, which includes all women, children, the elderly, sick, and even the soldier who has thrown down his arms in surrender, must not be attacked or threatened. This rules out all forms of indiscriminate warfare or "weapons of mass destruction." It is forbidden for anyone to deprive an enemy of the basic means of survival. Water supplies cannot be poisoned, food crops cannot be burned or destroyed whether in the fields or gathered into storage, and even trees must be spared because they provide food, shelter, and fuel. All "houses in which the name of God is mentioned," normally taken to refer to synagogues, churches, monasteries, and hermitages, "and those that dwell therein," must be shown respect and not damaged (provided that they do not become centers of open hostility to the Muslim community) (see Q. 22:39-40).

If it became clear that a *jihad* was necessary, then it could be called only by the legitimate Muslim ruler. Normally this was the Caliph, but such a power was exercised by others as the Islamic Empire spread and became less united by a single leadership. This has become a problem today, as there has been no Caliphate since 1924 and Muslims live in many different nation-states, some of which are led by Muslims but others not. A central question in contemporary Islam is to ask if a true *jihad* could be called in the current state of the worldwide Muslim community (*umma*). This does not stop some Muslim groups from using the rhetoric of *jihad*, but this is not justified under Islamic law.

If a *jihad* were called by a legitimate authority under all these conditions, then all Muslim men would be required to take part if needed. This is a *fard kifaya*, an obligation on the community that can be discharged by a subgroup, if that suffices. But if needed, all men must be ready to answer the call (Q. 2:216). Considering that the "just cause" for a *jihad* is to counter the oppression of evil that threatens oneself or others, one can see the weight of the obligation. If it is to protect the God-given Islamic way of life—the natural state of the human being— then not to resist such evil would give in to human degradation. In Islam, the use of force and violence is far too serious to be left to human initiative; therefore it must be used according to the laws of God.

These principles for regulating *jihad* bear many similarities with the just war theory developed in the Christian Middle Ages. It is remarkable to see recorded in history the way that *jihad* principles have guided Muslims in battle, as in the case of Salah al-Din (d. 1193) in the Crusades. That is not to say of course that on other occasions corrupt Muslim leaders have not used the rhetoric of *jihad* to support their wars, or that there have not been times when the rules of engagement in a legitimate *jihad* have been broken, but it is important to see clearly the principles drawn from the guidance of God.

Methods of warfare changed dramatically in the twentieth century in the (post-)Christian West. With the development of long-range artillery, bomber aircraft, and biological, chemical, and nuclear weapons, it is no surprise that modern warfare does not discriminate in the same way between combatants and non-combatants. Many more civilians are killed in modern warfare than was ever the case before. Christian and Muslim scholars have questioned whether such methods ever can meet the terms of a just war or the Muslim rules of engagement in *jihad*. Both Muslim and Christian political leaders are torn between the demands of the guidance of God and their perceived need to protect their people from aggression.

Indiscriminate killing is a feature also of terrorist attacks. This has brought with it the issue of the suicide bomber. Islamic tradition has always placed a high value on martyrdom as the ultimate act of obedience to the will of God, giving one's life if God so wills (Q. 9:38,111). Martyrdom is the complete recognition that we own nothing but God owns all, even our very lives. By tradition, the martyr was always assured a place in Paradise.

Some Muslims have made a case for suicide bombers as martyrs, but others have held that killing oneself in such a way is not permitted in Islam. This argument rests precisely on the understanding that our lives are not our own and so we are not entitled to kill ourselves; therefore suicide has always been forbidden in Islam (Q. 4:29). A martyr, they argue, is someone who stands for the cause of God even to the extent of not giving way if another comes to kill him or her. In the case of a martyr, death is accepted at the hands of another if it cannot be avoided. In the case of a suicide bomber, death is the means of killing others, and the person actually takes the initiative of terminating their own life as a weapon. This proactive suicide, they argue, is a rather different level of causality, and this makes such an act forbidden. Any bomb used against civil society kills indiscriminately; thus a suicide bomb used against civilians is forbidden.

It is interesting to note that no matter how hard pressed the young Muslim community was in the time of the Prophet, he did not launch a suicide attack. Of the many figures in the Hebrew Scriptures who appear in the Qur'an, Islamic tradition notes that Samson (Judges 16), the one who took his own life in destroying his enemies, is missing. We must remember that suicide bombers are a recent occurrence in Islamic history. The tactic was first used in the Lebanon in the 1980s against American forces but has become firmly established only in the Palestinian uprisings of the 1990s onward. Since then it has spread to Afghanistan, Egypt, Iraq, and the United States. Those Muslim scholars who have given a justification for these acts have argued that they are a legitimate form of warfare specifically against the overwhelming military superiority of what they see as the oppressors. A strong majority opinion among scholars on this question has been achieved only in the case of Palestinian attacks on Israel.

The journey within: Sufism

Much of this chapter may give the feeling that Islam is concerned only with law and the outer observance of the guidance of God. This outer observance is of course important in Islam, but the aim is to lead the believer into a constant state of God-consciousness, namely *taqwa*. God is not only awesome, tremendous, and utterly beyond our highest ideas; God is also closer to us than our jugular veins (Q. 50:16). There always has been another dimension to the spiritual quest in Islam, which took people in search of the inner power that could lead to meaning beyond the limits of this world. This was the quest for a direct personal relationship with God, a spiritual communion in which God sought out the individual by taking the initiative in offering repentance and mercy (Q. 9:118).

The mystical dimension of Islam is known as *tasawwuf*, which is both the journey into the depths of the human heart and also the ascent of the heart to God. There is a tradition that those who understand such things do not speak about them; that is left to those who do not understand. (Thus an obvious inference may be drawn from the existence of this section!) The terms "sufi" and "sufism" are often used as a more popular substitute for the technical term *tasawwuf*. The word *suf* means wool and is held by most to be a reference to the rough woollen garments favored by ascetics in the manner of Christian monks. Another less likely root of the meaning comes from *safa*, which brings in the idea of purification. Sufism is part of the Islamic tradition, being based squarely on the Qur'an and Sunna of Muhammad. It does not exist apart from that tradition. There are mystical dimensions to other faiths that may share common elements with Sufism, but Sufism stands on the foundation of the Islamic sources. This must be emphasized in light of the way that, in recent decades, the quest for meaning through Eastern spirituality has led people to explore elements of many traditions outside the contexts from which they come.

At the heart of the sufi understanding lies the Qur'anic command to remember God often or without ceasing (Q. 33:41). This is *dhikr*, the prayer of the heart, which we have already encountered and which is an extension of the spirit of *taqwa*. The sufi is one who seeks to enter more deeply into the remembrance of God, to such an extent that one lives constantly in the knowledge that one is in the presence of God (*ihsan*), that God may draw the believer into a "spiritual embrace." A key figure in sufi understanding is the *mi'raj*, the ascent of Muhammad to the presence of God during his *isra*, or night journey. In this encounter, Muhammad was given knowledge. Knowledge always purifies the receiver by drawing him or her closer to the source of all knowledge. The knowledge sought by the sufi is not intellectual knowledge but knowledge of the heart. This is a knowledge of absolute certainty, grasped as a whole in an intuitive sense and not through the use of reasoned argument (Q. 94:1). This knowledge is like a light that radiates through the recipient, who becomes translucent to the light of God. In this way, the spiritual quest of the Muslim is like a purifying ascent toward the divine presence, which is something of a *mi'raj*.

The Prophet Muhammad is the role model for all Muslim life. Within certain sufi understandings he is thought of as *al-insan al-kamil*, or the perfect human being. This term contains many shades of meaning. One of the ways Muhammad acts as a role model for sufi Muslims is by the relative simplicity of his lifestyle and his lack of concern for material wealth and possessions. Some hold that a group of people who had embraced a kind of spiritual poverty used to seek the company of Muhammad and thus became in effect the first sufis. Earlier we saw the different levels of meaning contained within the verses of the Qur'an, from the literal and outer, or *zahiri*, to the hidden and inner, or *batini*. It is understood by Muslims on the sufi way that Muhammad taught certain *batini* knowledge taken from the Qur'an to the members of this group, who were then able to pass it on to others and so down through the generations.

This tradition gives rise to an understanding of spiritual lineage, or *silsila*, among the sufis, whereby each contemporary would-be sufi must affiliate with a teacher, or *shaykh*, who in turn is affiliated with a chain of teachers who can trace themselves back to Muhammad himself. Each of these teachers has passed on the *batini* knowledge through the generations and is able to train new affiliates on the path toward spiritual awakening. Most of these *silsilas* trace themselves back through Ali, Muhammad's son-in-law and cousin, who was renowned for his knowledge, wisdom, and piety. One important *silsila* is traced back through Abu Bakr, the first Caliph, whose lifestyle is seen as a model of renunciation (*zuhd*). The term *faqir*, used for those who embrace poverty and simplicity on the sufi way, is linked back to the second Caliph Umar, who was noted for wearing a patched cloak. The underlying motif here is the richness of the Creator and the poverty of the human being, who stands in absolute need of God (Q. 35:15).

In the early years and occasionally in later centuries, some Muslims were respected for ascending the sufi path without a teacher or without being attached to a *silsila*. This is a reminder that God is not bound by custom and can draw people in the way that God knows best. A Qur'anic precedent for this is the figure of al-Khidr, or "The Green," a mysterious figure who became the guide to Moses (Q. 18:65). From the early centuries, Ibrahim ibn Adham (d. 778) is held to have been without a human teacher, as was ibn Arabi (d. 1240) in a later period. Caution is always advised by the saying that *Shaytan* becomes the guide of the person without a *shaykh*.

The city of Basra in Iraq gives us two examples of early sufis. Hasan al-Basri (642–728), central in the *isnad* of many Hadith, was a great scholar and theologian, was noted for his observance of the Shari'a, and had a reputation for renunciation and pious living. He is regarded as an example of a sufi *shaykh* who was right in the heart of the intellectual and legal tradition. Overlapping with Hasan al-Basri was one of the greatest women sufis, Rabi'a (713–752/801). Rabi'a and al-Basri are linked in many ways. Rabi'a was sought by many men in marriage but always refused their offers, as she was committed only to the love of God. She emphasized the love of God as the only acceptable motivation for a Muslim life and would not accept either the fear of hell or the hope of Paradise as worthy motivations for a Muslim.

The sufi way soon was developed into a systematic method, or *tariqa*. Just as the Shari'a guides the Muslim on the path of outer (*zahiri*) observance, the *tariqa* became the guide on the inner (*batini*) way. The two could not be separated: obedience without love is inhuman slavery, and love without obedience leads to chaos. Loving submission to the divine will goes together with the inner journey. The name of al-Junayd (d. 910) is always associated with the development of a systematic sufi theory. He insisted that the sufi remain within the bounds of the Shari'a, emphasizing that Shari'a is the "road that leads to the watering hole" from which eternal water might be drawn. He spoke of sufism as isolating the eternal from that which originates in time. He also developed the key doctrine of *fana*, usually translated loosely as annihilation or extinction, but carrying the sense of dying to the self but being alive in God, which leads to "abiding in God" (*baqa*).

Al-Junayd is buried in Baghdad and was a contemporary of al-Hallaj (*c.* 858–922), who was executed in the same city by crucifixion on the grounds that he had uttered heresy and blasphemed against God. Al-Hallaj spoke of the way in which the human being seeks God as being like a moth that is so attracted by the flame that it flies ever closer until finally it is consumed by it. His sense of *fana* led him to proclaim publicly *ana al-Haqq*, or "I am the Truth," which is one of the Names of God. Rumi (d. 1273), the great mystical poet, said that he understood the words to mean "I am naught, God is all," but the authorities in Baghdad at the time saw the words of al-Hallaj as blasphemy and sentenced him to death as a heretic. He refused to recant but cheerfully and prayerfully went to his death.

As centuries passed, the *tariqa*, or sufi way, became immensely complex and lies outside the realm of our present discussion. Important elements in it are the focus on the *silsila* that gives a chain of authenticity back through the generations to the Prophet, and within this context the relationship between the *shaykh* (fem. *shaykha*), or sufi guide, and the *murid*, or disciple. This relationship is much more intimate than that of a teacher and student. The *murid* gives over his or her will completely to the *shaykh*, "like the cadaver in the hands of the washers," by taking a *ba'ya* or bond of allegiance. The *shaykh* is able to guide the *murid* not only in terms of intellectual knowledge or experience of techniques but through a spiritual power, or *baraka*, that is held to come from having attained a higher state of being. The relationship with a *shaykh* is binding in this life and beyond. A *murid* does not move from *shaykh* to *shaykh*; even after the death of the *shaykh*, it is common not to take another but to retain that bond. Often *murids* would gather around the *shaykh* to live in a kind of retreat center, which came to be known by many names in different Muslim lands: in Arabic *zawiya* or *ribat*, in Persian *khanqah*, and in Turkish *tekke*.

Part of the system of the sufi way is to progress along a series of stations, or *maqamat*. In some systems there are twenty stations through which one must pass without missing any. The length of time one spends in a station would be under the direction of the *shaykh*, who would set exercises that are to be done until a certain spiritual character has been reached through the blessing of God. Such stations are given names like repentance (*tawbat*), conversion (*inabat*), renunciation (*zuhd*), and trust in God (*tawakkul*). Having passed through these stations, most sufis hold that they are never withdrawn once attained; one is then in a disposition to have a higher state bestowed by God. These states, or *ahwal*, are held to be more fleeting and have names such as love (*mahabba*) and yearning to be constantly with God (*shawq*).

A Sufi dancer.
Photo: Sally Messner.

Within these sufi systems, the practice of *dhikr* has been developed to encompass a variety of methods. Different sufi groups, also called *tariqas*, have particular methods of performing *dhikr*. These may consist of certain phrases that are repeated with the tongue and counted on a string of beads called a *misbah*, *tasbih*, or *subha*. Some groups make *dhikr* aloud in forms like chanting, either alone or in a sufi gathering or circle. Often *dhikr* involves the regulation of breath so that certain phrases are said as one breathes in and out. The tempo of both chanting and breathing can vary. Some groups avoid *dhikr* spoken or chanted aloud and concentrate instead on silent *dhikr*; other groups add music or rhythm (*sama*) to the chanting. The use of bodily movement has also been incorporated by some groups, this may be rhythmic swaying, bowing or jumping, or spinning around on an axis (the whirling of the *dervishes*). The use of music, movement, or control of the breath can lead to changes in the composition of blood gases and so dispose the devotee to an altered state of consciousness. This needs to be performed under the supervision of a *shaykh*.

Over the centuries, sufi Muslims have contributed a great deal of literature, both in poetry and prose. Much of this has become available in English in recent decades with awakened interest in Eastern spirituality. The poetry of ibn al-Farid (d. 1235) is widely read in the Arabic-speaking world; Farid ad-Din 'Attar (d. 1230) wrote an epic poem in Persian, *The Conference of the Birds*; and the outstanding Jalal ad-Din Rumi (1207–1273), the author of the six-volume *Mathnawi*, also must be mentioned. Many prose works take the form of manuals, metaphysical descriptions, systematic treatises, and pious exhortations. Four great names among such authors would be al-Ghazali (1058–1111), Abd al-Qadir al-Jilani (1077–1166), ibn Arabi (1165–1240), and Ibn Qayyim al-Jawziyya (1292–1350).

Not surprisingly, some Muslim individuals and groups want nothing to do with sufi practices or talk of stations or the *baraka* of *shaykhs*. They regard the whole issue as deviating from the pure practice of Islam, understood as being based on the Qur'an and the Sunna in a literal, or *zahiri*, way and regulated by the Shari'a. Such Muslims point to those sufis who have become so rapt in ecstasy that they have lost contact with the basic duties and practices of Islam; they also highlight the risk of exploiting the innocent. A small minority of sufis have taught that once one ascends higher on the sufi path the outer forms of the Shari'a no longer apply. The majority of sufi groups are adamant about the need to observe the full Shari'a at all times. Within the Shi'a tradition, many sufi practices are incorporated into the Muslim life of all believers.

Eventually great sufi groupings were established, each called a *tariqa* (often translated as Sufi Order, not in the sense of a monastic order but more an established system or path associated with the group and its teachers). Some are fairly limited geographically, like the Tijaniyya in North and West Africa, while others are spread around the world, like the Qadiri. Some are subgroupings of larger *tariqas*, and some great *shaykhs* are linked to several *tariqas* and are able to accept *murids* and train them in the methods of several groups. The *silsila* of each group and individual *shaykh* is highly prized and memorized as a spiritual bond going back through the centuries and on into Paradise.

Some of the most common and well-known *tariqas* are the Qadiriyya, founded by Abd al-Qadir al-Jilani (1078–1166); the Naqshbandiyya, founded by Muhammad Naqshband (d. 1389); the Badawiyya, founded by Sidi Ahmad al-Badawi (d. 1276) and prominent in Egypt; the Shadhiliyya, founded by ash-Shadhili (d. 1258) and mainly in North Africa; the Chistiyya, founded by Shaykh Muinuddin Chisti (d. 1236) and widespread throughout the Indian Subcontinent; the Bektashi, founded by Bektash Wali (d. 1338) and strong in Ottoman Turkey with some unusual practices and doctrines; the Mawlawiyya, founded by Jalal ad-Din Rumi (d. 1273) and mainly in Turkey; and the Ni'matullahiyya, founded by Shah Wali Ni'matullah, the largest Shi'a *tariqa*.

9

Islam and Other Faiths

All human beings are equal – all receive revelations and Prophets – Qur'an, Muhammad, and Islam are the criteria by which to measure other faiths – the duty to invite others to the way of Islam (*da'wa*) – status of the People of the Book (*Ahl al-Kitab*) – no compulsion in religion – Jews and Christians in the Islamic state – apostasy – God alone is the judge – classification of religions – polytheism – non-theism – nature religions – problems with historically later religions – privileged status of earlier revelations – no blanket judgments – the Jews – problems in accepting the Qur'an and the prophethood of Muhammad – treason in Madina – Jews accused of falsifying Scriptures and claiming ownership of God – Jewish-Muslim relations in history – Christians in the Arabian peninsula – Christians: the closest in affection to Muslims – controversy over the Son of God – God does not couple with human women – use of Son of God in Hebrew Scriptures – theological language of the Eternal Word of God and the incarnate Jesus – Christian and Muslim understandings of the Word of God – Muslim problems with the idea of incarnation – Muslim problems with any talk of the threeness of God – Trinity – the meaning of person/*personae*/ *prosopon* – models for talking about the Trinity – Jesus in the Qur'an – Prophet and Servant of God – born of the Virgin Mary – miracles – sent with the *Injil* – foretold the coming of Muhammad – did not die on the cross – taken alive into heaven – will return in the Last Days

Setting the scene

The Qur'an tells us that all humankind was created from a single pair (Q. 7:189) and so all human beings are fundamentally equal (Q. 49:13). The latter verse goes on to say that visible differences between human beings, which divide us into nations and peoples, are there so that we might know one another and benefit by that knowledge. Honor in the sight of God comes through being righteous, through living our humanity fully in accordance with the guidance of God. This message is reinforced in a Hadith that makes clear that the Arab is not superior to the non-Arab, nor the black person to the white person, and so on. The criterion for judgment among human beings is *taqwa*, God-consciousness.

The whole of creation was made to be *muslim* and to serve God alone. This unites humankind with the animal, vegetable, and mineral worlds in being called to worship and obey God as the only Sovereign

Lord. Should other beings be discovered on far distant planets, then the same would apply to them. Every created thing that exists is in a relationship of service to God and a fellowship in that service with every other created thing.

Human beings have the uniqueness of possessing free will, and all are equally called to be the Regent of God upon earth. To fulfill this high destiny, every human being stands in need of the guidance of God, and Islam holds that at least one Prophet has been sent to all peoples with essentially the same message (Q. 4:163-165, 6:42). Some of those Prophets and some of the Books that were sent down to them are known to us through the revelation of the Qur'an. This means, for example, that Moses and Jesus were *muslim* and taught *islam*. The attitude of a Muslim in encountering another faith must be to inquire what remains with those people from the revelation that was sent to them. It is a question of judgment whether a great religious teacher, like the Buddha, was a Prophet of God. Similarly, a Muslim must be open to the question of whether another ancient scripture, like the Vedas, contains some or all of the Book that was sent to the people of India as guidance from God.

The Qur'an calls itself *al-furqan*, the criterion for distinguishing right from wrong (Q. 25:1). Similarly, for Islam, Muhammad is the archetypal Prophet against whom others are measured. This gives Muslims a yardstick for making a judgment on what remains of the original revelation within another faith and of the authenticity of a possible earlier Prophet. Muslims have found within the traditional religions of Australia, Africa, and the Americas elements that resonate with some of the Qur'anic teaching. Elements of other faiths, such as human sacrifice, do not find a resonance in the Qur'an and thus are judged not to have been from the original revelation.

Possession of the Qur'an and the Sunna of Muhammad makes Islam the super-highway of God's guidance, as far as Muslims are concerned. All other faiths are at best meandering lanes by comparison with Islam. Some of their followers ultimately may be judged worthy by God, but the only straight path that assuredly leads to Paradise is Islam. The possession of this great gift of divine guidance brings with it a responsibility to share it with all humankind. As God wants all people to live as *muslims*, Muslims have always been concerned with offering the invitation to people to embrace Islam. This invitation is known as *da'wa*. Only God can move the heart of people to embrace Islam, but it is a duty to give *da'wa* to those who do not yet know the way of Islam. Muhammad is told in the Qur'an that he was sent as a "warner" to humankind, but it is not his responsibility if people do not accept the message and embrace Islam (Q. 2:119,272, 5:41). The gift of free will always makes it a possibility that people will reject the message, and then they must be left to the mercy of God, who alone is the judge (Q. 3:128-129, 109:1-6). People open to the faith can dispose themselves to receive it by living according to the guidance of Islam (Q. 49:14). We are told that God changes the condition only of those who change themselves (Q. 8:53).

The Qur'an gives guidance to Muslims who would give *da'wa* to people (Q. 16:125). This guidance is threefold: to use beautiful words, to use the best of arguments, and to do all with wisdom. In this way dirty tricks, polemical attacks, bitter words, and half-truths are all ruled out of the process. Wisdom here includes sensing what and how much to say at the appropriate time and place. These methods were highly successful in bringing Islam to the non-Arab world, where Muslims went to trade and spread the message.

During the initial spread of the Islamic Empire, Muslims distinquished between people that they encountered who were followers of an earlier revelation, or *Ahl al-Kitab*, and those who worshipped idols (something other than God). The phrase *Ahl al-Kitab* occurs many times in the Qur'an and normally is translated literally as "the People of the Book" (for example, Q. 3:20, 4:47, 5:65-66). Initially this meant Jews, Christians, and Sabeans. The identity of this third Qur'anic group never has been entirely clear. Some scholars have associated the term with the Mandeans of Southern Iraq and others with ancient Zoroastrians in Persia, who have also been identified as the Magians (Q. 22:17). When Islam reached Persia, the Zoroastrians were sometimes given *Ahl al-Kitab* status, as were Vedantic Hindus in India when the Muslims ruled there. The Qur'an makes clear that God made covenants with the Jews and Christians (Q. 5:12,14) to which God is faithful (Q. 9:111), and that "Our God and your God is one" (Q. 29:46), so the *Ahl al-Kitab* are allowed to continue in their religion as *dhimmi*, or protected people. The Islamic Empire did not tolerate idolatry within its borders, especially not on the Arabian Peninsula. Idol-worshippers were invited to embrace Islam, leave the territory, or face attack by the Muslim army.

The Qur'an says that "there is no compulsion in religion" (Q. 2:256), and this applied particularly to the *Ahl al-Kitab*. This does not mean freedom of religion in the sense that all religions are equal. Islam is the super-highway and therefore the best path for people to follow. The Islamic message corrects errors in the communities of the earlier revelations (Q. 4:46-47, 5:15-19). Jews and Christians are called to become Muslims (Q. 57:28).

Those who were given *dhimmi* status were allowed to practice their faith but not to seek converts, to parade their religion publicly, to build new churches, or to have a say in the governance of the Islamic Empire. They were exempted from military service and instead had to pay a poll tax, or *jizya*. At times they prospered under Islamic rule and at others they had to wear distinctive clothing, act with humility in the presence of a Muslim, and were forbidden to study the Qur'an. They could not have Muslim servants but could be servants to Muslims. Often they rose to high rank in administration, medicine, and scholarly pursuits. No Muslim was permitted to become a member of the *Ahl al-Kitab*, as it was unthinkable that someone should leave the clear guidance of the Qur'an for a defective earlier revelation. This would be apostasy, and, as we saw in chapter 4 with reference to the rebellion that followed the death of Muhammad, when apostasy is linked to treason, it is punishable by death (Q. 5:33, 33:60-62). Some Muslim scholars have drawn a distinction between simple apostasy and apostasy compounded by treason and/or vilification of the Qur'an and Muhammad. They have argued that simple apostasy is an offense against God that should be left to the judgment of God, whereas compounded apostasy in an Islamic state is an offense that carries the death penalty. Not all Muslims accept or are aware of this discussion, and so some simple apostates who become Christians in Muslim lands are persecuted.

There is a tolerant acceptance of those who follow the earlier revelations provided that they do not pose a threat or seek to undermine Islamic teachings (Q. 60:7-8). Muslims should not be contaminated by other religions. At the same time, "truth will always stand out clear from error" (Q. 2:256), and so Muslims are not afraid of rational investigation, resting their confidence on the Qur'an and the Sunna of Muhammad. Ultimately, God is the only judge; only God knows the inner disposition of the human heart. On the Day of Judgment, all things will be made clear, and people will see the error of their ways (Q. 5:14,48).

Classification of religions

The most detested sin in Islam is *shirk*, that is, to associate any created being or thing with God or to give God partners. This is the one sin that will not be forgiven by God (Q. 4:48). Even so, Muslims are counseled not to revile those who give partners to God for fear that they in turn would revile God (Q. 6:108). Islam grew within a context of idol-worship in pre-Islamic Arabia, and this became the criterion of following the guidance of the Qur'an and leaving such idolatry behind. All forms of idolatry are forbidden in Islam, not only the classical worshipping of a carved image but also worshipping anything instead of or alongside God. Nothing is allowed to come between the worshipper and God, who alone is worthy of worship. The modern worship of money, power, military might, high birth, clericalism, nationalism, or privilege is likewise condemned by Islam as a form of idolatry.

All forms of polytheism, that is, the worship of many gods, are by definition *shirk*, since God is one and unique, not like any created thing. Similarly a hierarchy of gods, or henotheism, is not permitted in Islam for the same reason, even if God is held to be the supreme god of the system. Many traditional religions, which often had images of their deities, were suspected by Muslims as being at least potentially polytheistic. Muslims traditionally had problems with some of the religions of India, which are generally grouped together under the term Hinduism. Some Hindus clearly worship God alone and use images only as ways of reminding devotees of some aspect of the Unseen God, sometimes called by the name Brahman. Other Hindus hold that there are many gods, and they worship certain ones in particular.

The question of Hinduism raises the issue: Who says what someone worships? If a particular group of Hindus bears witness that they worship the one God alone, is this acceptable in Islam? If someone includes an image in their worship, is that sufficient proof of *shirk*? This issue arises also with certain forms of Christianity in which it might be common for a devotee to bring flowers before a statue or icon, light a candle and place it there, and then kneel or stand in prayer. This might look to a Muslim like the worship of an idol. Who is to say? If one asks an individual worshipper, one might get an answer quite different from the teaching of a priest or scholar. The general Muslim disposition is to be extremely wary of anything that looks like idolatry. If a Christian took a group of Muslims to visit a church containing statues, icons, or the reserved sacrament, this would have to be explained, or else it would be open to deep a suspicion of *shirk*.

One interesting and problematic thing Muslims and Christians have in common is associating the worship of God with being at the tombs of holy people. Both faiths maintain absolutely that it is God alone who is worshipped. In both traditions, some would speak of asking the holy person to join them in a certain request to God in the hope that God would listen to the added prayer of such a "saint." We have seen that in Islam a certain timeless awareness returns to the person in their grave after burial. In the case of a holy person, this makes the site in which they are buried a holy place. In both traditions people make visits to such a place, and large numbers gather there at particular times of the year. Not surprisingly, there are others, both Christians and Muslims, who will have nothing to do with such practices. They regard them as dangerous and open to idolatry. At certain times in history, some Christian groups have broken down the tombs of saints. The same has happened in Islam. When the Wahhabis became strong in Saudi Arabia, large numbers of such tomb shrines were demolished.

Some religions do not engage in God-talk, claiming that speaking of God is an escape from ultimate reality. They generally are called non-theistic. Most schools of Buddhism are non-theistic, while some find it less difficult to compare Buddhist concepts with the concept of God in the Abrahamic religions. This has caused some Muslims to regard Buddhism as a philosophy of life and not a revealed religion at all. Some non-theistic religions speak in pantheistic terms, as though everything is god, and deny the existence of a creator beyond the creation. Some philosophies of life are positively atheistic, denying the existence of any divine being. Muslims find all such ideas to be deeply suspect in the light of the clear teaching of the Qur'an. How can such people be followers of a divine revelation if they deny or question the very existence of God? This has led to concern about atheism, humanism, secularism, rationalism, stoicism, and other similar philosophies.

For Islam, religion is revealed essentially by God both in Books and in the created world, in which people can read the signs of God. There is a natural religious sense in human beings that has led some people to construct religious ideas to explain the inexplicable in life. If these are human inventions and not attributable to divine revelation, then they are unacceptable in Islam. This tendency might be seen in nature religions that hold the powers of nature, the sun and other heavenly bodies, trees, water, certain animals, mountains, and various minerals to be worthy of worship. This would be seen as *shirk* and unacceptable in Islam. Some groups in this category would be forms of shamanism, Druids, pagans, and so on. Contemporary New Age movements often combine elements of nature traditions and so are a cause for concern for Muslims.

The Qur'an says that it is the last revelation and that there will be no more Prophets after Muhammad (Q. 5:3). When another religion claims a later revelation, such as the Mormons, or a Prophet after Muhammad, such as the Baha'is, this is against the clear teaching

Fig. 15. Classification of Religions

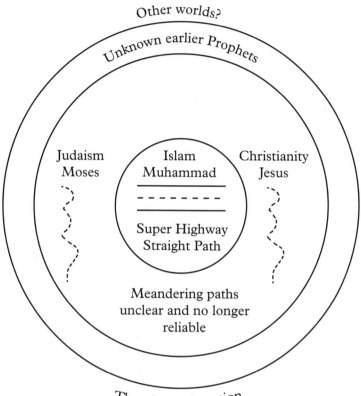

of the Qur'an and therefore unacceptable. The problems with the Ahmadiyya (or Qadianis) are dealt with in chapter 10. Muslims generally have been concerned about Sikhism. What is the status of the Sikh Holy Book, the Guru Granth Sahib? If Sikhs consider it a later revelation from God, then this would be unacceptable for Muslims. If it is the composition of pious teaching by the human Gurus, then it is not of the same status as the divinely revealed Qur'an. Similarly with the Sikh Gurus: Were they Prophets in the Islamic understanding of that term? If such a claim is made, that too would be unacceptable. If they were inspired holy men who taught people to live an upright life, then what is that alongside the sinless recipient of revelation, which is the definition of a Prophet?

Ahl al-Kitab

We have already encountered the Qur'anic term *Ahl al-Kitab*, which means the communities that follow the earlier revelations. Every Muslim is required to believe that Prophets like Moses and Jesus were true Prophets of God who received revelation in their Books and taught the true message of *islam* (Q. 2:136,285, 4:150-152). We have seen that the *Ahl al-Kitab* are to be given protected status in Islamic societies and allowed to practice their way of life. That they have a special status in Islam is demonstrated by three distinctive points. First, the food of the *Ahl al-Kitab* is theoretically halal for Muslims (Q. 5:5). This includes a recognition that the name of God is mentioned over animals when they are killed and therefore a recognition that they worship the one God. This still applies for Jewish kosher slaughter, but in modern societies there is grave uncertainty over the methods used and over the question of whether slaughtermen are Christians who mention the name of God in the process of killing an animal. Second, Sunni Muslim men are permitted to marry women from the *Ahl al-Kitab* but not from other religions (Q. 5:5). Such women are free to continue in their religion, which hardly would be permitted if they were not worshipping God. Third, Muhammad himself received a delegation of Christians from Najran in Yemen and allowed them to offer their prayers in his own mosque. He would not have permitted this if there was any question that they were worshipping God—"Our God and your God is one" (Q. 29:46).

The Qur'an refrains from giving a blanket judgment on the *Ahl al-Kitab* but always speaks of "a party among them" (Q. 3:113-116, 5:66). It is clear that a party among the *Ahl al-Kitab*, at the time of Muhammad, were acknowledged by the Qur'an to have held fast to the original teaching of the *islamic* faith that was given to their Prophet and contained in their Book. Others had deviated from this true path and gone astray in their worship, theology, and way of life. Those who followed faithfully the earlier revelations and bore the fruits of righteous deeds should not fear on the Day of Judgment (Q. 5:69). Most Muslim scholars hold that this acceptance of the validity of the earlier religions was terminated when Q. 3:85 was revealed. This verse is understood by them to mean that the worship of "anyone who follows a religion other than Islam," even though they are worshipping God, will not be accepted. They should leave the earlier ways, follow the clear guidance of the Qur'an, and accept the prophethood of Muhammad. A small minority of Muslim scholars have interpreted this verse to refer to *islam*, that is submission of all to God alone, and thus accepted the possibility of members of the *Ahl al-Kitab* finding favor with God without conversion to Islam. Ultimately God alone is the judge on the Day of Judgment, but the way of Islam is the straight path that leads to Paradise, and Muslims would want to invite everyone, including the *Ahl al-Kitab*, to follow it.

The Qur'an is the criterion in all things, and it raises challenges to Jews and Christians about the way they have followed their Books and Prophets. These need to be examined now in more detail.

The Jews

When Muhammad arrived in Madina in 622, he found there several Jewish clans. This would appear to be the first real interaction between the Prophet and organized Judaism. From the sources, we know that he expected these Jews to recognize that he was a Prophet of God and to accept the validity of the message he brought. Initially, the Jews and Muslims of Madina got on well together. They shared the same direction for prayer, as Muhammad oriented his community to worship in the direction of Jerusalem. In 624, about sixteen months after Muhammad's arrival in Madina, verses of the Qur'an were revealed instructing that the *qibla* (direction for prayer) for the Muslims be fixed on the Ka'ba (Q. 2:142-145). The mosque in Madina in use at that time is called now the Mosque of the Two Qiblas.

The Qur'an upheld the validity of the earlier revelations, but the purity of the message given to the Jews (and Christians) had been lost. They were called back to the straight path outlined in the Qur'an, and a reward from God was promised to those who accepted that guidance (Q. 3:199). The Jews had two problems in accepting the Qur'an and Muhammad. The Qur'an corrected some of their laws, and this meant accepting that their Scriptures were distorted; and the Hebrew Scriptures taught that Prophets only come from the Hebrew people, and Muhammad was not one of them.

The Jewish clans in Madina were included in the Constitution of Madina, which was drawn up by Muhammad in the early years of his time in the city. They were accorded the status of a religious community (*umma*) alongside the Muslims, and a mutual defense treaty was drawn up by which each agreed to defend the other and to take their respective stations in time of attack. This treaty was in place in 627, when Madina was under massive attack by the Makkans, who opposed Muhammad and sought to kill him and wipe out Islam. In the

famous Battle of the Ditch (or Trench) that year, it was found that one
of the Jewish clans, the Qurayza, had been plotting with the Makkans
against the Muslims. This was treason and a violation of the mutual
defense treaty. After the battle, the Muslims besieged the Qurayza,
and when they eventually surrendered, the men were executed and
the women and children sold into slavery, as was customary in cases of
treason at that time. After this treachery, Q. 5:82 was revealed, which
linked the Jews with the idolaters of Makka in terms of their hostility
to the believers. This experience left a bitter aftermath, and eventually
the remaining Jews, who were regarded as a kind of fifth column, were
sent into exile away from Madina (Q. 59:2-17).

Several challenges are leveled against the Jews to which a response
must be made. They are accused in Q. 57:29 of claiming exclusive
proprietorial rights over the mercy and grace of God. They are told that
God is not partial to any people but will bestow blessings according to
the will of God. In Q. 2:63-64, the Jews are accused of turning away
from the guidance of God that had been given to Moses on Mount
Sinai: "and if it had not been for the grace of God and his mercy
you would have been among the losers." The Jews were accused of
saying that God cannot change the law. Q. 2:75-81 makes even graver
accusations, that the Jews have knowingly falsified their Scriptures
by writing in passages and ascribing them to God and by changing
what was there in the original. They are accused of doing this in order
to "purchase a small gain" for themselves. Further they are accused
of hypocrisy, saying one thing when they are in company with the
Muslims and something else when they are alone. Finally they are
accused of arrogance, saying that the fires of hell will not touch them
or at worst only for a few days (Q. 2:80, 7:169). Of course, all of this
is, as the Qur'an points out, in disobedience to the original guidance
that was given to them.

These charges naturally have angered Jews, and it is easy to see why.
Orthodox Jews hold fast to the inviolable nature of the Torah that was
given to Moses and handed down unaltered within their community
until the present time. The problems for Progressive Jews in general
would also be diffcult, as they do not have the same understanding of
divine authorship of the Torah, seeing it more as an accumulation of
inspired wisdom without a single author. As to the specific charges,
they must be answered by Jewish scholars, and then Muslim scholars
must respond to such answers in the light of the Qur'an.

These troubled early years of Jewish-Muslim relations and the
accusations of the Qur'an did not render the two communities enemies
for all time. They were still recognized as the people of an earlier

revelation (*Ahl al-Kitab*) and as such accorded protected (*dhimmi*) status in Muslim lands. The balance of history would show that Jews fared better under Muslim rule down through the centuries than they did under Christian rule, especially in Europe. Many Jews fled Christian persecution and took refuge among Muslims, where they were treated with respect and hospitality. Many Jewish communities were found in Ottoman Turkey, Syria, Iraq, Iran, and throughout North Africa under Islamic rule. When Jews fled persecution by Christians in Eastern Europe in the late nineteenth and early twentieth centuries, the Palestinians, both Muslims and Christians, took them in and gave them shelter and land to settle. The present difficulties in Palestine stem from the early decades of the twentieth century when the Jews started to become more numerous and eventually to look for a permanent homeland in the Middle East. This was the age of colonialism and in the context of the rise of nation-states and a growing spirit of nationalism. In this spirit, the founders of the Zionist movement saw the need for a people, in this case the Jews, to have a land of their own. The struggle for an independent Israel and the wars that followed the 1948 creation of the state of Israel must not be allowed to tarnish a long and proud history of Jewish-Muslim tolerance and living together. Naturally, the dispossession of countless Palestinian homes and people since the creation of Israel means that this is a running sore that colors the whole perception of Jewish-Muslim relations in the modern period.

The Christians

Before going on to look at the Qur'anic verses about the Christians and Christian-Muslim relations, an introductory note is in order. An assumption has been made that many of those who read this book will be Christians or from a Christian background, while some others will be Muslims. Therefore, this section attempts to illustrate some of the theological problems between the two faiths to prompt Christians to think about the way that they speak with Muslims about their faith and to help Muslims see that the formulation of Christian doctrine is much more sophisticated and complex than it may appear.

As we saw in chapter 2, Muhammad's relations with individual Christians began before the first revelation of the Qur'an. When he was around twelve years old, he was on a journey to Damascus with his uncle Abu Talib. As they crossed the Syrian desert, they were intercepted by a Christian hermit called Bahira, who lived there. He spoke to Muhammad at length and then told his uncle to take good care of him as "the sign of Prophecy was on him." When Muhammad received the first revelation, it was confirmed by Waraqa ibn Nawfal, the Christian cousin of his wife Khadija. In 615, Muhammad sent a group of Muslims to seek refuge with the Christian King of Abyssinia, who took them in after recognizing that the message contained in the Qur'anic verses that they recited to him was close to his Christian faith. Finally, there was the delegation from the Christian community of Najran, who were received with hospitality by the Prophet in 631 and allowed to pray in his mosque in Madina.

Several different groups of Christians existed in the Arabian peninsula at this time. Probably these groups had taken refuge in the peninsula away from the centers of Byzantine orthodoxy. These communities had arisen in the course of disputes over the nature of Jesus (Christology) and the relationship of Jesus with God (trinitarian theology). It is important to make clear that the early Christian theologians were struggling to come to terms with the absolute transcendence of God, who is one and indivisible, and the experience that they had had in Jesus. They wanted to hang on to his humanity, in which he lived, taught, and eventually suffered death, and yet he was experienced as something more than an exceptionally good man and teacher.

In the early Christian centuries, deep divisions had developed in the Christian communities of the Roman Empire and Middle East. We tend to think of them now as theological controversies: "the orthodox" versus "the heretics." In reality, doctrinal differences were mixed up with questions about ecclesiastical and political authority. After the passage of another fifteen centuries, we can see that things then were far from simple and that few of these theological differences should have resulted in the dispersion of the Christian communion. In their various ways, they were struggling to express the belief that, in the created humanity of Jesus Christ, God had truly acted in the world, but in a way so as not to have compromised God's transcendent relationship with the creation.

In the centuries leading up to the rise of Islam, Christian theologians had been struggling to make clear their understanding of the place of Mary, the mother of Jesus. This cannot be separated from Christology. Those who wanted to defend the divine nature of Jesus developed for her the title of *theotokos*, or God-bearer. This led to an increased respect for her among the orthodox, while other Christians found this unacceptable. This may be part of the context of Qur'anic references to "God, Jesus, and Mary" (Q. 5:16). In addition, groups on the fringes of Christianity, like the Collyridians, had the unique belief in a "three-part God" comprising God, Jesus, and Mary. Such a doctrine never would have been accepted by any of the mainstream Christian traditions.

By contrast with the harsh words about the Jews contained in Q. 5:82, the same verse goes on to speak of "those who say, 'We are Christians,'" described as "the nearest in affection to the Believers." These Christians are characterized as having among them men devoted to learning and those who have renounced the world, "and they are not arrogant." We should note here the twin virtues of piety and wisdom, so highly prized by Islam. The same passage goes on in Q. 5:83-85 by noting that, like the King of Abyssinia whom tradition says later became a Muslim, these Christians affirmed the message of God contained in the Qur'an. Likewise, Christians are commended for having hearts full of tenderness and compassion (Q. 57:27), the followers of a Prophet marked by the same characteristics. At the same time, Christians are rebuked for having taken their priests as lords rather than God (Q. 9:31). This usually is interpreted as anti-clericalism, where priests have been seen as intermediaries between God and human beings, and also to refer to priests changing the law of God by reinterpreting it in new ways.

By the year 630, the Muslim army was preparing for battle with the forces of the Eastern Roman (or Byzantine) Empire. This was the context of Q. 9:1-29. Here, in verse 29, the Muslims are told to subdue the *Ahl al-Kitab* until they recognize the mastery of the Qur'an and way of Islam. As a token of this, they are to accept paying the *jizya* and living under Islamic rule. These Christians by contrast are characterized as "not believing in God and the Last Day" and refusing to accept the God-givenness of the Qur'an and the Prophethood of Muhammad. At the same time, Christians and Jews living in the Gulf of Aqaba region, who wanted to live in peace, agreed to a treaty with Muhammad.

Controversy over the "Son of God"

Qu'ran 9:30 speaks of the Jews calling Ezra a son of God and the Christians calling Jesus the Son of God. We are told, "This is a saying from their mouth; (in this) they but imitate what the unbelievers of old used to say." Such beliefs are worthy of the curse of God and are far from the truth. This verse must be read alongside Q. 112, which

makes it clear that God is one, unique, eternal, and unlike any creature, and that God "begets not nor is God begotten." Also Q. 4:171,
which says that God is one and "far exalted above having a son."

What did the "unbelievers of old" mean when they spoke of a Son
of God? The Qur'an was revealed in a context of polytheism among
the Arabs, who held that some of their gods were related (husbands/
wives, sons, daughters, big/little gods, tribal/family gods, and so on).
This was condemned explicitly in several passages in the Qur'an. God
has no wife or consort (Q. 72:3). God has no sons (Q. 2:116, 10:68,
19:91-92). And God has no daughters (Q. 6:100, 37:149-153). The
Arabs, who prized sons more highly than daughters, were rebuked for
wanting sons for themselves while relegating God to having daughters
(Q. 17:40, 16:57); the same verses point out that the angels are not
daughters of God.

We also know that the ancient Greeks used to believe that the gods
lived on Mount Olympus and periodically they would come down to
consort with human women and make them pregnant. We know, by
way of example, that the Greek god Zeus coupled with human virgins
to produce Dionysus, Apollo, and Minas, each of whom quite literally was called "the Son of God." Such a belief is utterly unacceptable
to Muslims, as the Qur'an affirms. Such a belief is, of course, also
totally unacceptable in orthodox Christianity, which never has held
that Jesus was the result of a coupling between God and Mary. The
Christian and Muslim traditions agree that God creates by a verbal
command: "'Be,' and it is" (Q. 3:47, 16:40). It was through hearing
and accepting the command of God that Mary became pregnant (see
Matt. 1:18-21, Luke 1:26-35).

The Hebrew Scriptures have a long and complex history of using
the title "Son of God." At various times, four different entities received
this title:

1. The whole of Israel (Exod. 4:22-23; Jer. 31:9; Hos. 11:1; the
response required was to promise obedience: Deut. 32:6; 1 Chron.
29:10; Jer. 3:4,19);
2. The King of Israel (2 Sam. 7:14; Pss. 2:7, 89:26; this connoted
adoption by God for obedient service, not divinization);
3. Angels (Gen. 6:2,4; Deut. 32:8; Job 1:6, 2:1, 38:7; Pss. 29:1, 82:6);
4. Righteous Israelites (Deut. 14:1; Isa. 43:6; Jer. 3:22; Ecclus. (Ben
Sira) 4:10).

The important thing to understand first is that the Hebrew usage is
a title and not a biological description. The title carried with it three
dimensions: first, election or adoption—the son was adopted as such

by the will of God and not through physical descent; second, obedience and dependence—the son was obedient to the father's will in all things, he was to imitate the character of the father and was totally dependent on him; third, representation—the son was to manifest the father, to have the qualities of the father, and to represent him and make him present. So the title Son of God is more like a job description than a biological description.

The writers of the New Testament and other early Christian scholars used this title for Jesus in order to express his uniqueness within the established tradition of the Hebrew scriptures. They took the intimate personal terms "Father" and "Son" from the Jewish usage to speak about this unique relationship. Any carnal relationship, such as between the Arab gods or Zeus and Dionysus, would be unthinkable for them. Islam has always avoided any use of personal terms for God, such as "father," precisely to avoid these difficulties. From a Christian perspective, it is important to note that Jesus applied this language of "father and son" to all believers, calling men and women to enter into the fullness of what it means to be Son of God.

When it comes to theological language, we need to distinguish between "the Eternal Word of God" and "the man Jesus," who is the Eternal Word of God incarnate. The eternal Word of God exists beyond time and therefore preexisted before the birth of Jesus from his mother, Mary. The human Jesus had a definite beginning, at his birth, but the Word of God is not created and exists beyond time. With this in mind, let us look at one theological statement.

The Nicene Creed, formulated and accepted in 381 and widely used by Christians, uses the term "begotten" of Jesus Christ twice, describing him as being "eternally begotten of the Father" and "begotten, not made." In so doing it is speaking of the Eternal Word of God and not referring to the human birth of Jesus from Mary. What is meant here? First, it is easier to restate what is *not* meant; it cannot mean that Jesus is begotten of the Father as Dionysus was begotten of Zeus. Second, the word "eternal" gives us an important context, referring to the transcendent world that is beyond time. It is a golden rule of theology that our earthly language, thought, and concepts are inadequate to speak about God in God's very self, because God is transcendent, totally other. This, like any other theological saying, is the best our earthly language can say about those things that are beyond our categories of comprehension. Third, there are two important truths of Christian faith being defended here: that Jesus Christ, as the Eternal Word of God, was not made or created, and that he is in an eternal relationship with the Father.

Although Jesus clearly was born of Mary at a certain time and in a certain place, the earthly Jesus, for Christians, is not the full story. We also need to speak of the eternal nature of the Word of God, which became incarnate in Jesus within time and space. Being eternal, the relationship between God and the Word of God, or between the Father and the Son, existed beyond time and therefore before creation began.

The author of the Fourth Gospel struggled to express this and turned to the Greek philosophical concept of *logos*. So Jesus came to be spoken of as the Eternal Word (*logos*) of God, who was present when the world was created and who is both God and distinguishable from God. This train of thought and language is a helpful way for Christians to try to speak with Muslims about Jesus. The Islamic tradition also has struggled to find an adequate way of speaking about the *Kalam Allah*, or the eternal, uncreated Speech of God. This leads to a channel of discussion about the way in which the *logos* was active before the human birth of Jesus, guiding and revealing knowledge of God to humankind. We have seen in chapter 3 how in Islamic understanding, the *Kalam Allah* as the unchanging guidance of God was sent down to the earth in various Books, in different earthly languages such as the Torah in Hebrew to Moses and the Qur'an in Arabic to Muhammad. It might be useful to think of the Qur'an and other revealed Books as the Word of God *inlibrate*, or in book form, although precisely what is understood by revelation and Word of God here would need further exploration. Christians would always want to hold that Jesus, as the Word of God *incarnate*, that is, in human form, is the fullness of the revelation of God.

This is not the place for a full-blown course in Christology—the theology of speaking about Christ—nor can we hope in this way to find a solution to the problems about Jesus that have beset Christians and Muslims through the centuries. But at least we can open up the issue and point to the need for clear thought and clear expression. The Qur'an says that Jesus, the son of Mary, is a creature created by God and no more (Q. 3:59), and Islam always has rejected the idea of incarnation. But we, likewise, would need to ask exactly what is being rejected and what exactly Christians are trying to say.

For Muslims, it is extremely difficult to think in terms of the incarnation of God in Jesus. The term usually used in Arabic to speak of this is *hulul*, or indwelling. Islam wants to avoid any talk of the mixing of divinity and humanity, because this necessarily would detract from God's transcendence. In Islam, the total otherness of God is paramount; it is impossible for God to *share* divinity with any *created* being or to think of Jesus as *part* of God. Of course, the three words in italics here understood literally have no place in the Christian doctrine of the incarnation. Any use of these words must be analogical. We can never use the verb "to share" literally when speaking of God's divinity, as sharing requires more than one being (I cannot share a cake with myself). God is one and not "many," and therefore we cannot speak literally of God sharing divinity with Jesus. When used literally, "to share" suggests a division of quantity, but it can also have a non-physical or analogical use, for example, when a mother's love is *shared* between her children without being diminished in any way. If she loves her daughter totally, it does not mean that she has no love left for her son. She can love him totally, also. Thus they both *share* in her love in a non-physical sense. Similarly, God is indivisible, and so we can never speak of Jesus as *part* of God, because that would be to suggest that God can be divided. Finally, as we have seen, although Jesus was born of Mary at a particular time, the *logos*, or Word of God, is eternal and not created. Therefore, in the Christian doctrine of the incarnation, God is not "sharing divinity with any created being"; it is much more subtle than that. Within the sufi tradition of Islam, attempts have been made to speak of the relationship of the human being—who becomes completely transparent to the light of God—with God. We have seen how terms like *fana* have been used and the troubles encountered by al-Hallaj. These relationships are not easily expressed in human concepts.

One other useful train of thought is to follow the Hebrew idea of the Son of God, where it is applied in the sense of the one most obedient to the Father, the one who makes the Father manifest by that very obedience. To see the Son is to "see" the Father (see John 14:7; Col. 1:15; Phil. 2:6; Heb. 3:3). In a colloquial expression, we might say that the Son is "a chip off the old block." If we follow this by asking what *logos* means here, we could say it is the self-communication or self-revelation of God. This prompts some interesting discussions with the *Kalam Allah* as the Speech of God.

Our intention here is not to play down the Christian understanding of Jesus or to render it in a way acceptable to the Qur'anic message and thus to Muslims. When dealing with eternal truths, we need many models to express our thought, knowing that all are ultimately inadequate. Finally, there may well be fundamentally irreconcilable understandings of the person and nature of Jesus between Christians and Muslims, but we need to guard our language to ensure that such differences are real and not caused by misunderstandings of speech.

The Trinity

The problem of speaking about Jesus as the Son of God leads directly to Qur'anic objections to any talk of "threeness" in God. The Qur'an makes clear: "Say not of God that God is one of three" (Q. 5:73). Also Q. 42:11: "there is nothing whatever like unto God." When Muslims hear Christians speaking about the Trinity, they hear a reference to "three gods," which of course is utterly condemned by the verse of the Qur'an cited here. This is compounded by phrases such as "God the Father, God the Son, and God the Holy Spirit" or "three persons yet one God." In fact, the early scholars of the Christian tradition developed the doctrine of the Trinity within Greek philosophical concepts *precisely* to stress the oneness of God and to avoid dividing up God or speaking of three gods. However, it must be admitted that some Christian popular perceptions of the Trinity fall far short of high philosophy and do lead people to talk in a way that sounds like "three gods."

Before going on to discuss the Trinity, it is fitting to notice how Christians came to use the title "Holy Spirit" to designate the reality of God at work in their lives. The concept of the Holy Spirit is drawn from the Hebrew word *ruach*, meaning wind, breath, and spirit. The early Hebrews lived as semi-nomads in the desert, where they experienced tremendous windstorms. Such winds were the most powerful, most unpredictable, most uncontrollable, and most irresistible thing that they knew. These winds were called *ruach*, and the term came to be associated with God's presence or power in their midst, therefore "God's Spirit." None knew where the *ruach* came from—it was invisible—but its power and effect could not possibly be denied.

Again, this is not the place for a thorough treatment of the Christian theology of Trinity. All we can do here is describe one way of speaking about the Trinity that deals directly with Muslim concerns about speaking of God as though God were one of three. Remember that the doctrine of the Trinity is immensely subtle and that any one description of it is inadequate. The following model is one such inadequate attempt, but it at least points in the right direction when Christians are in conversation on the matter with Muslims.

When Christians speak in English of God as "three persons," huge misunderstandings are possible. "I am a person, you are a person, and she is a person; that makes three persons, three people, or three beings." Our English language says as much, but when speaking of the Trinity, this is completely erroneous. The English word "person" used here is a translation of the Latin *persona*, which is itself a translation of the original Greek in which the doctrine was constructed. The original Greek used the word *prosopon*, a mask used in Greek theater. Greek theater did not use costumes for different characters; instead each actor held a mask, or *prosopon*, in front of their face and spoke through this. If an actor was playing more than one part, the other masks were held behind the back, and the equivalent of a costume change was made simply by bringing a new mask in front of the actor's face. The same actor then could be two or three different characters by wearing a different *prosopon*. This was what the original Greek meant when speaking of the three *prosopons* in reference to the one God. The problem with *prosopon* is that the word did not have a clearly defined meaning. The actor can only play one role at a time, so there could be no internal dialogue between the three *prosopons*. Thus the term *prosopon* was regarded as inadequate in the formulation of trinitarian theology.

In the search for a better term, the Greek theologians settled on speaking of God as one *ousia* and three *hypostases*. Here *ousia* is best translated as "substance," but *hypostases* is harder to translate. One possible translation is to speak of "modes of being." So we have a doctrine of "one substance and three modes of being." What is meant here by modes of being? We can think of a married woman with a family. She has one substance, there is only one of her, but she has three modes of being. At the same time, she is the daughter of her parents, the wife of her husband, and the mother of her children—three modes of being, each of which is really quite distinct, and yet she is the same woman. The ways in which a daughter relates to a parent, or a wife to her husband, or a mother to her child, are clearly not the same, and yet she is a single substance. We can even think of a relationship between one mode of being and another, when she calls on her daughter-parent relationship to inform her mother-child relationship. Thus we can speak of an internal dialogue within the single substance. This use of *hypostases* as mode of being proved inadequate because it did not distinguish sufficiently between the three *hypostases*. This deficiency led to the heresy of "modalism." A better translation of *hypostases* would be "self-subsistent reality." This would render the doctrine as "one substance yet three self-subsistent realities" or "three subjects," as in the subject of a sentence. Such a term allows us better to distinguish between the *hypostases* and allows for each to act in a distinct way.

Many other models have been used by Christians to grapple with this question. One is to think of the same liter of water (one substance) that when frozen is ice, when liquid is water, and when heated is steam.

The weakness with this model is that the water cannot be in all three states at one time. Another model is to think of the relationship between thought, word, and speech; or memory, intellect, and love. A helpful model used by the Greek Orthodox Church is to think of the Son as the visible aspect of the invisible Father. In the Greek icon tradition, one can paint the Son but not the Father. Hebrews 1:3 speaks of Jesus as "the reflection of God's glory and the exact imprint of God's very being," or in a phrase, "in thy light we see Light" (Ps. 36:9).

Each of these models can be used by Christians and Muslims to puzzle out what Christians are trying to express in the doctrine of the Trinity and then to weigh this against Qur'anic criticisms. Such attempts have been made in Christian-Muslim dialogue down through the centuries, and still the debate goes on! Two final points are worth bearing in mind: the goal of trinitarian theology was always to maintain the oneness of the transcendent God; such Christian theologies were not meant to be descriptions of God but to set codes of practice for speaking about God.

Jesus in the Qur'an

There are in total ninety-three references to Jesus in the Qur'an. He is affirmed as a Prophet (Q. 5:46-47), standing in the line of Prophets sent by God to humankind through the ages. As a Prophet, he led an exemplary life to be followed by the Children of Israel (Q. 43:57-59). The same verses make it clear that he was "no more than a servant" of God. Two issues follow from this point. First, the Qur'an sees Jesus as a Prophet to the Hebrew nation and not a universal Prophet sent to all humankind; that role is reserved for Muhammad. During the *mi'raj*, or Ascent into Heaven, Muhammad encountered all the earlier Prophets in Jerusalem, including Jesus, and they all lined up to pray behind him, thus showing that he is the Universal Prophet and the Seal of the Prophets. Second, as a *muslim*, the example of Jesus is applicable to all who follow the guidance as revealed by God, and thus many Muslims, especially within sufi circles, see Jesus as an example of an ascetic life, the inner way of love, and selfless devotion to God.

The birth and early years of Jesus are covered in two sections of the Qur'an (Q. 3:35-47 and 19:16-35). An angel was sent to Mary to announce that she would conceive and bear a son who would be a Prophet. Mary was a virgin and was made pregnant without any human intervention but simply by the command of God: "'Be' and it is." This is reminiscent of the manner in which the whole of creation came into being. Although Jesus is unique in being born of a virgin, the Islamic tradition has been at pains to point out that this is not a basis for any kind of divinity to be attributed to him; Adam and Eve had neither human mother nor father, and yet they were human and not divine.

Mary took herself off into a quiet place before the child was born. During her confinement, she was sustained with a stream of pure water and by dates falling from the tree against which she rested. A voice comforted her and told her to remain silent when she returned to her own people with her baby. Scholars have interpreted the verse variously as referring to either an angelic voice or the voice of Jesus from the womb. When she did return, she was met with amazement and questions about the origins of her child. As instructed, she remained silent and pointed to the infant, who spoke from his cradle to declare himself to be a Prophet of God.

Qur'an 4:171 makes clear that Jesus is "a word from God bestowed on Mary" and "a spirit proceeding from God"; these unique qualities are immediately preceded and followed by reminders that Jesus is not more than a Prophet of God and that God is "far exalted above having a son." Qur'an 2:253 speaks of Jesus being strengthened with the spirit and being given clear signs. Muslim scholars have understood this reference to the spirit to mean the Angel Gabriel. Part of the reference to clear signs is the miraculous birth and declaration of Prophethood from the cradle, but Jesus is also credited with working miracles (Q. 3:49). These miracles include making clay figures and then breathing life into them, healing the sick, revealing what lies hidden, and reviving the dead. The verse repeatedly states that such miracles are worked only by the permission of God and not through any independent power.

The most common title used for Jesus in the Qur'an is "Jesus, son of Mary." This emphasizes his virgin birth and is in contrast to any suggestion that he should be thought of as a son of God (Q. 5:72). Christians are admonished not to exaggerate the importance of Jesus by excessive claims (Q. 4:171, 5:77,112). As a Prophet, there can be no higher human status. As such, he must be respected by every Muslim, and the Jews are rebuked for failing to recognize him as such (Q. 2:87). In the Last Days, Jesus will return to earth to lead the forces of good in the great battle to vanquish evil. After the battle, he will rule the earth for a time according to the guidance of God, that is, in the way of Islam.

The Qur'an makes clear that Jesus, as a Prophet sent with a Book from God, was the recipient of a scripture called the *Injil*. Christian tradition knows nothing of the existence of such a scripture but the Qur'an is clear that it existed (Q. 5:46). At best, Christians have been careless in looking after such valuable guidance. At worst, down through the centuries it has been destroyed or corrupted. Theories relating to the *Injil* were discussed at some length in chapter 3.

In Qur'an 61:6, we are told that Jesus foretold the coming of a Messenger after him, whose name would be Ahmad, a form of the name Muhammad. Muslim scholars have searched the Christian Gospels for a possible reference to this. In the farewell discourse of the Fourth Gospel, we find several references to Jesus sending the *paracletos* after him (John 14:26, 15:26, 16:8,13-15). This Greek word is a technical term for the "counsel for the defense" and is generally translated into English as "the Comforter," the "Counselor," or "the Advocate." Christian tradition has seen this as a reference to the coming of the Holy Spirit. One theory put forward by some Muslim scholars to demonstrate that Jesus did foretell the coming of Muhammad is to say that *paracletos* is a corruption of the word *periclytos*, which means "the praised or trustworthy one," which when translated into Arabic would be *ahmad*. It has been suggested that if Greek were written like Hebrew and Arabic, without the vowels, then the two words would be written in the same way: *prclts*. The theory then is that the wrong vowels were inserted, either deliberately or by accident, to produce the wrong word. The difficulties with this explanation are that Greek was never written without the vowels and that Jesus spoke Aramaic and not Greek. Therefore, the Greek word was chosen by the Evangelist to convey the intended meaning. Leaving aside this discussion of the term *paracletos*, the truth of the Qur'an remains for Muslims, that Jesus foretold the coming of Muhammad. Qur'an 7:157 also mentions a foretelling of Muhammad in the Hebrew Scriptures, and Muslims have pointed to this in their reading of Deuteronomy 18:15-18 and other texts.

The Qur'an refers to the end of the earthly life of Jesus in Q. 4:157-159. Here we read that the Jews did not crucify Jesus or kill him but it only appeared that way. Jesus actually was "taken up" to God. Muslim scholars have interpreted this verse in different ways. Some have held that Jesus was not put upon the cross at all but that someone else was substituted for him and was crucified in his place. Others have held that he was indeed put upon the cross but was not crucified to death; instead he was taken down in a faint, revived, and then "taken up" by God. Still others have seen this as a rejection of the idea that the Jews killed Jesus, and that whatever happened was an act of God alone. A minority of scholars have held that God's "taking up" of Jesus actually referred to his death as an act of God; in this case, God "taking him up" would be a euphemism, a bit like we might describe someone's death as falling asleep. Whatever the verse may mean, scholars do not interpret it as Jesus' death and resurrection to eternal life.

As we have seen, Jesus is expected to return in the Last Days (Q. 43:61-68). At the end of the battle of good against evil and his Islamic reign, Jesus will die and be buried in the space reserved for him in Madina alongside the tomb of Muhammad. Shortly after this, the Last Trumpet will sound marking the end of the world, followed by the general resurrection of all, including Jesus.

How are Christians and Muslims to deal with this verse? For most Muslim scholars, the text of the Qur'an says that Jesus did not die but was taken up alive to God. To accept the Christian understanding of the death of Jesus on the cross and the resurrection from the dead would require them to deny the truthfulness of the Qur'an. This they cannot do. If Muslims admitted a single mistake in the Qur'an, it would destroy the Qur'an's infallibility and unaltered preservation throughout the centuries. For Christians, to accept that Jesus did not die on the cross rules out the possibility of resurrection to eternal life, the final victory over sin and evil, and the promise of life in the resurrected Christ for those who believe. Christians cannot omit the death and resurrection of Jesus from the Christian tradition. On this question neither side can "give way" to the other. The best we can do is ask that each side understand why the other cannot give up either the infallibility of the Qur'an or the death of Jesus on the cross and his resurrection to eternal life. We have here a disparity of accounts of a single event, the resolution of which appears to lie beyond human reach. The Qur'an promises that at the general resurrection and last judgment, the Prophets will be questioned about such matters and God will make all things clear (Q. 5:48,109,116-119, 19:37-40, 22:17,67-72).

Muslims in Britain, Western Europe, and the United States

Limitations of this chapter – Europe up to 1950 – 17th-century Britain: prisoners of war, Arabic in universities, diplomatic relations – 18th-century Britain: Muslim seamen – 19th-century Britain: merchants, wealthy Indian students, Quilliam and the Liverpool community, the Woking Mosque, beginnings of the Regent's Park Mosque – 1950 onward – Britain – 1962 Immigration Act – Kashmir – Bangladesh – East African Asians – immigrants from many former colonies – refugees – statistics on Pakistanis in Britain – demands of settled families – national representation – future predictions – France – Germany – Netherlands – Belgium – Denmark – Sweden – Norway – Switzerland – Austria – Italy – Spain – European issues: citizenship, education, radicalization, refugees, population expansion – groups of Sunni Muslims from the Subcontinent – background – Deobandis – Ahl-i Hadith – Barelvis – Modernists – Tablighi Jamaat – Jamaat-i Islami – Ahmadiyya Muslim Mission – a future perspective – United States – early history – immigration to America – Islamic organizations – African American Muslims – white converts – sectarian movements – Sufi movements – Islamic concerns

Most chapters in this book could be expanded easily to make a book in their own right. This chapter is no exception. Limits must be drawn somewhere, so nothing is included about Eastern Europe or other Western countries such as Canada or Australia. Nothing is said of European countries with small numbers of Muslims, such as Ireland, where the number is in the range of fifteen to twenty thousand, or Luxembourg where estimates are around seven thousand. Other mainland European countries are given only brief attention. There is no section devoted especially to European converts to Islam, although trends of conversion have been noted in other places. There is no way of estimating the number of European converts to Islam beyond saying that there are tens of thousands in Germany, almost certainly the largest number, and also many in Britain and France. In Britain, informed guesses usually put the figure between ten and forty thousand. Probably the number is in the middle of this range. As many people are confused over the various schools of Sunni Muslims in Britain, a special section is devoted to understanding these in light of their Subcontinental roots.

Overview of Muslims in Western Europe

Up to 1950

Muslim rule began in parts of Sicily in 827 and on the mainland beginning in 902. It ended with the Norman invasion (1060–1091). After that, many Muslims remained until they were sent into exile in Lucera, southern Italy, from 1224 to 1250. They came under pressure to convert to Christianity, and those that did not were killed in 1300. The end of Muslim rule in Spain was complete by 1492. Muslims remained, often as nominal converts to Christianity, until the Great Expulsion (1609–1614). The last record of a Muslim being executed by the Inquisition was in 1680. This marked the end of a Muslim presence in southern Europe.

Ottoman Turks moved into Bosnia and Bulgaria in the fifteenth century. This advance reached its limit in the well-known sieges of Vienna in 1529 and 1683. In 1878, the Austro-Hungarian Empire acquired Bosnia, and in 1912, Muslims achieved official status in the Empire as followers of a legally recognized religion. This status was reinvoked in 1979 by Muslims in Austria, who won the right to enjoy official recognition under Austrian law.

There are indications of British contact with the Muslim world from an early date, for example some coins from the reign of King Offa in the eighth century bearing the Arabic words "There is no god save God" on the one side and "Muhammad, the Messenger of God" on the other. The first records of Muslims in Britain date from the sixteenth century. At this time, British sailors and traders occasionally were taken prisoner by Muslims operating along the coast of the Mediterranean. Some of these captives were prisoners of war, and others were captured by pirates; they could well have ended up as galley slaves. Islam regards setting slaves free as a pious act (Q. 2:177; 5:89), and kindness is advocated toward prisoners of war, who may be open to converting to the way of Islam (Q. 8:70). One use for *zakat* funds is to free Muslim captives (Q. 9:60). It seems then that some of these British sailors converted to Islam, seeking to increase their chances of being set free and so of returning to Britain. Some of those who succeeded in winning their freedom and return converted back to Christianity once they were safely in Britain, but others remained Muslims.

Around this period, other aspects of the Muslim world attracted British people to convert. The first was that Muslim societies were more egalitarian and thus offered the opportunity for people to advance socially and materially. The second aspect was the higher degree of civilization that could be found in the Ottoman Empire, which appealed to those who became acquainted with it. One estimate of the numbers of Muslims in Britain by the seventeenth century speaks of a few thousand, another of "some forty 'Turks' in England" in 1627.

The same century saw developments on the academic front. The first manuscript of the Qur'an was deposited in the library of Cambridge University in 1631. The posts of Professor of Arabic were created at Oxford and Cambridge universities in the 1630s. The Qur'an was translated into English in 1649 from a French version by Alexander Ross. The first translation into English from an Arabic manuscript was completed by George Sale in 1734. Some scholars believe that the Islamic stress on the absolute oneness of God influenced the development of the Unitarian Christian movement in the seventeenth century.

The first record of a coffeehouse in London dates from 1652, and this led to the translation from Arabic of essays on the medicinal effects of coffee. In 1679 the first Turkish Baths were opened in London. In the reign of James I (r.1603–1625), diplomatic relations were established between Britain and the Ottoman Empire.

From 1760 on, Indian seamen were noted in numbers in the British merchant fleet, where people from Muslim lands generally were known collectively as *lascars*; they settled in numbers in British seaports. This trend increased after Britain annexed the port of Aden in Yemen in 1839. Aden served as a refueling station for British ships heading to East Africa, India, Australia, and East Asia. By the 1850s, communities of Muslim sailors were noted in Cardiff, Liverpool, London, Manchester, and South Shields. Again this trend increased after the opening of the Suez Canal in 1869. Most of these sailors were drawn from countries of the Empire such as India, Malaysia, Somalia, and Yemen. Groups of Pathans and Mirpuris from North India, present-day Pakistan, and Kashmir were recorded among sailors recruited in Bombay in the nineteenth century. By the outbreak of the 1914–1918 War, there were 296,000 men in the British merchant fleet, sixteen percent of whom were recorded as *lascars*, some 52,000. The largest groups of these were stokers from Somalia and Yemen. Some of these Muslim sailors married English women and raised families. Social pressures against such families often meant that they lived in close-knit communities with their own social customs. During the Great Depression in Britain in the 1920s and 1930s, large numbers of those settled, seafaring communities were repatriated, and the number of Muslims in Britain dropped significantly.

With the creation of such Muslim communities came merchants and traders in the nineteenth century to service their needs and the needs of the growing number of English people who had acquired Indian tastes in the days of the British Raj. Some returning English families brought Muslim servants with them; Queen Victoria, for instance, had Muslim servants. Trade between Britain and the Empire required offices in key cities such as Glasgow and Manchester. Groups of Indian peddlers carried on their trade in Britain in the early twentieth century and laid the foundations for later family migration. In the late eighteenth century, the first "Indian Vapour Baths and Shampooing Establishment" was created in Brighton, which came under royal patronage in the time of George IV, thus introducing the word "shampoo" into the English language. There were refugees also, such as a group of Turks in the late nineteenth century who opposed the Ottoman Sultans and founded the Turkish newspaper *Hurriyet* (Freedom) in London.

From the mid-nineteenth century onward, the sons of wealthy Indian families came to Britain to study, law especially. Some settled in Britain, such as Syed Ameer Ali, the lawyer and Muslim modernist writer who became a member of the Privy Council and was involved in building the East London Mosque. Other Muslim thinkers who became instrumental in the creation of Pakistan studied in Britain and then returned home, such as Muhammad Iqbal, who studied at Cambridge from 1905 to 1908, and Muhammad Ali Jinnah, who was called to the Bar at Lincoln's Inn in 1892.

One important English convert to Islam, Shaykh Abdullah (Henry William) Quilliam, a solicitor from the Isle of Man who had converted on his Ottoman travels in 1887, settled in Liverpool and established a Muslim community there. This community grew to include a mosque, a library, a reading room, schools for boys and girls, a museum, a press, and a literary society. In 1891 there were objections and riots by local Christians when the *adhan* was called from the *minaret*. Quilliam operated on the principle that his Muslim community belonged to the worldwide Muslim *umma*, and he established journals so that this message could be spread. In 1894, he was appointed as the official representative of the Ottoman Sultan in England, the *Shaykh al-Islam*. Quilliam believed in the need to reach out to the wider community, so he opened a home for unwanted children and established the tradition of a free lunch on Christmas Day for hundreds of the Liverpool poor. After his departure from England in 1908, following more anti-Muslim sentiments, the center declined and eventually ceased to exist. After Turkey's defeat alongside Germany in the 1914–1918 War, a polemical campaign was launched against Muslims, who were held to be disloyal to Britain and therefore not to be trusted. Much of the rhetoric used, for example that by Lloyd George, had the same tone as the anti-Catholic and anti-Irish sentiments of the time.

The first purpose-built mosque in England was the Shahjehan Mosque in Woking, opened in 1889. The costs had been met by the Muslim rulers of Bhopal, India, so the name was taken from the princess of that state, Shah Jehan Begum. Under the influence of the London barrister Khwaja Kamaluddin in 1912, it temporarily became a center for the Ahmadiyya and was associated closely with the breakaway of the Lahori Ahmadiyya. But in 1935, it broke all ties to the Ahmadiyya movement and returned to being a Sunni mosque. It became a custom at Woking to rotate the *imams* for Friday prayers between the different schools of law so that all groups could be kept together as a single community. A cemetery was established nearby to receive the bodies of Muslim soldiers who had died of their wounds in Britain during the 1914–1918 War.

The Woking Mosque was associated with Muslims from the upper classes in Britain. Its founding director was G. W. Leitner, formerly of the Punjab University. Syed Ameer Ali was a supporter as were emminent translators of the Qur'an into English, Muhammad Marmaduke Pickthall and Abdullah Yusuf Ali. Lord Headley, who founded the British Muslim Society in 1914, was heavily involved. It was the aim of such upper-class Muslims to present Islam in a comprehensible and attractive way to their own kind; to this end they established a journal. They often supported modernist interpretations of Islam, such as the *fatwa* from Muhammad Abduh, the Rector of al-Azhar University in Cairo, who taught that under particular circumstances meat that had not been slaughtered in the Muslim fashion could be *halal* for Muslims. They sought to lead new converts gradually from their pre-Muslim lifestyles into a fuller observance of the Shari'a, for example in matters such as regular observance of *salat*, fasting during Ramadan, and abstention from alcohol.

A Central Mosque had been established in Paris in 1926 through the close links of France with Muslim parts of its empire in North Africa. The Paris mosque prompted a move to establish a Central Mosque in London. In 1928, the Nizam of Hyderabad, together with Lord Headley, set up the London Nizamiah Mosque Trust to this end, but little happened until the early 1940s. King George VI gave a grant of land in Regent's Park for an Islamic center in exchange for a parcel of land in Cairo to build an Anglican Cathedral. In 1944, an Islamic Cultural Center was opened, and after the war the ambassadors of Muslim countries together formed the Central London Mosque Trust to oversee the development of the project. A foundation stone was laid in 1954, but the Suez Crisis led to wrangles over plans and planning permission. The mosque eventually was completed and opened in 1977.

1950 onward

Britain

In the period after the 1939–1945 War, Britain actively recruited manual workers from the New Commonwealth to help rebuild the country and staff the boom in industry. The first places of recruitment were the Caribbean Islands, with groups arriving from the late 1940s onward. As part of the break-up of the empire, the 1948 Nationality Act was passed, giving all imperial subjects the right of free entry to Britain. One of the arguments used to attract migrant workers was that men from the Caribbean and the Indian Subcontinent had fought with the British in the war; a popular slogan was "you know us and we know you." During the 1950s, people began to be recruited from the Indian Subcontinent, and migration totaled about ten thousand men per year at this stage.

This period of free access and migrant workers was halted by the passing of the Commonwealth Immigration Act in 1962. The purpose of this Act was to restrict and regularize the situation, but it had two effects. It caused a large increase in numbers of those who wanted to become settled in Britain before the Act came into law. And it shifted the emphasis from a migrant labor force of men who left their families behind to earn quick money to send home, to a settled group of immigrants who were told that such migratory practices had to end and that they had to choose between remaining permanently in Britain or returning permanently to their countries of birth. As there were few prospects in their homelands, many made the decision to settle in Britain permanently and arranged for their families to join them.

In the three years from 1960 to 1962, more immigrants came to Britain than in the whole of the previous sixty years. People knew that such a law was under discussion, and many made concerted efforts to "beat the Act." In 1961, 130,000 people migrated to Britain, and in the six months before the Act came into force on 1 July 1962, 80,000 people arrived. This had a profound effect on the character of the immigrant settlements, which was transformed from working men in

The Mecca Masjid in
Hyderabad, India.
Photo: David Coward.

temporary lodgings to settled communities of men, women, and children. From this time on, the direct immigration of unskilled labor technically was halted, but there were considerable opportunities for people applying to join family members who had already settled in Britain. This brought an extended family (*biradari*) dimension to the nature of immigration, and chains were established linking particular settlements in Britain with villages and families from the countries of origin. This was a contributory factor in the passing of new legislation in 1965, which reduced the voucher system so that no one country could account for more than fifteen percent, in effect an annual limit of 8,500 at that time. This was seen by many to be directed against those wanting to come from the Indian Subcontinent.

The recruitment from the Subcontinent was not evenly spread geographically. People had been disturbed by the 1947 Partition, when nine million are believed to have migrated across the future border between Pakistan (East and West) and India. Some estimates put the deaths associated with this migration at around one million. For those who had lost their traditional family lands, especially those in the Punjab, which saw the worst of the killing, there was little to keep them home when opportunity beckoned from Britain. Significant numbers left Gujarat State at this time, and, after the 1948 Indian invasion of Hyderabad, Deccan, a number of Muslim professionals and businesspeople came to Britain.

The largest concentration of Muslims from the Subcontinent came from Kashmir, a state whose future was left unresolved by the British withdrawal. Political leadership was in the hands of Hindus and Sikhs, but the majority of people were Muslim. A United Nations Resolution called for a referendum to decide Kashmir's future as part of either Pakistan or India, but this never took place, and an armed standoff has existed ever since, with two wars between India and Pakistan being sparked by this issue. In 1960, a major project was started in the Kashmiri district of Mirpur on the border with Pakistan. The Mangla Dam was to be built by flooding the valley, thus incurring the loss of around 250 villages. This would provide massive amounts of electricity to fuel the Pakistani cities of West Punjab. Those whose homes were lost were compensated and given virgin forest to resettle and develop into new towns and villages. Just at this time, Britain was seeking labor, and so the Mirpur District became an obvious recruiting ground where people already were used to temporary migrant work. Others came from the Punjab and the North-West Frontier Province of Pakistan, as well as from cities like Karachi, where many migrants from India had settled in the new Pakistan.

The Sylhet and Chittagong areas of North India, later to become East Pakistan after the Partition, had a long tradition of men migrating for work and an association with British shipping, so these also became natural recruiting grounds. East Pakistan gained its independence from (West) Pakistan in the war of 1971 and from then on took the name Bangladesh. Of those who migrated to Britain after the Partition and the 1971 War of Independence, ninety-five percent were from the Sylhet District.

With the coming of independence in Africa in the early 1960s, Britain also experienced a process of "Africanization" that led, among other things, to the migration of East African Asians from Uganda, Kenya, and Tanzania. In 1968, there were attempts to restrict the migration of Asian people from Kenya, but those who came settled and began making significant contributions to society. A new law passed in 1971 favored those who had a British-born parent or grandparent. This directly favored immigrants from Australia, Canada, and New Zealand over against those from the Subcontinent, Africa, or the West Indies. This was the time of the Uganda crisis, when President Idi Amin gave notice to Ugandan Asians to leave immediately. The British conscience was touched at this, and huge efforts were made to secure a new future for them in Britain and elsewhere against the tide of contemporary legislation. A total of 21,000 Ugandan Asians were resettled. Many white, middle-class British families opened their homes to give them temporary accommodation, partly on humanitarian grounds but also due to the recognition of the contribution made by earlier migrants from other East African countries.

Many of the Ugandans were the descendants of families that had been taken from India to the East African colonies by the British. They had been skilled artisans and made up the managerial classes in several countries. Their natural links with Britain were strong. Many among them were Sikhs and Hindus as well as various schools of Muslims. Many had been prosperous in Africa and had experience as professionals or in business. They brought a natural entrepreneurial flare to their new country.

In addition to Muslims from the Subcontinent, groups immigrated to Britain from Malaysia, West Africa, Somalia, and Yemen, all of whom had close ties to Britain or, like those from Morocco, were naturally in search of work. A significant group of Turkish Cypriots came to Britain after independence in 1960 and again after its partition in 1974. Beginning in the 1960s, a steady stream of Arab students arrived in Britain to study and then stayed on, contributing richly to British life. Many Arabs were attracted to settle in London after the 1973 oil crisis, and they have had a major impact on financial, real estate, and business life. Their economic power has led to good relations with successive British governments, which have been keen to encourage their investment. A number of Iranians left around the time of the Islamic Revolution in 1979 and settled in Britain. Further groups of Iranian, Iraqi, and Lebanese refugees came to Britain during and after the Lebanese Civil War and the Iran-Iraq war in the 1970s and 1980s.

Later, fighting in the Balkans brought groups from Bosnia and Kosovo. Kurds were fleeing discrimination in Turkey. War in Somalia and the Sudan brought refugees. There has been a steady flow of Palestinian refugees since the creation of the State of Israel in 1948. Many Iraqis came to Britain to escape Saddam Hussein's regime, and the war in Afghanistan brought another wave of refugees.

An indication of the changing nature of the Muslim communities in Britain can be seen in a comparison between 1961, when women made up only fifteen percent of the people of Pakistani birth in Britain, and 1981, when women were fifty percent of the British Pakistani community. The figures for all people in Britain of Pakistani heritage demonstrate this trend. In the census of 1951, there were 5,000. In 1961, 24,900 of whom only 1.2 percent were born in Britain. By 1971 this figure had risen to 170,000 with 23.5 percent British born. Figures for 1981 were 360,000 (37.5 percent British born) and 1991, 640,000 (47 percent British born). In the latest census of 2001, the population of Pakistani heritage had risen to 747,285, of whom 410,861 (55 percent) were born in Britain.

With the arrival of families, there was a demand for school places, medical facilities (especially midwifery), food and clothing shops, second-language provision in schools, and, for adult migrants, housing and community facilities. Many new mosques were established at this time. Many were converted from houses or commercial properties. Some applied for official registration as places of worship, but this was not a requirement. In the mid-1960s, an average of seven mosque registrations was made annually. By the mid-1970s, the number had risen to between twenty and thirty a year. By the year 2000, it was estimated that Britain had at least one thousand mosques, and some put the figure considerably higher. Many of the first generation of converted-house mosques had become too small and the communities were sufficiently established to be able to undertake the construction of purpose-built mosques, which act as focal points for the community and make the statement that Muslim communities are now a permanent part of the British landscape. There currently are ten such purpose-built mosques in Birmingham alone. These second-generation mosques are used mainly for *salat*, education, funerals, and festivals. A new third generation of mosques has started to appear, in which a whole array of community service facilities are included. The new East London Mosque is an examply of this construction.

Education is a key issue in the development of any society. Progress can be seen in three broad trends. First, the growth of cultural sensitivity to Muslim needs in terms of school uniform adaptations. These include girls wearing trousers and loose-fitting trouser suits in the Subcontinent style (*shalwar/kameez*). When requested, nearly all secondary schools and many primary schools will permit girls to wear a headscarf as part of their school uniform. Increasingly, provisions are made for single-sex sports activities, halal meat is provided for school lunches, and an awareness is shown for pupils who wish to fast during Ramadan. Second, there was a change in religious education in schools from 1975 onwards to introduce multi-faith syllabuses. Educationalists now saw school Religious Education as learning about and learning from different faiths rather than nurturing children in the religion of their families. This trend was enshrined in the Education Reform Act of 1988, which required teaching about Christianity and the other principal faiths in society. Third, certain adaptations in the wider curriculum introduced Arabic and other community languages as well as a less Eurocentric understanding of history, geography, and science. All that being said, Britain has made slow progress in developing worship facilities for non-Christians as a normal school provision.

Nurturing children in their own particular faith is seen increasingly as the responsibility of the religious communities rather than the school. For Muslims, this has meant the creation of hundreds of mosque and community-based *madrasas* that cater to children from five years old and up. Here, children memorize some parts of the Qur'an in Arabic so that they can pray and learn the basic tenets and practices of their faith, some of the history of Islam, and their cultural heritage.

The effect of the Immigration Acts, which were designed to regulate migratory workers, has been a lasting change in British society as a country of immigration. Because Commonwealth citizens merely had to register to receive British citizenship—often dual citizenship in the case of Pakistan—so in a couple of decades Britain had a settled Muslim population that enjoyed all the rights of full citizens of the country. Muslims have become active in local and national politics, where they are found in city councils and have started to enter both houses of parliament. Many Muslims are now on school boards of governors and on all manner of public representative bodies. A tiny but vocal group of Muslims, called Hizb ut-Tahrir (The Party of Liberation), has been campaigning for a return of the Caliphate and arguing that Muslims are forbidden to vote in British elections. There exists within the Muslim community, as with other faiths, a tension of how to be obedient to the rule of God when this is at variance with the law of the land. The twentieth-century British tradition of the right conscientiously to object, even to the extent of refusing to go to war, has given grounds for the use of conscience in such matters. Throughout the last century, campaigners made public protests against what they perceived to be unjust laws and, if necessary, accepted prison rather than give way, for example, women's suffrage, anti-nuclear weapons campaigns, and animal-rights activists.

Muslim entry into public life can be seen in attempts to bring about national bodies to represent the Muslim voice in various ways. The earliest of these was the Union of Muslim Organisations, founded in 1970, which sought, as its name suggests, to coordinate a wide spectrum of Muslim organizations. In the mid-1980s, the Council of Mosques of the United Kingdom was formed with backing from the Muslim World League. With its strong connections to Saudi Arabian Islam, it attracted only certain groups of Muslims. A second body, the Council of Imams and Mosques, was founded shortly thereafter with a membership drawn more from the Barelvi communities that would not join the former. This process led to the Muslim Parliament, founded by Kalim Siddiqi in 1992. He attracted publicity as a shrewd journalist, but the movement had limited impact, especially after his death in 1996. The Muslim Council of Britain, founded in 1996, is the most widely representative of these umbrella bodies so far. Its prominence increased by developing good relations with the government; however, this very strength has resulted in some Muslims questioning its independence.

The 2001 census included for the first time a voluntary question about religious affiliation. The question invited people to indicate to which religious group they belonged. This put the figure of Muslims in the United Kingdom at 1,591,126. Muslims make up nine percent of the total population of Greater London and similarly fourteen percent of the total population of Birmingham. In these two cities, the Muslim population is more diverse than in some northern regions where the dominance of the Subcontinent is more obvious. Of these British Muslims, fifty-two percent were younger than than twenty-five years, compared to thirty-one percent in the total population, and only six percent were older than sixty years, compared to twenty-one percent in the total population. Given the age profile of these communities, it is obvious that they will increase significantly in size in the next couple of decades simply by virtue of marrying and having children. The best estimate using 1991 census figures indicate that the Muslim population of Britain would have to double before it reached demographic stability; that is, the same number being born as dying.

France

The French Muslim population, the largest in Western Europe (estimated in 2000 between four and five million), shows strong links with the former French colonies in North Africa and Francophone West Africa (especially Senegal and Mali). The first waves of migrant workers came after the 1939–1945 War, from Algeria, Morocco, and Tunisia. These increased significantly after the Algerian War of Independence. A significant Algerian group, often referred to as the "Harkis," had such close links with the French colonial rulers there that they had to leave after independence and so were repatriated to France. Groups of Turks began to arrive in the early 1970s. The French Muslim communities are located largely in the industrial regions around Paris, Marseilles, Lyon, and Lille. Attempts at getting French Muslims to organize themselves into a body to interact with the heavily centralized French governmental system are ongoing.

Germany

Germany and Turkey have a long history of foreign relations, so Turkey was an obvious place to seek workers from the late 1950s onward. An official Turkish-German agreement was made in 1962 to regularize the flow of temporary male workers (*Gastarbeiter*). A large increase in the early 1970s was linked to economic prosperity, but it included many women workers and families. Additional workers were recruited from Morocco, Bosnia, and Pakistan. In addition, refugees came from Turkey (many Kurds) and Iran, as well as Arabs, mainly from Palestine and Lebanon. West Berlin had a strangely cosmopolitan mixture, as many refugees arrived in East Germany and were then sent over into West Berlin. The main areas of settlement were the traditional industrial cities of Berlin, Düsseldorf, Duisburg, Essen, Frankfurt am Main, Hamburg, Köln (Cologne), München (Munich), and Stuttgart. In 2000, the Muslim population of Germany was estimated at three million.

After the fall of the Ottoman Empire and the forced secularization of Turkey from 1924 onward, many of those who came to Germany and other lands were Muslim by cultural background but without any connection to the religious dimensions of Islam. Some proclaimed themselves secular or atheist. This makes any simple correlation between "Turk" and "Muslim" problematic. In addition, many of the Kurds who migrated were Alawites, the descendants of a Shi'a sect of Islam with a significantly different culture and outlook. Some groups had left Turkey in protest at its secularization, like the members of the Süleymançi movement. Others had close links with Islamic Movement groups in Turkey, such as the Milli Görüs. The Turkish government did not want to lose touch with the Turkish communities in Western Europe and so started to run mosques and send approved *imams* and religious teachers through its official Department for Religious Affairs (normally known for short as the Diyanet).

Other European countries

Smaller Muslim communities exist in all European countries. Numerically the most significant are the following. In the Netherlands (1999: 700,000), colonial links provided immigrants from Indonesia and Suriname, as well as Turkey, Morocco, Tunisia, and ex-Yugoslavia. Belgium (1999: 370,000) has significant communities from Morocco and Turkey, especially in Brussels and Liege, and the industrial regions around Antwerp and Limburg. Denmark (2000: 150,000) took immigrants from Turkey, Pakistan, and North Africa in the late 1960s, as well as refugees from the war between Iran and Iraq and the Lebanese Civil War. Sweden (2000: 250–300,000) has Turkish and ex-Yugoslavian communities as well as immigrants from Morocco, Pakistan, and Egypt, and a number of war refugees. Similarly, Norway (2000: 100–150,000) took in Pakistanis, Turks, and Moroccans in the mid-1970s and later refugees from ex-Yugoslavia, Somalia, India, and Iran. Switzerland (2000: 310,000) attracted migrant workers from Turkey and ex-Yugoslavia to its German-speaking cantons, and from North Africa to its French-speaking cantons. Austria (1997: 300,000) has a significant Turkish population as well as its long established relations with Bosnia. With its position in the Mediterranean, Italy (2000: 700,000) tended to attract significant numbers of migrant workers from North Africa and Albania. Similarly, Spain (1999: 300–400,000) has attracted Muslims mainly from North Africa.

Each country in Europe has its own approach to granting citizenship. In Britain and France this is part of the legacy of colonialism, and children born in both these countries automatically received citizenship. The Scandinavian countries generally allowed applications for naturalization after a period of being settled in the country. In 1998, Germany introduced provisions for citizenship for children born to settled families. In other countries, like Switzerland, it remains difficult to obtain citizenship. Once someone is a citizen of one country of the European Union, then they have the right to move to any other country within the EU. This has heralded a trend of internal European migration, in which, for example, a Somali family that has received citizenship in Belgium, Holland, or Sweden might decide to migrate to Britain to join other members of their extended family who have settled there.

Developments in education have already been indicated in the case of Britain. Again, patterns vary throughout Europe. In France, with its strict separation between religion and state, religious education does not figure into the state curriculum. Germany traditionally has permitted the major churches to run religious education classes within the educational system. There now are developments in the direction of extending the same provisions to Muslims. Norway and Sweden are considering the incorporation of multi-faith religious education in schools. In countries that have funded schools sponsored by religious communities, such as Belgium, this provision has been granted also to Muslims. This discussion often turns on the process of official recognition of a religious body by the state. Such recognition was granted in Belgium in 1974 and in Spain in 1992. The recognition of Islam as a formal religious body granted in the nineteenth century was reestablished in 1979 in Austria, where, in addition to religious education, Muslims also enjoy access rights to state media broadcasts.

Because many first-generation migrants to Europe had limited formal education, they tended to work in unskilled jobs. They were more concerned with getting established and dealing with racial discrimination than gaining access to further and higher education. This had its effect in the second generation, and only now in the third generation have levels of academic achievement drawn closer to national averages. This connects, of course, with poverty and poor housing conditions. The formation of monocultural quarters in cities where migrants were concentrated was both caused by and led to racial tensions. Many of the Muslim religious leaders imported with the immigrants were ill at ease in European society and poorly equipped religiously to deal with the issues raised. All these factors, together with world events, have contributed to an isolation and discontent among certain elements of young Muslims in Europe. A small but significant number of them thus become ready targets for radical Muslim groups.

Across Western Europe, the last decade has seen an increased number of Muslims arriving as refugees and asylum-seekers from Afghanistan, Bosnia, Chechnya, Ethiopia, Iran, Iraq, Kosovo, Nigeria, Somalia, and many other countries. Some estimates put the percentage of Muslims among refugees in Europe as high as seventy percent, and the majority of refugees worldwide are Muslims. It is important to remember that most refugees worldwide only cross one international border and settle in a neighboring country. For example, Pakistan has around two million refugees, most of them from Afghanistan. In this context, the number of refugees in Europe is relatively small and tends to comprise younger and more educated people who have the initiative and means to make their way to Europe. United Nations figures for migrants worldwide, that is, people living outside their country of birth, indicates the scale of this trend. In 1965 there were 75 million migrants; 1975, 84 million; 1985, 105 million; 1990, 120 million; and 2000, 150 million migrants.

These trends must be placed alongside the decline in birthrates among most indigenous Europeans, people living longer, and the needs of an aging population. It generally is believed that 2.2 children per woman are needed to maintain the size of the population. The European Union figure is 1.4 children per woman, and in the United Kingdom, 1.64. Coupled with the comparative youth of former immigrant communities, we can conclude that further increases in Muslim populations in many European countries are likely in the coming decades.

Subcontinental Sunni Muslims

During the eighteenth century, there were various revival and reform movements around the Muslim world. In the Indian Subcontinent, this coincided with the collapse of the Mughal Empire and British colonization. The Mughals went from controlling most of India to controlling only a small territory around their capital in Delhi. This was the time of Shah Waliullah (1703–62), the great Indian reformer of the age. He refocused attention on the Qur'an and the Sunna as the principal sources of Islam as he sought to rid Indian Islam of what he held to be the philosophical and cultural additions it had attracted. An important goal for him was to emphasize those elements of Islam that would help it survive political decline.

He was followed in this vein by Sayyid Ahmad of Rai Bareli (d. 1831), who founded the Tariqa Muhammadiyya. Sayyid Ahmad targeted Shi'a practices and the intercession of *pirs* (spiritual masters) in particular. He wanted a form of Islam purified from what he called "Hindu influence." Although he was brought up in Delhi, he moved to the North-West Frontier Province, where he set up a Muslim community run on the principles of Shari'a. This trend is often referred to as "Indian Wahhabism," taking its name from a similar reform movement led by Muhammad ibn Abd al-Wahhab (1703–1792) in the Arabian peninsula.

The impact of British rule in India on Muslims in the nineteenth century was far-reaching. The rise of the East India Company made trade much more important. Trade tended to be dominated by Hindus and led to a decline in the power of the traditional Muslim landlords. The British abolished grants to religious teachers and institutions that had been funded by the Mughals. The Shari'a was reduced to the sphere of personal law with the introduction of Anglo-Muhammadan Law. Civil and criminal law was in the hands of the British, who established their own law officers. British values tended to dominate public life for the ruling elite, and Islam was reduced to private religion.

After the 1857–1858 Indian Mutiny, or First War for Indian Independence (depending on the perspective), Delhi was sacked and the Mughal Emperor forced to abdicate. The dominant question now became how to survive as a Muslim community under British rule. This led to the formation of various movements.

Deobandis

The Deobandi Movement's founders, Muhammad Qasim Nanutavi and Rashid Ahmad Gangohi, found the answer in education. They founded a center for Islamic studies in the town of Deoband in Saharanpur District, about ninety miles northeast of Delhi, regarded today as one of the foremost centers of Sunni learning in the world. From this base, they established a chain of *madrasas* (schools) throughout India and wherever their followers migrated around the world. By the centenary of the foundation of Deoband in 1967, there were 8,934 affiliated *madrasas* worldwide.

The principles underlying this movement were a return to the purity of the Qur'an and the Hadith as the two principal sources of Islam and an avoidance of elements associated with Hindu and British values. They emphasized the importance of the Hanafi School of Sunni

Shari'a and avoided anything that might be drawn from Shi'a practices. A restricted form of sufi practice was permitted, but there was to be no intercession of *pirs*. Great emphasis was laid on literacy, so they tended to attract educated urban Muslims. Many classical texts were translated into Urdu and published widely. They drew only on funds supplied by followers and accepted no government funds; they wished to have as little as possible to do with British administration. In the absence of an Islamic state, they emphasized personal responsibility for living a Muslim life.

As the Deobandi movement spread, it emphasized outreach to other Muslims (*da'wa*), especially through education. Part of the genius of the movement was establishing a bureaucratic structure that did not rely on charismatic leaders. This ensured that the survival of the movement would not be threatened by the deaths of individual teachers. They established a Dar al-Ifta (Office of Legal Rulings) at Deoband, so that questions would receive an orthodox, learned response. *Bihishti Zevar*, a book by Maulana Ashraf Ali Thanvi on the duties of a Muslim woman, first published in 1890 and continuously in print ever since, attracted a huge following, as did other books of this kind. In 1919, the Deobandi established the Jamiat ul-Ulama-i Hind, a body that was to represent the views of the scholars (*ulama*). When discussions of the formation of Pakistan began, they stressed the importance of the rule of the *ulama*, according to the principles of Islam, as opposed to the "secular Muslims," who were largely British educated. After the formation of Pakistan, a new branch of the Jamiat was formed there, the Jamiat ul-Ulama-i Islam.

There are similarities between the Deobandi Movement in the Subcontinent, the Muhammadiyya Movement in Indonesia, and the Salafiyya worldwide. Their strengths lay in their development of book-based Islam with the need for education and literacy, their structure linking back to the headquarters at Deoband, their emphasis on personal piety rather than politics, and their solid stance within the Hanafi School of Law. The same trends can be observed in the diaspora, such as in Britain and America, where they have emphasized the development of educated, personally responsible Muslims and the importance of educational establishments linked into the Deoband system. Currently they have the largest and best organized *madrasas* in England, at Dewsbury and Bury, where they are training a new generation of *imams*.

Ahl-i Hadith

The Ahl-i Hadith movement in Delhi, India, grew out of the same situation the Deobandis had experienced. They tended to come from the social elite, as represented by their founders Maulana Nazir Hussain Dehlvi and Nawab Siddiq Hasan Khan of Bhupal. As their name (the People of the Hadith) suggests, they lay great emphasis on the purification of Islam by referring directly to the Qur'an and the Hadith. They recognize all schools of law from a scholarly perspective but prefer to work directly with the principal sources, stressing the consensus (*ijma*) of the *ulama*. They established their own mosques, *madrasas*, and journals, and in 1912 the All-India Ahl-i Hadith Conference. The men have a particular style of untrimmed beards and their own customs during the *salat*, such as reciting *Surat al-Fatiha* with the *imam*, holding their hands above the navel when standing and then raising them to their heads before making the profound bow, and saying the "amen" aloud.

The Ahl-i Hadith lay great stress on individual responsibility. They are scrupulous about the calculation and payment of *zakat* and encourage people to make the *Hajj* if at all possible. They condemn all expressions of sufism and work on a close interpretation of the Shari'a. They advocate simple marriage ceremonies and small dowries for brides. They are the inheritors of the tradition of Sayyid Ahmad of Rai Bareli in India and are linked to the Wahhabis of present Saudi Arabia. In the diaspora, they attract educated Muslims and have a tradition of running extensive educational and publishing programs. They are often linked with the distribution of books on Islamic subjects and can be a focal point for Muslims of a similar tradition from other parts of the world, such as Salafis. Their British headquarters are in Birmingham, where they run bookshops and seminars and organize *da'wa*.

Barelvis

The name Barelvi comes from Bareilly in North India, the native town of Ahmad Riza Khan (1856–1921), but they often prefer to be known by the more Islamic title, the Ahl-i Sunnat wa al-Jamaat (the People of the Sunna and the Authentic Community). This name implies their self-perception of being part of an international majority movement within Sunni Islam grounded within the ongoing tradition. Within this community there is a much greater stress on the customary practices that have been handed down and sanctioned by tradition. They permit praiseworthy innovations within Islam, following the majority position, provided that they are in keeping with the Qur'an and the Sunna. They embrace sufi etiquette and practice, are the traditional custodians of the shrines of the Friends of God (*awliya*) in the Subcontinent, and have developed an understanding of the intercession of both Muhammad and the *awliya*. As such, there has always been a certain tension between them and more puritanical groups. The Barelvis traditionally have been associated with rural Islam and sacred sites around India and Pakistan. They are strongly linked with sufi *tariqas*, especially the Qadiri, Naqshbandi, and Chisti.

Among the Ahl-i Sunnat wa al-Jamaat, great emphasis is laid upon the person of the Prophet Muhammad, who is understood to be both human and super-human, since he is the embodiment of the *Nur Muhammadi*, or the Light of Muhammad. It is held that a light was created from the Light of God before the creation began. This was the *Nur Muhammadi* that dwelled in all the earlier Prophets and came to the fullness of its indwelling in Muhammad. Muhammad is understood to have had knowledge of the unseen (*ilm al-ghayb*) and to have been able to intercede for believers. The Friends of God (*awliya*) were translucent to the Light of God and are also intercessors. The annual celebration of the *Mawlid un-Nabi*, or the Birthday of the Prophet, is marked with processions, speeches in his praise, and prayers for his intercession. The death anniversaries of the Friends of God (*urs*) are celebrated by huge gatherings at their shrines, where their intercession can also be sought. For many, the eleventh of each lunar month is important and is celebrated with gatherings for prayer and communal food, after the practice of the great sufi Abdul Qadir Jilani (d. Baghdad 1166).

The Barelvis generally had a better relationship with the British in India and were in favor of the founding of Pakistan. Their principal organization there is the Jamiat al-Ulama-i Pakistan, although they tend not to favor centralized umbrella groups. Each individual spiritual leader (*pir*) and the center associated with him tend to be the focus for those who follow him. The Barelvis were strong in the villages from which most of the immigrants to Britain from Pakistan and Kashmir came, and so they are the majority among those communities settled in Britain. They have developed some organizations of mosque communities and among their *ulama*. Important mosques tend to be centered around the representative of an established *pir* in the Subcontinent, who has a role as spiritual guide to the local community.

"Modernists"

Another reaction to the presence of the British in India in the nineteenth century was to seek to reconcile Islam and Muslims with British rule and civilization. Figures such as Sayyid Ahmad Khan (1817–1898) are associated with such a tendency and are generally referred to collectively as Modernists, but they were much more individual thinkers of influence rather than founders of movements. Sayyid Ahmad Khan held that nothing in the achievements of Western civilization was contrary to Islam. He appealed directly to the Qur'an and the Hadith and sought to reinterpret them in a way that reconciled the revealed Word with modern science. In this he argued that, as both reason and revelation have the same source, the two, *when properly understood*, must be in harmony. Part of his method was to distinguish the central Islamic message from the historical context of seventh-century Arabia. He reinterpreted miracles metaphorically.

Another figure who received much of his higher education in Europe was Muhammad Iqbal (d. 1938), widely recognized as a hugely influential philosopher-poet. He wrote poetry extensively in Persian and Urdu as well as prose works in English, such as *The Reconstruction of Religious Thought in Islam*. He stressed the consensus (*ijma*) of the whole community, not just the *ulama*, and so was able to see a vision for a modern democratic state in Pakistan. Important institutions associated with such individuals are the Muhammadan Anglo-Oriental College founded at Aligarh in 1877 on the model of an Oxbridge College and later transformed into Aligarh Muslim University; similarly, the All-India Muslim Educational Conference founded in 1886, and the All-India Muslim League founded in 1906.

Tablighi Jamaat

The Tablighi Jamaat, or Company of Preachers, is also known as the Faith Movement (Tahrik-i Iman). It was founded by Maulana Muhammad Ilyas (1885–1944), a graduate of Deoband, and so the two movements are closely associated. Maulana Ilyas had a vision of reviving the piety and practice of Islam among Muslims. To do this, he developed the idea of sending out groups of ordinary Muslims under a leader (*amir*), with one of a scholarly nature to guide the others (*mu'allim*), to visit people in their homes and call them to meetings where they would be exhorted to live an Islamic life. The method of doing this in groups was part of the spirit of the movement; it taught people to live in collective groups and to have respect for one another.

The aim of these groups was to revive Muslims in their faith: "always by persuasion; never by compulsion." This required building up mutual love and a zeal to acquire and transmit knowledge of the Qur'an and the Sunna. People were encouraged to "enjoin the right and forbid the wrong" in their own circles and then in the wider community. The movement did not engage in political discussion or permit religious controversy, but sought to promote a personal commitment to Shari'a and a sincere intention to put it into practice. In keeping with the Deoband connection, sufi practices were restricted.

Part of the genius of the movement, and an important element in its success, is that it stresses the gift of time by ordinary Muslims to "go on Tabligh." People moved by a pious response to this call will devote their free time and holidays to join a group and travel to another town or village with the message. The group lives simply and commits all its actions to God in prayer frequently during the day by communal *du'a*. They will lodge in a mosque or similar community hall. The activity of going on Tabligh is as much a spiritual renewal for the members as for the people to whom they go. Many Muslims arrange their jobs so that they can give substantial periods of time to the work. Annual camps to train and strengthen members attract enormous gatherings. The movement has expanded beyond communities of Subcontinental origin and is strong in North Africa and across mainland Europe, where it is known as *Foi et Pratique*.

Jamaat-i Islami

The Jamaat-i Islami is the Subcontinental form of a much wider Islamic Movement that embraces Arab groups such as al-Ikhwan al-Muslimun (The Muslim Brotherhood), founded in Egypt by Hasan al-Banna (1906–49) in 1928, and Turkish groups such as Milli Görüs, closely associated with Neçmettin Erbakan. For them, part of the question was how to be a Muslim in the face of Western civilization. They saw the need to work within the modern nation-state, within which attaining political power was the key to returning fully to the original form and content of Islam as a complete way of life. Through working within the existing democratic structures, they hoped to gain power and then establish laws that conformed to the Shari'a and led the masses toward a closer following of Islam.

The founder of Jamaat-i Islami, Sayyid Abul Ala Maududi (1903–1979), was a journalist by profession and self-taught in Arabic and Islamic studies. In 1932, he took over as editor of *Tarjuman al-Qur'an*, a periodical that became his most influential means of disseminating his message. This was targeted at the Muslim intelligentsia. The goal was to divert them from aspiring to Western values by showing them that Islam was a superior code of life for culture, political systems, economic systems, and modes of education.

Maududi worked on the principle of the sovereignty of God in all things. The Shari'a is a complete code of life without any need to borrow things from the West. Achieving political power is an essential tool in putting the divinely ordained systems into operation. The Islamic state must be created and cannot rest until it is universal. Such a state is to be run by those who comprehend its spirit and embrace its theology; *dhimmis* will be given their rightful place in the state. God is the author of all laws but uses the state as the *khalifa* on earth to implement those laws. It is the duty of informed Muslim citizens of the state to interpret the laws of God within the framework of the Shari'a, and so a theory of "theo-democracy" was developed to give political power to the right-thinking people under God. The leader of the state (*Amir*) should be elected by the people to ensure their confidence in his rule.

The Jamaat-i Islami has a highly developed organization in Pakistan with its headquarters in Lahore. Its power base lies with the urban middle classes in all cities and major towns. It has integrated parts of the organization in other places around the world where Pakistanis have migrated in numbers. Several organizations in Britain stem from this movement, although some have developed beyond the original inspirational founders. One such organization is the United Kingdom's Islamic Mission, which runs mosques offering community facilities, Islamic education for children, and good relations with local government. In 1971, the former East Pakistan gained independence as Bangladesh, and so Dawatul-Islam was founded as the umbrella organization for Jamaat-i Islami activities among Bangladeshis.

"Ahmadiyya Muslim Mission"

Within this context, it must be noted that the Ahmadiyya claim to be Muslim but have been formally declared non-Muslims by the *ulama* of Pakistan and around the world. It is important to understand the origins and tenets of this movement and why it has been declared outside the pale of Islam.

In 1889, Mirza Ghulam Ahmad of Qadian (1839–1908), a sort of Mahdi figure, declared himself to be a "minor prophet" who had come to rejuvenate Islam. He did not claim to have received a new revelation but to bring a new interpretation of the Qur'an that had been revealed to the Prophet Muhammad. The basis for such a distinction lies within Islamic tradition. Some Prophets, such as Harun (Aaron), were sent to reinforce and implement the revelation given to a major Prophet, in Harun's case to Musa (Moses). The orthodox Islamic understanding is that Muhammad was the last in the chain of all prophecy, and so it did not accept this description of Ghulam Ahmad as a minor prophet. Ghulam Ahmad also claimed that Jesus did not die on the cross but only swooned; that he later was revived and went in search of the lost tribes of Israel in Afghanistan and Kashmir; and that his grave is held to have been located in Srinagar, Kashmir. This broke the orthodox Islamic understanding of Jesus being "taken up" to God. Finally, Ghulam Ahmad claimed that the only acceptable form of *jihad* from his time onward was the spiritual *jihad* of passing on the message of Islam. After the death of Ghulam Ahmad, a party among the Ahmadiyya led by the respected Qur'an translator and commentator Maulana Muhammad Ali distanced themselves from his claims to be a minor prophet and held him only to have been a *mujaddid*, or renewer of Islam. The concept of a *mujaddid* is upheld in orthodox Sunni Islam, where such a person is thought to be sent by God at the beginning of each new Islamic century. But orthodoxy did not accept such a claim for Ghulam Ahmad. The group that proclaimed him only a *mujaddid* came to be called Lahori Ahmadiyya, and the main group often is referred to as Qadianis.

The Qadianis are well organized worldwide and have their own satellite television station with a transmitter in Britain and studios in Frankfurt am Main. They are committed to *da'wa* and have made a significant number of converts in Africa. They are active in *da'wa* to Muslims in the diaspora and are not welcome in the gatherings of orthodox Muslim groups. In 1973, they were legally declared non-Muslims by the Pakistani government of Zulfiqar Ali Bhutto. Since that time they have been subject to a number of proscriptions under Pakistani law to prevent them from operating under the guise of Islam. They eventually moved their international headquarters to London.

A future perspective

There are many hopeful signs for the future of Muslims in Europe. For one thing, many of the old rivalries between the various groups of the Subcontinent are breaking down, and the young generation are seeking a direct understanding of Islam rather than the cultural forms that their grandparents brought with them. As more and more young Muslims are educated in Europe, they have access to a wider range of scholarly materials, many of which now are being translated into English. The Internet plays a large role in connecting Muslims worldwide and allowing people to see beyond the narrow confines of their original communities. The same questions of how to live a Muslim life in the twenty-first century are being addressed not only in the West but throughout the Muslim world as well. Muslim scholars are giving serious thought to the development of a way of being Muslim as a minority in a non-Muslim country (*fiqh al-aqalliyat*).

An important part is being played by British convert scholars, such as Timothy Winter (Abdal Hakim Murad) in Cambridge. He combines an extensive classical training in the Islamic sciences with a profound understanding of living as a Muslim in Britain. In this way, deeper understandings of the traditions of Islam are made available for a generation of English-speaking Muslims. Such trends can also be seen among two American scholars: Nuh Ha Mim Keller, who concentrates on translating classical works for an English-speaking audience, and Shaykh Hamza Yusuf, who has an extensive following through his many taped talks for young Muslims in the West. Tariq Ramadan, currently based in Switzerland, writes extensively in French and English, exploring what it means to be a Muslim in Europe. Some of their works are listed in the Further Reading section.

Positive relations with Muslims from the Arab world have led to substantial endowments and sponsorships for centers of Islamic studies at various British universities. New lectureships have been established, and several of them have been filled with Muslim scholars who are Western converts to Islam. This injection of Arab money at a mainstream university level has no parallel in mainland Europe. Similarly, for more than twenty years, Zaki Badawi has been pioneering independent higher studies at his Muslim College in London. In the same vein, the contribution of Yusuf Islam to Muslim schools must be noted.

The importance of English as a new lingua franca for Muslims worldwide is critical. Recently, this has been enhanced by the Internet, but for decades books have been translated into English and new works written, published, and then exported from Britain. At a popular level, many of the younger generation of British Muslims owe their knowledge of Islam to English-language audio and video cassettes, which are available in large numbers.

Muslim women especially are taking active roles in claiming the position that Islam gives them as distinct from the restricted lives many of their grandmothers endured. Women's study circles are forming in many areas, and women are dealing directly with the sources and learning how to challenge men on the basis of the Qur'an and the Sunna. Among them are Muslim women such as Aisha Bewley, who specializes in translation from Arabic to English, and Ruqaiyyah Waris Maqsood, who has become established as a popular author. It is often mothers who ensure that the Islamic education of their children is more balanced and open to the liberating message of Islam than they themselves received. Denied the cultural cushion that "we are all Muslims here," they place a greater stress on personal faith and commitment. Many are asking, What difference does it make to be Muslim in this society?

This same question is being explored by groups such as the Islamic Society of Britain, which attracts a "thirty-something" educated membership and seeks to engage the broader society. It has promoted a series of Islam Awareness Weeks to make some of the cultural, socio-political aspects of Islam better understood. Speakers are trained and presentations developed to break down stereotypes and raise awareness of Islam as a complete way of life. Within this context, we should mention the glossy Muslim lifestyle magazine *emel*, which attracts a mixed audience of Muslims and other people.

The international relief and development agency Islamic Relief, founded in Birmingham in 1984, is now a major player on the world stage and a member of the Disasters Emergency Committee. Islamic Relief originally intended to respond to major disasters on a humanitarian basis; it now has seen the need to articulate the full range of humanitarian concerns based on Islamic principles, such as development education, advocacy, and awareness. Such work does a great deal to counter false images and provides an Islamic voice in discussions on the issues addressed by national and international agencies. In keeping with its principles, it actively seeks to work in partnership with Christian agencies and other bodies.

The growing awareness that being a Muslim in the West should include interaction with other faiths can be seen in the development of interfaith activity at the Islamic Foundation in Leicester. This organization has developed considerably from its original mix of publishing materials to promote an understanding of Islam. Now its material includes specialist units in interfaith relations, support for new Muslims, and studies on European Islam. It did pioneering work in developing Islamic economics in Britain and has now moved on to create a center for higher studies in partnership with British universities. It offers courses in partnership with Christian bodies to train a generation of specialist Muslim chaplains to work in the public sector.

Critical Muslim journalism has been established through the monthly magazine *Q-News*, which provides a platform to explore a whole range of issues in an investigative way covering the concerns of a new generation of British Muslims. An Association of Muslim Researchers has been founded to promote interdisciplinary academic interaction. There is now a variety of discussion groups running on the Internet that cater to a wide spectrum of opinion.

The emphasis in the media on "rogue elements" among Muslims worldwide has forced a greater media awareness and a desire not to let such elements speak for Muslims as a whole. Radical elements are challenged directly and shown for the shallowness of their arguments. The most important of these elements is Hizb ut-Tahrir (the Party of Liberation), a popular Islamic movement founded in Palestine in 1953, which has gained some support among young British Muslims since the early 1990s with its uncompromising call for a revival of the Caliphate to replace the modern system of nation-states.

A greater engagement with politics in general has been prompted by acts such as the American "war on terrorism" in Afghanistan and Iraq. A huge development in Britain was the Stop the War Coalition, in which Muslims, often led by women, learned to make concerted efforts with people who did not necessarily share their ideology, such as socialists, trade unionists, Green activists, and Christians. There has been a greater emphasis on Muslims getting into positions of influence in society, not only in politics but also in the professions, in business and education, and as government advisers. This dovetails with a greater presence of Muslims in all forms of the media, in sports, and in popular music and entertainment.

An important development is taking place in the work undertaken by mosques. The new generation of mosques has moved on beyond prayer and education to be involved in many social projects to improve school attendance and achievement, face the growing issue of drug abuse, help people find employment, support working mothers and the elderly without families, and engage with youth culture. Often such projects are staffed by trained workers and run in partnership with the state.

Alongside this runs a trend toward the secularization of Muslim youth. Sometimes this is a distancing from Islam itself, sometimes a rejection of the cultural baggage of their grandparents, and sometimes a view that says, "I am Muslim but I will define the limits of my faith and practice." For many of the older generation, this is a troubling and unacceptable trend. Others are adopting a more gradualist approach that says "half a loaf is better than no bread." Some who were only culturally Muslim have been reawakened to their Muslim identity and inspired to explore the richness of their heritage. The classical Muslim theological position holds that all those who confess the *Shahada* are Muslims, even if by their lifestyle some might consider them "bad Muslims." The judgment on any individual is a matter for God and not for other human beings. This position has led to initiatives that seek to be open to and inclusive of all who claim to be Muslim, whatever their observance of the Shari'a.

The migration of Muslims to Europe, whether through economic necessity or as refugees fleeing problems in their country of birth, has led Muslims into an interesting situation. The guidance of the Qur'an to those who cannot practice their Islam fully in a given location is to "make *hijra*," or migrate to a country where they can be Muslims without hindrance (Q. 4:97). The reality is that many Muslims in Europe have moved from societies that might on the surface be thought better disposed to an Islamic way of life. Will Europe's Muslims make *hijra* and move to a Muslim-majority country elsewhere? This seems highly improbable for the overwhelming majority, given the quality of life they are able to lead in Europe and the religious freedom that has been established in recent centuries as part of European life. What then is the solution for pious Muslims? It must be to find a way of being Muslim as a minority in Europe that is acceptable to them and to their fellow citizens, blending together in a harmonious way a life filled with *taqwa*, loyalty to the country in which they live, and solidarity with fellow believers around the world. Most important, they will seek to find favor with God on the awesome Day of Judgment.

Many of the Muslims who have come to live in the West and who have thought about these things see in the story of the Prophet Joseph's time in Egypt a model of the kind of life they should seek to live. The story is recounted in Sura 12 of the Qur'an. Here we read that the man who bought him as a slave gave orders that his life should be made agreeable in his new land (v. 21). Joseph established a reputation in Egypt for his integrity and honor (v. 23), his resistance to the temptations to sin found there (v. 24), his commitment to telling the truth (v. 26), and his steadfastness in faith (vv. 37–38). He took God as his protector (v. 101), trusting God to preserve him in time of temptation (v. 33), full of patience (v. 90) and never giving up hope in the mercy of God (v. 87). He knew that he should prefer the reward of heaven over all else (v. 57) and by his life bear witness to the message with which he had been sent (vv. 39–40). The quality of his life should provoke the admiration of others (v. 51), and thus he should invite them to belief in God (v. 108).

Muslims in the United States

Yvonne Yazbeck Haddad and Jane I. Smith

With some five to six million adherents in the United States today, and with numerous Islamic institutions—mosques, centers, schools, publishing houses, and welfare organizations—located across the continent, Islam is clearly an American religion. The community is made up of immigrants and their descendants, African American and white converts, and sojourners (students, diplomats, visitors, and business people). Some two-thirds either have recently arrived from overseas or are second- and third-generation Americans. Most of the rest are African Americans, belonging to Sunni Islam or any number of sectarian movements.

The Muslim community in North America is growing through immigration, conversion, and procreation, and a few decades from now, there might well be more Muslims than Jews in the United States. Most of the major cities of the United States have Muslim populations, with the largest concentrations located in New York City, Chicago, Los Angeles, and Houston. The majority of Muslims in America (about eighty percent) are not associated with organized religious institutions. They continue to identify themselves as Muslims, however, and often come together to celebrate special occasions, such as the end of Ramadan and the annual pilgrimage to Makka. Sunnis may celebrate Milad al-Nabi (the birthday of the Prophet) and Shi'as, 'Ashura (the commemoration of the death of Ali). They also share with their coreligionists many of the general concerns related to life in American society.

Early History

Increasing evidence is being uncovered by Muslims to suggest that there is a long history of Muslim activity in America. A few scholars have argued for a pre-Columbian presence, as well as for early West African explorations in the Caribbean. It seems fairly certain that some Spanish Muslim sailors acted as guides for discoverers from Spain and Portugal and that perhaps thousands of *Moriscos* (Spaniards who clandestinely retained their Muslim identity after 1492) came to the Americas in the 1500s, most of whom subsequently disappeared through persecution and assimilation.

From the seventeenth to the nineteenth century, a major transfer of
Muslim population to America took place. Perhaps as much as one-
fifth of the Africans brought in the slave trade were Muslim. At first they
may have attempted to practice their religion, but most were forced to
convert to Christianity. Little remains of the records of these Muslim
slaves aside from a few narratives and a Qur'an apparently written
down from memory. We do hear of some Muslim revolts, such as those
in 1758 in Haiti and 1835 in Brazil. The virtual disappearance of earlier
African Muslims in America because of intense persecution has been
reversed in the twentieth century by the growth of African American
Islam and the increase in immigration from continental Africa.

Immigration to America

Regular Muslim emigration to America from various parts of the
Islamic world began in the late nineteenth century, with Arabs from the
Ottoman Empire comprising the majority. The first wave of immigrants
came around 1875 from what then was Syria and was divided later
into the countries of Syria, Lebanon, Jordan, and Palestine. These
Muslims were mainly unskilled and uneducated peasants who hoped
to become financially successful in America, at least in relative terms,
and then to return to their homeland. Opportunities were limited,
however, and most were forced to become migrant, factory, or mine
workers or peddlers, while others became grocers, shopkeepers, and
petty merchants. Some decided to homestead in areas of the Midwest,
while others ended up serving as cheap labor on work gangs. Many
never realized their dreams either of earning a fortune in the new
land or of returning home, but those who made it became an impetus
for further emigration of their compatriots. Immigration laws of this
period allowed only persons who were "Negroid" or "Caucasian";
Arabs were considered to belong to neither category. In 1824, the
United States, through the Quota system, restricted emigration from
the Middle East to one hundred per year. In the same year, the courts
ruled that Syrians were "white" and thus fit to become citizens.

Between the mid-1940s and the mid-1960s new immigrants began
to arrive, propelled by very different circumstances abroad. Many of
those who came were much better educated than the earlier immigrants, often leaving to escape political oppression. The largest contin-
gent were Palestinians leaving after the creation of the state of Israel,
Egyptians whose property had been confiscated in the nationaliza-
tion policies of Gamal Abdel Nasser, Iraqis who wanted to leave after
the revolution of 1948, and Muslims from Eastern Europe trying to
escape the ravages of World War II or of communist rule.

Changes in immigration policies of the United States in the 1960s placed the needs of the labor market and the potential of immigrants to fulfill those needs over racial or ethnic restrictions. The third wave, still in progress, began around 1967. Those arriving in this last influx for the most part have been well educated, Westernized, and generally fluent in English, coming for reasons such as professional advancement and in many cases the desire to settle in America and to achieve economic and social status. Exceptions to the general trend are the less well educated, often illiterate and unskilled, workers from Yemen and Palestine and some Shi'a from Lebanon. Increased numbers of Muslims have come to Canada from the former British colonies of Uganda and Rhodesia (Zimbabwe). Many Indo-Pakistanis and some Africans have moved to Canada, some of whom subsequently have settled in the United States. There are significant numbers of immigrants and sojourners, refugees and asylum seekers, who have come to escape difficult social, economic, and political circumstances in their home countries, including Iranians leaving as a result of the overthrow of the shah; Lebanese emigrating after the invasion of their country by Israel; Afghans and Somalis, among others, escaping from civil war or famine; Kurds, Palestinians, and Iraqis fleeing after the Gulf War and Operation Iraqi Freedom.

Mosque in the United Arab Emirates. Photo: Angela Pierce.

In the mid-twentieth century, immigrant Muslims from the Middle East generally were committed to Arab socialism or nationalism and were more secular than religious in orientation. Since the 1970s, immigrants have reflected the growing Islamic consciousness that has developed as a result of American foreign policy in Muslim nations. More recently, however, commitments have changed dramatically. Far greater numbers of immigrants from such areas as Southeast Asia and the Arab world are Islamically committed. These Muslims, the majority of whom are well-educated professionals, are interested in establishing a solid religious community in their adopted country. Mosque building has increased substantially, owing both to the commitments of the members of the Islamic community and to the donations coming from oil-rich Gulf countries for the construction of religious establishments in America.

Over the past several decades a number of factors have led to a rapid growth in Islamic institutions and organizations in America. The Muslim population itself has increased markedly; the community is searching for ways in which to establish roots and provide instruction for its children. A series of events, however, has created an atmosphere in which Islam has been criticized and defiled. The Iranian Revolution of 1979; the Israeli invasion of Lebanon in 1982; the bombing of Libya in 1986; the controversy surrounding the publication of Salman

Rushdie's novel *The Satanic Verses* in 1989; the Gulf War in 1991; the bombing of the World Trade Center in 1993; the attacks of 9/11 and subsequent bombings in Madrid and London; and the insurgency that has arisen as a result of the U.S. occupation of Iraq have led to sharp critiques of Islam on the part of the media and the American public. Despite this, the number of Muslim institutions in the United States has risen to more than 2,400, of which more than 1,300 are mosques and Islamic centers.

Islamic Organizations

The earliest immigrants to continental America often were single, young, and usually not well informed about Islamic practices or doctrines. Busy with their economic pursuits and often seeing their stay in America as only temporary, they did not attempt to locate religious communities or identify structures for worship. Gradually, however, small groups gathered for prayer, often led by someone in the community not educated in the essentials of the faith. A number of communities began to consider the importance of establishing a mosque in their area, and soon new structures were built as they began to develop Islamic organizations and institutions. Finding or erecting buildings to serve as mosques or Islamic centers began in the 1920s and 1930s; by 1952 more than twenty mosques formed the Federation of Islamic Associations (FIA) in the United States and Canada. At its peak about fifty mosques were part of the FIA.

Immigrants of the 1960s committed to an Islamist perspective found the FIA to be too Americanized. When their efforts to Islamize these mosques and make them conform to institutions in Pakistan and Egypt failed, they initiated their own organizations to meet their own specific needs.

The Muslim Student Association in the United States and Canada (MSA) was founded in 1963 by a small group of students to provide service to the hundreds of thousands of Muslim students from overseas enrolled on American campuses, many of whom would return to play major leadership roles in national and international Islamic movements. The MSA regularly sponsors Friday and other prayers on college campuses and establishes Islamic libraries and other services for students. The organization is international in perspective and advocates an Islam that transcends all linguistic, ethnic, and racial distinctions. Particular needs of students from specific countries initiated nation-specific groups, such as the Muslim

Student Association Persian Speaking Group, founded in the late 1970s by a group of Iranian students. Other linguistically oriented student organizations that cater to specific ethnic identities include the Muslim Arab Youth Association and a group for Malaysian students.

The Islamic Medical Association was formed by alumni of the MSA in 1967 as a locus for Muslim health professionals to meet, exchange information, and provide services to others in the community. Similar organizations are the Association of Muslim Scientists and Engineers, begun in 1969 for the promotion of scientific research based on Islamic principles, and the Association of Muslim Social Scientists, started in 1972 as a professional, academic, educational, and cultural organization to promote Islamic thought. All of these associations sponsor annual publications and conferences.

In 1978, the Council of Masajid of the United States was established by representatives of the Muslim World League with a membership of twenty mosques. It was consolidated with the Council of Masajid of Canada, formed in 1983, as the Continental Council of Masajid of North America, with goals of aiding local mosques in their educational and outreach programs, helping them acquire permanent buildings for mosques, perpetuating Islamic culture, and facilitating communications with non-Muslims. By 1985, 151 mosques in the United States and Canada were affiliates. Its sponsorship by a Saudi-based organization, the Muslim World League, led some to be concerned about foreign intervention in American Muslim affairs. The organization has ceased to exist, and many of the mosques have become independent.

The Islamic Society of North America (ISNA) is an umbrella organization created in 1982 by the board and alumni of MSA who decided to settle in North America; they were interested in addressing the needs of the Muslim community in the United States. The MSA became a subsidiary group focusing primarily on the needs of students. Headquartered in Plainfield, Indiana, the ISNA provides assistance to students and other Muslims living in America through meetings and conferences, publication of the journal *Islamic Horizons*, and helping to negotiate an authentic Islamic presence in North America. More than three hundred and fifty mosques and Islamic centers were at one time affiliated with the organization. During the Gulf War, ISNA lost its financial support from overseas. Later, under the leadership of Sayyid Syeed, it focused on raising funds from American Muslims. It continues to provide leadership training and holds an annual convention that attracts up to 40,000 Muslims from the United States and Canada.

Shi'a Muslims

Although most of the Muslims who emigrate to America are Sunni, there is also a sizable community of Shi'a who are beginning to gain greater recognition as a separate and identifiable segment of the Islamic population, with sixty-nine mosques and Islamic centers throughout the United States, concentrated in New York, Detroit, Washington, Los Angeles, and Chicago, as well as several major cities in Canada. Until fairly recently little attention was paid to the Shi'a presence, in part because of the attempt by Muslims themselves to present Islam as a unified whole and in part because there were relatively few Shi'a among the immigrant population. That situation changed noticeably after the 1979 revolution in Iran. As a result of the revolution and the costly war between Iran and Iraq, a large number of Iranians have left the Middle East to come to the United States. The Lebanese civil war and the Israeli invasions of Lebanon in 1982 also displaced many Shi'a, who now have settled in such areas as Dearborn, Michigan. Operation Desert Storm brought more from Iraq.

Shi'a immigrants in the late nineteenth and early twentieth centuries tended to be uneducated and relatively impoverished workers, as was true of Sunnis emigrating at that time. Many of the more recent arrivals from Iran are from the better-educated middle and upper-middle classes. Most are members of the Ithna 'Ashari (Twelver) branch of Islam, who believe that the twelfth imam disappeared in the tenth century and will return at the end of time to establish justice in the world. In the meantime, Twelvers acknowledge the authority of their religious scholars in Iran and Iraq. Substantial numbers of Iranian Shi'a have settled in areas of Texas and southern California, where they await the time when Prince Reza Pahlavi, son of the late shah, will be restored to power in Iran. The Twelver Shi'a operate an Islamic seminary located in Medina, New York. It provides a four-year course of Islamic instruction for male students (studying to be imams) at the Jami'a Wali al-'Asr and for female students (who want to have a teaching career) at Madrasah al-Khadija al-Kubra.

Among other Shi'a groups in America are the Isma'iliyah (Seveners), who believe that Prince Karim Aga Kahn (b. 1936) is the forty-ninth hereditary imam. They have established a thriving community of more than eighty thousand in Canada, especially in Vancouver and Toronto, and have small communities scattered throughout the United States, especially in New York and California. Isma'ilis place a very high premium on education. They have a strong organizational structure and have been able to replicate their institutions effectively in the United States. There are also small pockets of 'Alawiyun from

Syria, Lebanon, and Turkey, and Zaydiyah from Yemen. There is a small Druze community in the United States, the majority of whose members are of Lebanese origin with a few individuals from Syria, Palestine, and Jordan. The Druze originally grew out of Isma'ili Shiism. Some Druze in America today identify themselves as Muslims, although others reject that association. The largest Druze concentration is in Los Angeles, with chapters of the American Druze Society in a number of other cities.

African American Muslims

Roughly a third of the Muslims in continental America are African Americans who have decided to join either mainstream Islam or one of the sectarian movements directly or loosely identified with Islamic doctrines. The earliest to claim a Muslim connection were the followers of Timothy Drew (1886–1929), who changed his name to Noble Drew Ali and began to preach that Christianity is the religion of whites and that the true religion for "Asiatics" (blacks) is Islam. In 1913, in Newark, New Jersey, he founded the Moorish American Science Temple, whose Koran is entirely different from the Holy Qur'an of Islam. The movement spread to such major cities as Detroit and Philadelphia, eventually weakening after the death of its founder; remnants of the community remain today in over seventy major cities.

Islam as a truly American phenomenon first caught the attention of the United States with the rise of the Nation of Islam. In 1929, a person probably of either Turkish or Iranian origin by the name of W. D. Fard began to preach in Detroit on the theme of Islam as true identity for African Americans. Calling them real Muslims who in this country have been separated from their homeland, he became the first spokesperson for what came to be known as "The Lost-Found Nation of Islam in the Wilderness of North America," or simply the Nation of Islam. Fard's preaching was heard by one Elijah Poole, born in Georgia in 1897, who assumed the name Elijah Muhammad and soon became the leader of the movement and its "Messenger of God." After the disappearance of Fard, Elijah Muhammad preached the necessity of bringing blacks in America to an understanding of their true nature as Muslims and helping the community regain its self-respect, ethical integrity, and economic independence from whites.

Nation of Islam doctrines were in many ways antithetical to Islam. Elijah taught that the white man is the devil and the black man is good, and that the only way to success for blacks is to separate themselves from their longtime oppressors. His emphasis on ethical responsibility, hard work, and moral uprightness, as well as identification of the root causes of the suffering of blacks, was extremely appealing to many in the African American community. Many of the former followers of Noble Drew Ali, as well as some of the followers of Marcus Garvey, rallied to the call of the Nation of Islam to assume their identity as Muslims.

Although the center of Nation of Islam activity has been in Chicago, temples were established in depressed black areas of a number of metropolitan cities. The message appealed to those needing a way out of their difficult circumstances, including some blacks incarcerated in large urban prisons. Prison ministry has been and continues to be one of the most effective means of recruiting African Americans to Islam. The Nation also was attractive to a number of persons who occupied leadership positions in the African American community, including the educated and professional elite. Several branches were established in the Caribbean and Canada.

By the 1960s, international difficulties began to disrupt the community. Malcolm X (1925–1965), the most prominent and articulate of the Nation of Islam leaders, had converted to Islam in prison and become a deeply committed follower of Elijah Muhammad. A combination of personal disillusionment with his leader and his experience on the pilgrimage of a universal Islam inclusive of all persons and races led Malcolm X to a final break with the Nation of Islam. He was assassinated at a religious rally in 1965; two Nation of Islam members were convicted of the murder.

With the death of Elijah Muhammad in 1975, the leadership of the movement was assumed by his son Wallace, under the name of Warith Deen Mohammed. He began to lead the community away from the separatist teachings of his father and closer to the egalitarian understanding of Sunni Islam. He preached that Elijah Muhammad's message had been essential to the recovery of the black community in America at the time, a necessary transitional step in their movement from slave mentality toward accepting true Islam. Having received a classical Islamic education, Warith Deen Mohammed assumed the title of *mujaddid* (renewer of faith) and immediately led the movement through a number of name changes, from "Nation of Islam" to "The American Bilalian Community" after the first black convert to Islam under the prophet Muhammad to "The World Community of Islam in the West" in 1976 to "The American Muslim Mission" in 1980 and later, the Muslim American Society. In 1985, the community was urged to integrate into mainstream Sunni immigrant Islam. He later changed the name to Ministry of W. Deen Mohammed and later to American Society of Muslims in order to distinguish his group from a predominantly Arab immigrant organization named Muslim American Society. Warith Deen Mohammed's broadcasts are heard every weekend on more than thirty radio stations across the country.

Elijah Muhammad's Nation of Islam instituted a nationwide system of education known as the University of Islam, later restructured under his son as the Sister Clara Muhammad Schools. Today it includes more than fifty institutions across the country. These schools offer a curriculum of Islamic studies as well as basic instruction for elementary and sometimes high school students. The individual schools are not responsible to any central authority, but they generally offer a fairly uniform curriculum.

The Nation of Islam as a separate group continues under the leadership of Minister Louis Farrakhan. Concerted efforts continue to be made to establish a strong black economic system in which members can be free of the dominant white structures. Nation of Islam members also have taken active leadership roles in local community efforts to keep neighborhoods free of drugs and drug-related crime. Farrakhan's movement is based in Chicago, but three other groups lay claim to being the authentic Nation of Islam under different leaders in Baltimore, Detroit, and Atlanta.

Other Muslim groups have attracted African Americans to Sunni Islam. One that drew considerable attention in the 1960s was known as the Darul Islam movement. Initially formed in the late 1940s and early 1950s, the group established the first Darul Islam mosque in Brooklyn in 1962. It grew fairly rapidly, disbanded because of internal disagreements, and reformed in the early 1970s under the leadership of Imam Yahya. Darul Islam members have had occasional problems with local police; the brotherhood developed what was called a ministry of defense and a parliamentary force called Ra'd (Thunder). By the middle of the 1970s, thirty-one mosque-based Sunni African American communities had chosen to affiliate with the Darul Islam movement, mainly in the larger cities of the East Coast and a few in the Caribbean. In 1980, Imam Yahya abdicated his leadership of the group; many of his former followers have started local groups, and some have come under the influence of a Sufi organization. Other African American Sunni organizations include the Hanafi movement, the Islamic Party of North America, the Union of Brothers, and the Islamic People's Movement, centered in the Caribbean and with a mosque in Washington, D.C.

African American and immigrant Muslims for the most part have maintained separate communities in the United States, although there are increasing efforts at cooperation, conversation, and some common worship and social activities. With the return of most of the former members of the Nation of Islam to the fold of Sunni Islam under Warith Deen Mohammed, significant issues remain to be resolved between the two communities. Some African Americans believe that they are more diligent than their immigrant brothers and sisters in observing the strict codes of diet, dress, and other forms of observance. Immigrants, however, often tend to think that as lifelong Muslims they have a better understanding of Islam than do those who recently have converted. African Americans are a product of American society and are looking for ways to function as equals in the American context; they often feel that they are the most appropriate ones to interpret Islam to non-Muslims. Many immigrant Muslims acknowledge that they might not yet understand American society but still are reluctant to delegate the negotiation of the place of Islam in America to African Americans.

White Converts to Islam

Leaders in the Islamic community estimate that there are some 45,000 to 80,000 white converts in America. Among the earliest was Alexander Russell Webb (d. 1916), U.S. consul to the Philippines at the end of the nineteenth century. Disenchanted with Christianity, Webb began a correspondence with Mirza Ghulam Ahmad, leader of the Ahmadiyah in Lahore, and eventually became an articulate spokesperson for Islam in America. He published a journal called *The Moslem World* as well as several texts about Islam.

The majority of white converts to Islam are women who have married Muslim men and decided to adopt the faith themselves. In some cases women convert before finding a marriage partner out of the conviction that women are held in higher esteem in Islam than in American society in general. A number of Americans who have found themselves at odds either with their own religious tradition or denomination or with the prevailing norms of American culture have looked to Islam to provide alternatives. Sometimes they choose to affiliate with established Sufi or mystical schools of thought operating in the American context. Muslims often prefer the term "revert" to "convert," suggesting that one returns to the natural state of submission.

Sectarian Movements

The Ahmadiyah movement, an Indo-Pakistani missionary community that for many years has been active in translating the Qur'an into the world's major languages, began sending agents to America for the express purpose of converting the West to its version of Islam. Failing in early efforts to convert the white population and Sunni Muslims to their doctrines, the Ahmadiyah began to target the African American community. Considered a heretical movement by most Muslims, Ahmadi groups are found in a number of the larger cities of the United States. Since the 1960s, both the Qadiani (with headquarters in Washington, D.C.) and the Lahori (with headquarters in California) groups have established several mosques in the United States.

Another offshoot of Islam found in America is the Baha'i religion. Founded by Baha' Allah in Iran in the mid-nineteenth century, Baha'i faith was first brought to the United States in 1892. The largest community is in the Chicago area, with the temple and national Baha'i archives found in Wilmette, Illinois. Like other immigrant groups, Baha'is struggle to determine their distinctive identity in the American context.

Among the growing number of African American sectarian movements calling themselves Islamic is that identified as the Five Percenters. A splinter group from the Nation of Islam formed in 1964 under Clarence "Pudding" 13X, they believe that they are the chosen five percent of humanity. They see eighty-five percent of humankind as doomed to self-destruction; another ten percent has right knowledge and power but uses it to deceive the majority. It is the five percent who are living a truly righteous Islamic life, manifesting the divine nature of the black man, who is identified by Allah. The headquarters of the group was in Harlem, although the Five Percenters have branches in major U.S. cities and in many prisons. Five Percenters were highly visible in the rap music industry, using the quick and complicated form of rap lyrics to spread the five percent ideology, called the Science of Supreme Mathematics. While they later decided that they were not Muslims, some rappers continue to write and perform "Islamic rap."

The sectarian Ansaru Allah Community was founded in 1970 by Isa Muhammad, born York and known variously as Isa al Haadi al-Mahdi and As Sayyid al Imam Isa al-Mahdi. Isa Muhammad was influenced by the black power movements of the 1960s, and his teachings reflect a disenchantment with the culture of the United States, which he considers to be racist. A prolific writer, Isa consistently has presented himself as the divinely inspired interpreter of the true message of the Qur'an and in the direct lineage of the Sudanese Mahdi, Muhammad Ahmad ibn 'Abd Allah. Isa Muhammad is noted for changing and transforming his teachings over time. He moved from doctrines of black supremacy to a much closer affiliation with the egalitarian teachings of Islam and back to the original teachings on race with special invective against "pale Arab" Muslims. Later he identified himself as Rabboni Yashu'a. The original headquarters of the group was in Brooklyn, with branches in a number of major cities, including Philadelphia and Los Angeles. Members maintained an active ministry in the penal system and were seen selling his publications in such prominent places as Times Square in New York City. In the middle of the 1990s, he moved his headquarters to rural Georgia and established a settlement. He is currently serving a jail sentence as a convicted sex offender for having sex with the young girls in his group as part of their initiation.

Sufi Movements

Although many of the Sufi groups were not recognized by immigrant Sunni Muslims as legitimate, many have become an acknowledged part of the complex fabric of Muslim life in America. The resurgence of interest among young Americans in religions of the East, most prevalent in the 1960s, contributed to the popularity of these Sufi movements, some of whose members have relatively little knowledge of or even interest in classical Islamic doctrines and practices. Some American converts did not even realize that Sufism has any connection with Islam.

Among the most influential Sufi orders are the Qadiriyah, which is embodied in the Bawa Muhaiyaddeen Fellowship located in Philadelphia. The fellowship has more than two thousand converts, primarily from the highly educated Christian and Jewish middle- and upper-middle classes. Members engage in Sufi sessions and listen to taped teachings of the now-deceased Bawa Muhaiyaddeen, whose burial site is considered by some immigrants as a wali (saint) shrine. Sufi convert groups are found also in upstate New York, California, Texas, Michigan, and New Mexico.

Some immigrants have perpetuated the Sufi tariqahs (literally "ways") of their countries of origin. These include the Bektashis, the most thriving of which is the Albanian tekke (building for Sufi activities) in Detroit (with a resident Sufi shaykh), the Shadhiliyah, the Ishraqiyah (among Iranians), and the Naqshbandiyah (among Syrians and Turks).

The Muslim community became increasingly wary of Sufis at the end of the last millennium, when Sheikh Muhammad Hisham Kabbani of the Naqshabandi order in Lebanon became prominent in the United States. He founded what he called the Islamic Supreme

Council of America in 1997 and sought to bring Muslims under his aegis. He was rejected initially by the Salafis, who consider Sufism a deviant expression of the faith. He became notorious when in a lecture at the Department of State he accused eighty percent of mosques in the United States of being under extremist control. The concern about the Sufi agenda has increased with the publication of the Rand Report of 2003, which recommended that the United States government promote the dissemination of Sufi teachings in an effort to contain the Islamist movement and create a moderate Islam.

Meanwhile, Sufism has increased in popularity among the college-age children of immigrants as they search for a moderate Islam in the post-9/11 atmosphere in the United States. Popular Sufi converts such as Hamza Yusuf of the Zaytuna Institute in Hayward, California, and Nuh Ha Mim Keller, who has an elaborate educational institution in Amman, Jordan, attract young seekers who at times take a year or two off their academic studies to immerse themselves in Islamic knowledge.

Islamic Concerns

A number of particular problems face Muslims in America, among them the need for trained religious leadership, opportunities for observing requirements of the faith such as prayer and fasting, and matters related to social interactions. Of particular concern to both mainstream and sectarian groups is the education of children. Not all Muslims agree that parochial education is the right answer, but more than two hundred Islamic day schools have been established, and others are being planned. Hundreds of Sunday schools function to instruct youth in the basics of the Islamic faith. There is a need to establish an accredited school of Islamic education to train imams for mosque leadership and chaplains for hospitals, prisons, and the military. The School of Islamic Social Sciences in Northern Virginia has attempted to fill this vacuum; it recently has received accreditation from the state of Virginia. Hartford Seminary in Connecticut offers several programs, including online degree programs.

With each wave of immigration, the initial challenge continues to be whether to try to assimilate into American society and to what degree. Muslims want to be acknowledged as full members of American society, whether as representatives of their respective national groupings, as members of the community of Islam, or simply as American citizens. At the same time some Muslims have become increasingly aware that the prevailing culture often is inimical to their own understanding of

Islam; in order to be true to their beliefs it may be necessary not only to maintain social practice and observance in line with the dictates of Islam but also to develop alternative forms of economics and education. Often national ties and the bond of a common language seem to unite Muslims in America more than specific religious affiliation, making the establishment of religious associations and organizations difficult. In some areas there are tensions between conservative groups and those who wish to accommodate more flexibly to American customs, as well as between those who strive to be more strictly Islamic, and thus uniform in practice, and others who want to maintain the variations of their own particular cultures.

The Social Security system in the United States, for example, has raised questions about the necessity of paying the *zakat* (alms). The fact that Islam does not allow interest on loans causes problems for Muslims using the American banking system. Meantime, Muslims have devised creative ways to finance their homes and businesses while observing Islamic restrictions on usury. Recently an Islamic bank was opened in Michigan. Other issues include observing dietary restrictions that tend to set Muslims apart, hindering the social integration considered important by Americans for professional advancement. A number of efforts have been made by Islamic organizations to acquaint Americans with Islamic contributions to art, science, and culture. Muslims in general continue to enjoy the context of freedom of association and expression in America at the same time that they are concerned over the discrimination that nonetheless exists, the fact that Muslims often have difficulty finding employment, and certain aspects of American foreign policy in the Middle East.

Among the issues of deep concern to Muslims have been the persistent and heightening instances of prejudice in North America against Islam, Arabs, and Muslims. This has encouraged many Muslims over the years to keep a low profile. Muslims have expressed concern about the distorted and inaccurate picture of Islam presented by the media and the biased treatment of Muslims in textbooks, news coverage, and entertainment programming. Some Muslims have been engaged in providing more reliable information. Several Muslim groups have developed television programs on Muslim faith and practice that are aired in the United States and also are distributed worldwide. They publish numerous magazines, books, and audio and videotapes on the Muslim experience.

The American Muslim Community Post 9/11

The events of 9/11, and the resulting rise in anti-Muslim feelings among the American populace, have offered a particular challenge to Muslims, who had believed that they were on their way to being recognized as full members of American society. They have had to find ways to counter the negative press about Islam and to prove that they are patriotic and conscientious citizens. Some American opinion makers, along with right-wing political and religious leaders, have argued publicly that the presence of Muslims in the West is a potential threat not only to Western democracy, liberalism, pluralism, and tolerance, but also to the West itself. The tendency of American policy makers to refer to the world as divided between good and evil, democratic and despotic, with the clear implication that extremist Muslims fit the second category, has made even more difficult the challenge to American Muslims to present Islam as a moderate religion.

The Bush Administration adopted several measures in its attempts to combat terrorism. The most problematic for Muslims has been HR3162, commonly known as the USA PATRIOT (Providing Appropriate Tools Required to Intercept and Obstruct Terrorism) Act of October 24, 2001. The measure has served to remove liberties and legal protections for Muslims and Arabs in the United States by sanctioning the monitoring of individuals, organizations, and institutions without cause and without judicial approval. Nongovernmental organizations, as well as civic, charitable, and religious organizations, have been constantly monitored. By monitoring charities and organizations that support efforts to help the needy overseas out of fear that they might transfer funds to terrorist organizations, the government has circumscribed one of the basic responsibilities of Muslims, that of charitable giving. These measures tend to be viewed by Arabs and Muslims as being specifically anti-Muslim rather than generally anti-terrorist.

Muslims are working to develop mutual systems of support, including political action committees, to combat anti-Muslim views. Some Muslims have initiated conversations with members of Christian and Jewish religious communities for the purpose of providing more accurate data about the nature of Islam in this country and abroad. The Muslim community has begun coalition building with human rights, religious rights, and civil rights groups. Relating to non-Muslims has become a priority for the children of the immigrant generation, reflected in their invitations to members of churches and synagogues to visit the mosques and engage in dialogue.

Muslims pose a challenge to America's vision of itself. They are demanding that America live up to its public professed values of pluralism and freedom of speech and religion and make room for its Muslim citizens, allowing them to define what it means to be American and Muslim. It remains to be seen if American society, given its democratic and pluralistic principles, will allow for a non-Judeo-Christian religion with a distinctive culture and alternate values to flourish in its midst.

Mosque Maryam in Chicago, Illinois. National Center and Headquarters for the Nation of Islam. Photo: James Brand

The Mother Mosque of America in Cedar Rapids, Iowa. The first mosque built in the United States. Photo: Amy and Jason Cooper

Further Reading

A note of caution

All books and Web sites come from a certain perspective. It is important both to read critically and to look around at a range of opinions. If a book has been translated, edited, or abridged, be aware that someone else is coming between you and the original. Almost anyone can set up a Web site giving personal opinions, and some of them lack balance in the positions they offer. No one will agree with everything they read, so be critical and be aware!

Web sites

Dr. Gary Bunt of the University of Wales, Lampeter, has produced two invaluable guides to Islamic Internet sites:
Gary Bunt. *Virtually Islamic: Computer-Mediated Communication and Cyber Islamic Environments.* Cardiff: University of Wales Press, 2000.
Gary Bunt. *Islam in the Digital Age: E-jihad, Online Fatwas, and Cyber Islamic Environments.* London: Pluto, 2003. He maintains a homepage with a regularly updated list of Web sites, called "Pathways," with short descriptions: www.virtuallyislamic.com.

Another site with well-researched Internet links is run by Prof. Alan Godlas of the University of Georgia: www.arches.uga.edu/~godlas/. This provides links for research into a variety of Islamic topics and is updated with listings of current academic research on Islam.

A *fatwa* service run by the school of Yusuf al-Qaradawi can be found at: www.islamonline.net.

A great source of information on aspects of Muslim culture and civilization can be found at: www.muslimheritage.com.

The homepage of the Muslim Council of Britain can be found at: www.mcb.org.uk/direct.

Books

Copies of the Qur'an

Copies of the Qur'an in Arabic and English with footnotes are printed in Saudi Arabia for free distribution. The translation is based on that of Abdullah Yusuf Ali, but both it and the footnotes have been revised by a team of scholars approved by the publishers. It is often possible to obtain free copies by asking at mosques. Many translations are published in English, and those mentioned in this book are noted here.

Abdullah Yusuf Ali. *The Holy Qur'an.* Revised with English footnotes. Birmingham: IPCI, 1998.
Mir Ahmed Ali. *Holy Qur'an.* New York: Tahrike Tarsile Qur'an, 1988.

ЫЙЫЙЫЙЫЙЫЙЫЙЫЙЫЙЫЙ

ЫЙ

ЫЙ

Muhammad Asad. *The Message of the Qur'an*. Gibraltar: Dar al-Andalus, 1984.
Abdalhaqq and Aisha Bewley. *The Noble Qur'an*. London: Madinah Press, 1999.
Kenneth Cragg. *Readings in the Qur'an*. London: Collins, 1988.
M. A. S. Abdel Haleem. *The Qur'an*. Oxford: Oxford University Press, 2004.
T. B. Irvine. *The Noble Qur'an*. Brattleboro: Vt.: Amana, 1992.
T. B. Irvine et al. *The Qur'an: Basic Teachings*. Leicester: Islamic Foundation, 1979.
Marmaduke Pickthall. *The Meaning of the Glorious Koran*. New York: Dorset, n.d.

Introductions to the Qur'an

Farid Esack. *The Qur'an: A Short Introduction*. Oxford: Oneworld, 2002.
Muhammad Abdel Haleem. *Understanding the Qur'an: Themes and Style*. London: Tauris, 1999.
Jacques Jomier. *The Great Themes of the Qur'an*. London: SCM Press, 1997.
Imam Nawawi. *Etiquette with the Qur'an*. Trans. Musa Furber. Chicago: Starlatch, 2003.
Fazlur Rahman. *Major Themes of the Qur'an*. Minneapolis: Bibliotheca Islamica, 1980.
Neal Robinson. *Discovering the Qur'an*. London: SCM Press, 2003.
Anton Wessels. *Understanding the Qur'an*. London: SCM Press, 2000.

Qur'an Commentaries

Mahmoud Ayoub. *The Qur'an and Its Interpreters*. 2 vols. to date. Albany: SUNY Press, 1984–.
Abdul Kalam Azad. *The Tarjuman al-Qur'an*. 3 vols. New Delhi: Kitab Bhavan, 1990.
Abdul Majid Daryabadi. *Tafsir-ul-Qur'an*. 3 vols. Karachi: Darul Ishaat, 1991. Abridged into one vol. as *The Glorious Qur'an*. Leicester: Islamic Foundation, 2001.
Fadhlalla Haeri. *Keys to the Qur'an*. 5 vols. Reading: Garnett, 1993.
Ibn Kathir. *Tafsir ibn Kathir*. Abridged into 10 vols. to date. London: Al-Firdous, 1996–.
Abul A'la Mawdudi. *Towards Understanding the Qur'an*. 7 vols. to date. Leicester: Islamic Foundation, 1988–.
Al-Qurtubi. *Tafsir al-Qurtubi*. One vol. to date. London: Dar al-Taqwa, 2003–.
Sayyid Qutb. *In the Shade of the Qur'an*. 10 vols. to date. Leicester: Islamic Foundation, 1999–.
Muhammad Shafi. *Ma'ariful Qur'an*. 7 vols. to date. Karachi: Maktaba-e-Darul-'Uloom, 1996–.
Al-Tabari. *The Commentary on the Qur'an*. Abridged, 1 vol. to date. Oxford: Oxford University Press, 1987–.
Al-Tabataba'i. *Al-Mizan: An Exegesis of the Qur'an*. 7 vols. to date. Tehran: World Organization for Islamic Services, 1983–.
Shabbir Ahmad 'Usmani. *The Noble Qur'an*. 3 vols. Karachi: Darul-Isha'at, 1999.

General Introductions to Islam

Mahmoud Ayoub. *Islam: Faith and History*. Oxford: Oneworld, 2004.
Daniel Brown. *A New Introduction to Islam*. Oxford: Blackwell, 2004.
Frederick M. Denny. *An Introduction to Islam*. New York: Macmillan, 1994.
John Kaltner. *Islam: What Non-Muslims Should Know*. Facets. Minneapolis:
    Fortress Press, 2003
Seyyed Hossein Nasr. *Ideals and Realities of Islam*. London: Unwin, 1988.
_____. *The Heart of Islam*. San Francisco: HarperCollins, 2002.
Fazlur Rahman. *Islam*. Chicago: Chicago University Press, 1979.
David Waines. *An Introduction to Islam*. Cambridge: Cambridge University
    Press, 1995.

Hadith Studies

Thomas Cleary, trans. *The Wisdom of the Prophet: The Sayings of Muhammad*.
    Shambala Classics, 2001.
Ezzeddin Ibrahim and Denys Johnson-Davies, trans. *Forty Hadith Qudsi*.
    Lebanon: Dar al-Koran al-Kareem, 1980.
Ezzeddin Ibrahim and Denys Johnson-Davies, trans. *An-Nawawi's Forty
    Hadith*. Damascus: Holy Koran Publishing House, 1976.
Muhammad Zubayr Siddiqi. *Hadith Literature: Its Origin, Development, and
    Special Features*. Cambridge: Islamic Texts Society, 1993.

The Life of Muhammad

Khalid Alavi. *Muhammad, the Prophet of Islam*. Islamabad: International
    Islamic University, 2002.
Karen Armstrong. *Muhammad: A Biography of the Prophet*. London: Phoenix, 1991.
Aisha Bewley, trans. *Muhammad, Messenger of Allah: Ash-Shifa of Qadi 'Iyad*.
    Inverness: Madinah Press, 1998.
Martin Lings. *Muhammad: His Life Based on the Earliest Sources*. Cambridge:
    Islamic Texts Society, 1983.
F. E. Peters. *Muhammad and the Origins of Islam*. Albany: SUNY Press, 1994.
Annemarie Schimmel. *And Muhammad Is His Messenger: The Veneration of the
    Prophet in Islamic Piety*. Chapel Hill: University of North Carolina Press, 1985.
Montgomery Watt. *Muhammad at Mecca*. Oxford: Oxford University Press, 1979.
Montgomery Watt. *Muhammad at Medina*. Oxford: Oxford University Press, 1981.

Shi'a Islam

Farhad Daftary. *The Isma'ilis: Their History and Doctrine*. Cambridge: Cambridge
    University Press, 1992.
Heinz Halm. *Shiism*. Edinburgh: Edinburgh University Press, 1991.
S. H. M. Jafri. *The Origins and Early Development of Shi'a Islam*. Oxford: Oxford
    University Press, 2000.
Moojan Momen. *An Introduction to Shi'i Islam*. New Haven: Yale University
    Press, 1985.
Yann Richard. *Shi'ite Islam*. Oxford: Blackwell, 1995.

Ja'far Sobhani. *Doctrines of Shi'i Islam: A Compendium of Imami Beliefs and Practices*. London: Tauris, 2001.
Sayyid M. Husayn Tabataba'i. *Shi'ite Islam*. Albany: SUNY Press, 1977.

History

Karen Armstrong. *Islam: A Short History*. London: Phoenix, 2002.
Richard Fletcher. *Moorish Spain*. London: Phoenix, 2001.
Carole Hillenbrand. *The Crusades: Islamic Perspectives*. Edinburgh: Edinburgh University Press, 1999.
Philip Hitti. *History of the Arabs*. London: Macmillan, 1985.
Marshall Hodgeson. *The Venture of Islam*. 3 vols. Chicago: Chicago University Press, 1974.
J. Hoeberichts. *Francis and Islam*. Quincy, Ill.: Franciscan, 1997.
Hugh Kennedy. *An Historical Atlas of Islam*. Leiden: Brill, 2002.
Ira Lapidus. *A History of Islamic Societies*. Cambridge: Cambridge University Press, 2002.
María Rosa Menocal. *Ornament of the World: How Muslims, Jews, and Christians Created a Culture of Tolerance in Medieval Spain*. Boston: Little, Brown, 2003.
P. H. Newby. *Saladin in His Time*. London: Phoenix, 2001.
Syed Azizur Rahman. *The Story of Islamic Spain*. New Delhi: Goodword, 2001.
Steven Runciman. *A History of the Crusades*. 3 vols. London: Penguin, 1991.
Reinhard Schulze. *A Modern History of the Islamic World*. London: Tauris, 2000.
M. A. Shaban. *Islamic History: A New Interpretation*. 2 vols. Cambridge: Cambridge University Press, 1990.
Tamara Sonn. *A Brief History of Islam*. Oxford: Blackwell, 2004.
Montgomery Watt and Pierre Cachia. *A History of Islamic Spain*. Edinburgh: Edinburgh University Press, 1992.

Philosophy

Peter Adamson and Richard Taylor, eds. *The Cambridge Companion to Arabic Philosophy*. Cambridge: Cambridge University Press, 2005.
Lenn E. Goodman. *Avicenna*. London: Routledge, 1992.
Oliver Leaman. *A Brief Introduction to Islamic Philosophy*. Cambridge: Polity, 1999.
Oliver Leaman. *An Introduction to Classical Islamic Philosophy*. Cambridge: Cambridge University Press, 2002.
Seyyed Hossein Nasr and Oliver Leaman, eds. *History of Islamic Philosophy*. 2 vols. London: Routledge, 1996.
Ian Richard Netton. *Al-Farabi and His School*. London: Routledge, 1992.
Dominique Urvoy. *Ibn Rushd (Averroes)*. London: Routledge, 1991.

Theology

Binyamin Abrahamov. *Islamic Theology: Traditionalism and Rationalism*. Edinburgh: Edinburgh University Press, 1998.
Majid Fakhry. *Islamic Philosophy, Theology, and Mysticism: A Short Introduction*. Oxford: Oneworld, 2000.

Charles Kurzman, ed. *Liberal Islam: A Sourcebook.* Oxford: Oxford University Press, 1998.

Charles Kurzman, ed. *Modernist Islam 1840–1940: A Sourcebook.* Oxford: Oxford University Press, 2002.

Richard Martin et al. *Defenders of Reason in Islam.* Oxford: Oneworld, 2003.

F. E. Peters. *A Reader on Classical Islam.* Princeton: Princeton University Press, 1994.

Montgomery Watt. *Islamic Philosophy and Theology.* Edinburgh: Edinburgh University Press, 1979.

Montgomery Watt, trans. *Islamic Creeds: A Selection.* Edinburgh: Edinburgh University Press, 1994.

Law

Laleh Bakhtiar, trans. *Encyclopedia of Islamic Law: A Compendium of the Major Schools.* Chicago: Kazi Publications, 1995.

Mawil Izzi Dien. *Islamic Law: From Historical Foundations to Contemporary Practice.* Edinburgh: Edinburgh University Press, 2004.

Khaled Abou El Fadl. *Speaking in God's Name: Islamic Law, Authority, and Women.* Oxford: Oneworld, 2001.

Mohammad Hashim Kamali. *Principles of Islamic Jurisprudence.* Cambridge: Islamic Texts Society, 2003.

Nuh H. M. Keller, trans. *The Reliance of the Traveller: A Classic Manual of Islamic Sacred Law.* Evanston, Ill.: Sunna, 1994.

Contemporary Thought

Ibrahim Abu-Rabi, ed. *On the Life and Thought of Bediuzzaman Said Nursi.* Albany: SUNY Press, 2003.

Mohammed Arkoun. *Rethinking Islam: Common Questions, Uncommon Answers.* Oxford: Westview Press, 1994.

Clinton Bennett. *Muslims and Modernity: An Introduction to the Issues and Debates.* London: Continuum, 2005.

Farid Esack. *On Being a Muslim: Finding a Religious Path in the World Today.* Oxford: Oneworld, 1999.

John Cooper et al., eds. *Islam and Modernity: Muslim Intellectuals Respond.* London: Tauris, 1998.

Carl Ernst. *Rethinking Islam in the Contemporary World.* Edinburgh: Ediburgh University Press, 2004.

John Esposito and John Voll. *Makers of Contemporary Islam.* Oxford: Oxford University Press, 2001.

Joseph Lumbard. *Islam, Fundamentalism, and the Betrayal of Tradition: Essays by Western Muslim Scholars.* Bloomington: World Wisdom, 2004.

Yusuf al-Qaradawi. *Islamic Awakening: Between Rejection and Extremism.* Herndon, Va.: Zain International, 1991.

Yusuf al-Qaradawi. *Priorities of the Islamic Movement in the Coming Phase.*
   Swansea: Awakening, 2000.
Fazlur Rahman. *Islam and Modernity: Transformation of an Intellectual Tradition.*
   Chicago: University of Chicago Press, 1982.
Fazlur Rahman. *Revival and Reform in Islam: A Study of Islamic Fundamentalism.*
   Oxford: Oneworld, 2000.
Abdulaziz Sachedina. *The Islamic Roots of Democratic Pluralism.* Oxford:
   Oxford University Press, 2001.
Omid Safi, ed. *Progressive Muslims: On Justice, Gender, and Pluralism.* Oxford:
   Oneworld, 2003.
Abdolkarim Soroush. *Reason, Freedom, and Democracy in Islam.* Oxford:
   Oxford University Press, 2000.
Suha Taji-Farouki and Basheer Nafi. *Islamic Thought in the Twentieth Century.*
   London: Tauris, 2004.
Kate Zebiri. *Mahmud Shaltut and Islamic Modernism.* Oxford: Clarendon
   Press, 1993.

Women in Islam

Leila Ahmed. *Women and Gender in Islam.* New Haven: Yale University Press,
   1992.
Fadwa El Guindi. *Veil: Modesty, Privacy, and Resistance.* Oxford: Berg, 2000.
Fatima Mernissi. *Women and Islam: An Historical and Theological Enquiry.*
   Oxford: Blackwell, 1995.
Ziba Mir-Hosseini. *Islam and Gender: The Religious Debate in Contemporary
   Iran.* Princeton: Princeton University Press, 1990.
Anne Sofie Roald. *Women in Islam: The Western Experience.* London: Routledge,
   2001.
Barbara Stowasser. *Women in the Qur'an, Traditions, and Interpretation.* Oxford:
   Oxford University Press, 1994.
Amina Wadud. *Qur'an and Woman: Rereading the Sacred Texts from a Woman's
   Perspective.* Oxford: Oxford University Press, 1999.
Mai Yamani, ed. *Feminism and Islam: Legal and Literary Perspectives.* Reading:
   Ithaca, 1996.

Sufism

William Chittick. *Sufism: A Short Introduction.* Oxford: Oneworld, 2000.
Alexander Knysh. *Islamic Mysticism: A Short History.* Leiden: Brill, 2000.
Martin Lings. *What is Sufism?* Cambridge: Islamic Texts Society, 1993.
Annemarie Schimmel. *Mystical Dimensions of Islam.* Chapel Hill: University
   of North Carolina Press, 1975.
Hamza Yusuf, trans. *Purification of the Heart: Signs, Symptoms, and Cures of
   the Spiritual Diseases of the Heart.* Chicago: Starlatch, 2004.

Islam and Other Faiths

Ghulam Haider Aasi. *Muslim Understanding of Other Religions*. Islamabad: International Islamic University, 1999.

Hasan Askari. *Spiritual Quest: An Inter-Religious Dimension*. Leeds: Seven Mirrors, 1991.

Ismail Raji al-Faruqi. *Islam and Other Faiths*. Leicester: Islamic Foundation, 1998.

Yohannan Friedmann. *Tolerance and Coercion in Islam: Interfaith Relations in the Muslim Tradition*. Cambridge: Cambridge University Press, 2003.

Hugh Goddard. *Christians and Muslims: From Double Standards to Mutual Understanding*. London: Curzon, 1995.

Hugh Goddard. *A History of Christian-Muslim Relations*. Edinburgh: Edinburgh University Press, 2000.

Tarif Khalidi, ed. *The Muslim Jesus: Sayings and Stories in Islamic Literature*. London: Harvard University Press, 2001.

Geoffrey Parrinder. *Jesus in the Qur'an*. London: Sheldon Press, 1965.

Kate Zebiri. *Muslims and Christians Face to Face*. Oxford: Oneworld, 1997.

Neal Robinson. *Christ in Islam and Christianity: The Representation of Jesus in the Qur'an and the Classical Muslim Commentaries*. London: Macmillan, 1991.

Ataullah Siddiqui. *Christian-Muslim Dialogue in the Twentieth Century*. London: Macmillan, 1997.

Jacques Waardenburg. *Muslims and Others: Relations in Context*. Berlin, New York: de Gruyter, 2003.

Jacques Waardenburg, ed. *Muslim Perceptions of Other Religions: A Historical Survey*. Oxford: Oxford University Press, 1999.

Christian Views of Islam

Michael Nazir Ali. *Frontiers in Muslim-Christian Encounter*. Oxford: Regnum Books, 1987.

Michael Nazir Ali. *Islam: a Christian Perspective*. Exeter: Paternoster, 1983.

Marcus Braybrooke. *What We Can Learn from Islam*. Alresford: John Hunt, 2002.

Stuart Brown. *The Nearest in Affection: Towards a Christian Understanding of Islam*. Geneva: WCC, 1994.

Colin Chapman. *Cross and Crescent: Responding to the Challenge of Islam*. Leicester: Inter-Varsity, 1995.

Kenneth Cragg. *Muhammad and the Christian: A Question of Response*. Oxford: Oneworld, 1999.

Christine Mallouhi. *Waging Peace on Islam*. London: Monarch, 2000.

Steven Masood. *The Bible and the Qur'an: A Question of Integrity*. Carlisle: Paternoster, 2001.

Chawkat Moucarry. *Faith to Faith: Christianity and Islam in Dialogue*. Leicester: Inter-Varsity, 2001.

Pontifical Council for Interreligious Dialogue. *Guidelines for Dialogue between Christians and Muslims*. New York: Paulist Press, 1990.

Douglas Pratt. *The Challenge of Islam: Encounters in Interfaith Dialogue*. Aldershot: Ashgate, 2005.

Andrew Wingate. *Encounter in the Spirit: Muslim-Christian Meetings in Birmingham*. Geneva: WCC, 1988.

South Asian Islam

Barbara Daly Metcalf. *Islamic Revival in British India: Deoband, 1860–1900*. New Delhi: Oxford University Press, 2003.

Francis Robinson. *Varieties of South Asian Islam*. Warwick: ESRC, 1988.

Usha Sanyal. *Devotional Islam and Politics in British India: Ahmad Riza Khan Barelvi and His Movement, 1870–1920*. Delhi: Oxford University Press, 1999.

Wilfred Cantwell Smith. *Modern Islam in India*. Lahore: Ashraf, 1969.

Pnina Werbner. *Pilgrims of Love: The Anthropology of a Global Sufi Cult*. London: Hurst, 2003.

Muhammad Qasim Zaman. *The Ulama in Contemporary Islam: Custodians of Change*. Princeton: Princeton University Press, 2002.

World Overview

Mervyn Hiskett. *The Course of Islam in Africa*. Edinburgh: Edinburgh University Press, 1994.

Ahmed Rashid. *Jihad: The Rise of Militant Islam in Central Asia*. London: Yale University Press, 2002.

Barry Rubin, ed. *Revolutionaries and Reformers: Contemporary Islamist Movements in the Middle East*. Albany: SUNY Press, 2003.

Jane I. Smith. *Islam in America*. New York: Columbia University Press, 2000.

David Westerlund and Ingvar Svanberg, eds. *Islam Outside the Arab World*. London: Curzon, 1999.

Muslims in Europe

Jørgen Nielsen. *Muslims in Western Europe*. Edinburgh: Edinburgh University Press, 2005.

Tariq Ramadan. *Western Muslims and the Future of Islam*. Oxford: Oxford University Press, 2004.

Anne Sofie Roald. *New Muslims in the European Context: The Experience of Scandinavian Converts*. Leiden: Brill, 2004.

Muslims in Britain

Tahir Abbas, ed. *Muslim Britain: Communities under Pressure*. London: Zed, 2005.
Humayun Ansari. *The Infidel Within: Muslims in Britain since 1800*. London: Hurst, 2004.
Philip Lewis. *Islamic Britain: Religion, Politics, and Identity Amongst British Muslims*. London: Tauris, 2002.
Nabil Matar. *Islam in Britain 1558–1685*. Cambridge: Cambridge University Press, 1998.
Tariq Modood. *Multicultural Politics: Racism, Ethnicity, and Muslims in Britain*. Edinburgh: Edinburgh University Press, 2005.
M. Siddique Seddon et al. *British Muslims between Assimilation and Segregation: Historical, Legal, and Social Realities*. Leicester: Islamic Foundation, 2004.

Muslims in the United States

Allan D. Austin, ed. *African Muslims in Antebellum America: A Sourcebook*. New York: Garland, 1984.
Edward E. Curtis. *Islam in Black America: Identity, Liberation, and Difference in African-American Islamic Thought*. Albany: SUNY Press, 2002.
Yvonne Yazbeck Haddad, ed. *The Muslims of America*. New York: Oxford University Press, 1991.
Yvonne Yazbeck Haddad and Adair T. Lummis. *Islamic Values in the United States: A Comparative Study*. New York: Oxford University Press, 1987.
Yvonne Yazbeck Haddad and Jane I. Smith. *Mission to America: Five Islamic Sectarian Communities in North America*. Gainsville: University Press of Florida, 1993.
Yvonne Yazbeck Haddad and Jane I. Smith, eds. *Muslim Communities in North America*. Albany: SUNY Press, 1994.
Yvonne Yazbeck Haddad, Jane I. Smith, and Kathleen Moore. *Muslim Women in America: The Challenge of Islamic Identity Today*. New York: Oxford University Press, 2006.
Asma Gull Hasan. *American Muslims: The New Generation*. London: Continuum, 2001.
Karen Isaksen Leonard. *Muslims in the United States: The State of Research*. New York: Russell Sage Foundation, 2003.
Aminah Beverly McCloud. *African American Islam*. London: Routledge, 1995.
Richard Brent Turner. *Islam in the African American Experience*. Indianapolis: Indiana University Press, 2003.
Jane I. Smith. *Islam in America*. New York: Columbia University Press, 2003.
Earle H. Waugh, Baha Abu-Laban, and Regula B. Qureshi, eds. *The Muslim Community in North America*. Edmonton: University of Alberta Press, 1983.
Earle H. Waugh, Sharon McIrvin Abu-Laban, and Regula B. Qureshi, eds. *Muslim Families in North America*. Edmonton: University of Alberta Press, 1991.
Raymond Brady Williams. *Religions of Immigrants from India and Pakistan*. Cambridge and New York: Cambridge University Press, 1988.

Glossary

Abbasids: The second dynasty of Sunni Islam, based in Baghdad from 750 to 1258 C.E.

'abd: The Loving Servant of God.

Abdallah: Male name meaning Servant of God.

adhan: The call to prayer before each *salat*.

Ahl al-Bayt: The Family of the Prophet Muhammad.

Ahl al-Kitab: The People of the Book or Earlier Revelations, that is, Jews and Christians.

ahwal: In sufi traditions, a higher state of being bestowed by God.

akhira: The afterlife.

alim: A scholar of the Islamic sciences.

al-Andalus: The Arabic name for Islamic Spain.

ansar: The first group of Muslims in Madina, who welcomed the *muhajirun* in 622.

'aqiqa: The ceremonies surrounding the seventh day after birth.

asbab al-nuzul: The occasions of revelation that record the contexts in which portions of the Qur'an were revealed.

Ashura Day: The tenth of Muharram, on which the martyrdom of Imam Husayn is commemorated.

'awra: A woman's attractive charms.

aya: Literally "a sign," used for the verses of the Qur'an.

Ayatollah: Literally "Sign of God," the highest level of religious scholars in Ithna Ashari Shi'a Islam.

ba'ya: The bond of allegiance made by a *murid* to a *shaykh*.

baqa: Sufi term for abiding in God.

baraka: A blessing from God. In sufi terms a spiritual power that comes from having attained a higher state of being.

barzakh: Life in the grave in a state of timeless awareness.

basmala: The Arabic expression *Bism' Allah al-Rahman al-Rahim*, In the name of God, the Merciful, the Compassionate.

batini: Esoteric or hidden dimensions to the interpretation of the Qur'an.

bila kayf: "Ask not how."

Bohras: A branch of the Sevener or Isma'ili Shi'a Muslims.

al-buraq: The mysterious mount that carried Muhammad on his miraculous night journey (*isra*) from Makka to Jerusalem.

Caliph: The traditional leader of Sunni Muslims.

daff: A simple drum.

da'i: Someone who makes *da'wa*, inviting others to follow the path of Islam.

da'if: In Hadith studies, a Hadith with a weakness in its *isnad*.

al-Dajjal: The Great Impostor who will lead the forces of evil in the Last Days.

da'wa: The invitation to others to follow the way of Islam.

dervish: A sufi practitioner.

dhikr: The remembrance of God in the heart.

dhimmis: Literally "the protected people," the status given to Jews and Christians in the Islamic Empire.

din al-fitra: The natural God-given way of life.

du'a: Informal prayers of supplication.

Eid: Another spelling for 'Id.

fana: Sufi term for dying to self but being alive in God.

faqih: A scholar who specializes in Islamic law.

faqir: A sufi who embraces a life of poverty and simplicity.

fard: A compulsory act.

fard 'ayn: An act that is compulsory for all Muslims.

fard kifaya: A compulsory duty that can be discharged by a group of Muslims on behalf of all Muslims.

fatwa: A learned opinion based on personal judgment by a recognized authority in Islamic law.

fiqh: The science of law.

al-Furqan: The Criterion, name given to the Qur'an.

Ghadir: The oasis at which Muhammad is believed by.

ghayba: Occultation, the hidden existence of the Twelfth Imam.

ghusl: The major ablution requiring a complete bath or shower.

hadd: The limit, a punishment prescribed by the Qur'an.

Hadith: A tradition of Muhammad; something he said, taught, did, or an action he approved.

hadith qudsi: Sayings from God given to Muhammad that were not part of the Qur'an.

hafiz: Title given to a male who has memorized the whole Qur'an.

hafizah: Title given to a female who has memorized the whole Qur'an.

Hajj: The annual pilgrimage to Makka.

al-Hajj: Title given to a man who has performed the *Hajj*.

al-Hajjah: Title given to a woman who has performed the *Hajj*.

halal: Something that is compulsory or fit for Muslim usage.

hamd: Praised.

al-hamdu li 'llah: All praise/thanks be to God.

hanif: Seeker; one who worshipped one God alone but was in search of deeper knowledge.

haqa'iq: Spiritual truths contained in the Qur'an that are accessible only to the Prophet and Imams.

haram: An action or thing that is forbidden.

hasan: In Hadith studies, a beautiful and reliable Hadith.

al-Hawiya: Literally "the Abyss," one of the names for hell.

Hijra: The migration of Muhammad and early Muslims from Makka to Madina in 622 C.E.

al-Huda: The Guidance, name given to the Qur'an.

hulul: Indwelling.

'al-Hutama: Literally "that which shatters," one of the names for hell.

ibada: The worship of God.

'ibarah: A literary understanding of the Qur'an.

'Id al-Adha: The Festival of Sacrifice that comes at the end of the *Hajj* commemorating the sacrifice of Ibrahim and Isma'il.

'Id al-Fitr: The Festival of Fast-Breaking at the end of the fasting month of Ramadan.

'idda: The waiting period after divorce during which a woman cannot remarry.

iftar: The light meal with which the fast is broken during Ramadan.

ihram: The two sheets used as clothing by men on the *Hajj*.

ihsan: To live in the constant watchfulness of God.

ijma: A consensus on a point of Shari'a.

ijtihad: An intellectual striving to solve a question.

ilham: Divine inspiration.

ilm al-kalam: The science of theology.

Imam: Among Shi'a Muslims, the infallible leader of the Muslim community in succession to Muhammad.

imam: The person who leads the congregation in *salat*.

imam khatib: A scholar who delivers the address (*khutba*) at Friday Prayers.

iman: Faith or belief.

inabat: A station on the sufi way: conversion.

infaq: The economic principle of the circulation of wealth.

Injil: The Book that was sent to the Prophet 'Isa.

al-insan al-kamil: The perfect human being.

Insha'a Allah: God willing.

iqama: The call that *salat* is about to begin.

iqra: "Recite," the command given to Muhammad by the Angel Jibril.

isharah: A meaning alluded to in the Qur'an that is accessible only to scholars.

Islam: The way of life based on the revelation of the Qur'an and teaching of Muhammad.

islam: The state of perfect harmony between God and all creation.

Isma'ilis: The Seveners among the Shi'a, who disagreed with the majority over the identity of the Seventh Imam.

Isma'ilis (Nizari): The group of Isma'ilis who accept the Aga Khan as the Living Imam.

isnad: The chain of transmitters of a Hadith.

isra: The miraculous night journey of Muhammad from Makka to Jerusalem.

Ithna Ashari: The Twelvers, the largest branch of Shi'a Muslims, who recognize Twelve Imams.

i'tikaf: The practice of remaining in seclusion during the last ten days of Ramadan.

Ja'fari School: The *madhhab* school of law, followed by Ithna Ashari Shi'a Muslims.

Jahannam: Literally "the Depths," one of the names for hell.

al-Jahim: Literally "the place for idolaters," one of the names for hell.

ja'iz: A neutral act that carries neither reward nor punishment.

al-Janna: Literally "the Garden" or Paradise.

Jibril: The Arabic form of the name Gabriel, the messenger angel.

jihad: To struggle on the path of God to establish goodness and root out evil and oppression.

al-jihad al-akbar: The constant struggle against the wayward self, "the greater jihad."

al-jihad al-asghar: The legitimate use of force in defense, "the lesser jihad."

jinn: A third order of sentient beings, created of fire, that inhabit a parallel universe to human beings.

jizya: A tax paid by Christians and Jews in the Islamic Empire in lieu of military service.

Jum'a Masjid: A principal mosque in which the main Friday congregational prayer is held.

juz: One-thirtieth part of the Qur'an.

Ka'ba: The cuboid building in the center of Makka built by Ibrahim and Isma'il, the earthly focus of prayer.

Kalam Allah: The eternal transcendent Speech of God.

Karbala: The site of Imam Husayn's martyrdom in 680.

khafd: The Arabic word for female circumcision.

khalifa: The Regent of God on earth.

khanqah: A sufi residential spiritual center.

khitan: The circumcision of boys.

al-Khumm: Shi'a Muslims to have nominated Ali as his successor.

khums: The Fifth or twenty percent payment in Shi'a Islam.

khutba: An address given at the Friday prayers (*Salat al-Jum'a*).

kiswa: Embroidered black cloth that covers the Ka'ba.

Koran: Another spelling of Qur'an.

kunya: An addition to someone's name signifying that they are the father or mother of . . . (the child's name).

laqab: An addition to someone's name giving their place of birth, profession, or place where they have studied.

lata'if: A hidden meaning in a Qur'anic verse accessible only to the most pious.

al-Lawh al-Mahfuz: The Preserved Tablet that contains the *Kalam Allah* in the transcendent world.

Laylat al-Mi'raj: The Night of the Ascension of the Prophet, which commemorates Muhammad's *isra* and *mi'raj*.

Laylat al-Qadr: The Night of Power or Destiny, which celebrates the first revelation of the Qur'an.

Laza: Literally "the Great Furnace," one of the names for hell.

madhhab: A school of law.

Madina: The city in Arabia in which Muhammad established the first Muslim community and in which he is buried.

madrasa: An Islamic school or center of learning.

mahabba: A sufi higher state of being; love.

al-Mahdi: The Rightly Guided One who will appear in the Last Days. In Shi'a Islam, associated with the Hidden Imam.

mahr: The dowry given to the bride by her husband.

mahram: A person's close relations with whom marriage is not permitted.

Makka: City in Arabia, the birthplace of Muhammad, the site of the Ka'ba, and the location of the *Hajj*.

makruh: An action that is disapproved.

maqamat: A sufi term for a station on the path of spiritual growth.

Masjid al-Nabi: The Prophet's Mosque in Madina.

masun: A recommended act.

matn: The body of teaching contained in a Hadith.

Mawlid al-Nabi: The Festival of the Birthday of Muhammad.

Mecca: Another spelling for Makka.

Medina: Another spelling for Madina.

mihrab: A niche built into the *qibla* wall in a mosque in which the imam will stand to lead prayers.

minaret: A tall tower from which the *adhan* (call to prayer) is called.

minbar: The platform in a mosque from which the *khutba* is given.

mi'raj: The ascent into heaven of Muhammad when he made his night journey (*isra*) from Makka to Jerusalem.

misbah: The prayer beads used by Muslims.

miswak: A small piece of fibrous wood used for cleaning the teeth.

Moslem: Another spelling for Muslim.

mu'adhdhin: The person who calls Muslims to prayer (Arabic spelling).

mubah: A neutral act that carries neither reward nor punishment.

muezzin: The person who calls Muslims to prayer (common spelling).

mufti: A scholar recognized by others as being capable of giving an independent learned opinion (*fatwa*) on a legal question.

muhajirun: The group of early Muslims that migrated with Muhammad from Makka to Madina in 622.

Muhammad: Born c. 570 C.E., the last in the chain of Prophets.

Muharram: The month in which the martyrdom of Imam Husayn is commemorated by Shi'a Muslims with intense mourning.

mujtahid: A scholar qualified to perform *ijtihad*.

murid: A sufi "disciple" attached to a *shaykh*.

al-Mushaf: The Recitation, name given to the Qur'an.

Muslim: A *muslim* who follows the guidance of the Qur'an and the Sunna of Muhammad.

muslim: Something or someone who is in perfect harmony with God.

mut'a: Temporary marriage permitted only in Shi'a Islam.

nabi: A Prophet, normally one not sent with a Book but who comes to reinforce an earlier revelation.

nafs: The soul, spirit, inner self of a human being.

al-Nar: Literally "the Fire," one of the names for hell.

nasab: An addition to someone's name, "son or daughter of...(their father's name)".

nasheed: A song in praise of the Prophet Muhammad.

nikah: The marriage ceremony.

nisab: The basic allowance before *zakat* is liable.

niyya: The intention that precedes any action.

nushuz: A violation of religious duties by either partner in marriage.

Prophet: A human being chosen by God to receive revelation, live it out in an exemplary way, and lead others on the same path.

qadi: A judge.

Qari: A person who has mastered the technical styles for the recitation of the Qur'an in public.

qibla: The direction to be faced in formal prayer (*salat*), toward the Ka'ba in Makka.

qiyas: Analogical reasoning.

Qur'an: The Book that was revealed to Muhammad, 610–632 C.E.

qurban: The meat of the animal sacrificed at 'Id al-Adha, which is to be given to the poor.

qurbani: A sum of money sent to buy an animal to be sacrificed for the poor as *qurban*.

rak'a (pl. rak'at): The cycle of recitation, movements, and prayers that comprises one unit of *salat*.

Ramadan: The fasting month in the Islamic calendar.

Rashidun: The "Rightly Guided Caliphs" according to the Sunnis, the first four Caliphs in succession to Muhammad.

rasul: Messenger; a Prophet sent with a revealed Book.

ra'y: Personal judgment.

riba: Economic exploitation, giving or taking interest.

ribat: A sufi residential spiritual center.

ridda: Literally "apostasy," but specifically referring to the rebellion of some Arab clans after the death of Muhammad.

sabr: The virtue of patience.

sadaqa: Bearing one another's burdens, the principle of charity.

safa: A possible root for the word "Sufi," connoting purification.

sahih: In Hadith studies, a sound Hadith without defects.

Sa'ir: Literally "the blazing inferno," one of the names for hell.

salam alaykum: Traditional Muslim greeting: May you come ever more completely into the state of *islam*; more commonly, "Peace be with you."

salat: The five-times-a-day formal prayers.

salat al-'asr: The late afternoon prayer.

salat al-fajr: The prayer before sunrise.

salat al-'isha: The night prayer.

salat al-janaza: The funeral prayers.

Salat al-Jum'a: Friday prayers, the principal congregational prayer of the week on Friday early afternoon.

salat al-maghrib: The prayer directly after sunset.

salat al-zuhr: The prayer just after the sun has passed its zenith.

sama: Generally, music; technically in Sufi circles: a spiritual concert.

Saqar: Literally "the scorching fire," one of the names for hell.

sawm: Fasting during the month of Ramadan.

sa'y: Running between two hills in Makka, a rite during the *Hajj*.

sayyid: A blood descendant of Muhammad.

Shahada: The principal statement of faith: I bear witness that there is no god save God, Muhammad is the Messenger of God.

Shari'a: A pathway or complete code of life based on the Qur'an and the Sunna of Muhammad.

sharif: A blood descendant of Muhammad.

shawq: A sufi higher state of being: yearning to be constantly with God.

shaykh: A male sufi teacher.

shaykhah: A female sufi teacher.

Shaytan: The Satan figure of Islam, a fallen *jinn*; Iblis.

Shi'a: The minority group among Muslims (ten percent of the total) who hold that leaders (Imams) must come from the Ahl al-Bayt.

shirk: To associate partners with God.

shukr: Thankfulness, gratitude.

sifat: The attributes of God.

silsila: A sufi spiritual lineage linking a *shaykh* back to Muhammad.

sipara: One-thirtieth part of the Qur'an.

sira: The biography of Muhammad.

subha: The prayer beads used by Muslims.

Subhan Allah: "All glory be to God."

suf: Literally "wool," most likely the root of the word "sufi."

Sufism: The mystical dimension of Islam.

Suhuf: The Book sent to the Prophet Ibrahim.

Sunna: The way of life of Muhammad.

sunna: A recommended act.

Sunni: The largest grouping among Muslims, approximately ninety percent of the total.

sura: A chapter in the Qur'an.

tafsir: Commentary written on the Qur'an.

tafsir bi al-ra'y: A commentary based on rational judgment.

tafsir ma'thur: A commentary based on the Hadith of Muhammad.

talaq: The process of divorce by simple repudiation by the husband.

al-Tanzil: That which was sent down, name given to the Qur'an.

tanzil: Literally "the sending down," used to describe the revelation of a Book.

taqlid: Faithful following of an earlier legal ruling.

taqwa: God-consciousness.

tarawih: The prayers each night during Ramadan in which Sunni Muslims recite daily one-thirtieth part of the Qur'an.

tariqa: A sufi order.

tarwiz: A portion of the Qur'an written on parchment contained in a leather pouch and worn by a Muslim.

tasawwuf: The mystical dimension of Islam.

tasbih: The prayer beads used by Muslims.

Taurat: The Book sent to the Prophet Musa.

tawaf: Walking around the Ka'ba seven times as part of the rites of the *Hajj*.

tawakkul: A station on the sufi way: trust in God.

tawba: Repentance.

tawbat: A station on the sufi way: repentance.

tawhid: The absolute oneness of God.

tawil: The "allegorical" interpretation of the Qur'an.

tekke: A sufi residential spiritual center.

ulama: The body of scholars (pl. of *alim*).

Umayyads: The first dynasty of Sunni Islam, based in Damascus from 661 to 750 C.E.

umma: The united worldwide community of Muslims.

ummi: "Unlettered" or "without book learning," the state of Muhammad before the Qur'an was revealed to him.

umra: The minor pilgrimage to Makka.

usul al-fiqh: Principles of jurisprudence.

wahy: The technical term used for revelation.

wajib: A compulsory act.

wali: Literally "a Friend of God," someone of outstanding piety.

waqf: A charitable trust.

wudu: The ritual ablution that must be made before formal prayer or handling the Qur'an.

Zabur: The Book that was sent to the Prophet Daud.

zahiri: The literalist school of Qur'anic commentary.

zakat: Purification of wealth by passing on two and a half percent of surplus wealth each year to those in need.

zakat al-fitr: A payment to those in need before the celebration of 'Id al-Fitr; the cost of one meal per person in the household.

Zamzam: The spring in Makka that was miraculously provided by God for Isma'il and Hagar.

zawiya: A sufi residential spiritual center.

Zaydis: The Fivers among the Shi'a, who recognized a different Fifth Imam to the majority.

zuhd: A station on the sufi way: renunciation.

Index

The Madina Mosque in Cardiff, Wales. Plans are underway to a construct a beautiful, new purpose-built mosque in the coming years. Photo: David Messner.